GW00417379

RUSSIA

RAINE
LDOVA

TURKEY

CYPRUS

SYRIA
LEB
JOR

BYA   EGYPT

HAD   SUDAN

CAR   ETHIOPIA

NGO   UGAN KENYA
ZAIRE
                TANZANIA

OLA ZAMBIA MALAWI

BIA   ZIMB MOZ MADAGASCAR MAURITIUS
BOT
        SWAZI
SOUTH LESOTHO
AFRICA

RUSSIA

KAZAKHSTAN   MONGOLIA

GEORGIA
TURKEY ARM AZERB   UZBEK KIRGIZ   N. KOREA
            TURKMEN TAJIK   S. KOREA JAPAN
IRAQ   IRAN   AFGH   CHINA
KUWAIT   BHU
BAH QATAR PAKISTAN NEPAL   HONG
SAUDI   UAE   B'DESH   KONG TAIWAN
ARABIA   OMAN   INDIA MYANMAR LAOS   MACAO
ERITREA YEMEN   THAILAND VIETNAM
DJIB   CAMBODIA   PHILIPPINES
SOMALIA   SRI   BRUNEI
                     LANKA   MALAYSIA
                                   SING
                                        INDONESIA   PAPUA
                                                           NEW GUINEA

                                                                        FIJI

                     AUSTRALIA

                                                           NEW ZEALAND

The Economist

POCKET WORLD IN FIGURES

The Economist

=== POCKET ===
WORLD IN
FIGURES

THE ECONOMIST IN ASSOCIATION WITH
PROFILE BOOKS LTD

Published by Profile Books Ltd,
62 Queen Anne Street, London W1M 9LA

First published by The Economist Books Ltd 1991

Copyright © The Economist Newspaper Ltd, 1991, 1992,
1993, 1994, 1995, 1996, 1997

Material researched and compiled by
Robert Eves, Andrew Gilbert, Carol Howard, Stella Jones,
Liz Mann, Dianne Martin, David McKelvey, Justene McNeice,
Henrietta Nelder, Nick Wiseman

Design and makeup Jonathan Harley

The greatest care has been taken in compiling this book. However,
no responsibility can be accepted by the publishers or compilers
for the accuracy of the information presented.

Printed in Italy by
LEGO S.p.a. - Vicenza - Italy

A CIP catalogue record for this book is available
from the British Library

ISBN 1 86197 015 3

Contents

CONTENTS

CONTENTS

a   At the time of going to press Zaire had been renamed the Democratic Republic of Congo but had not been officially recognised by many countries.

Notes

This edition of the annual *Economist Pocket World in Figures* has been expanded to include a larger number of countries. The country profiles cover some 63 major countries, including Russia and Ukraine, and a selection of statistics for the other ex-Soviet republics. The world rankings consider 171: all those with a population of at least 1m or a GDP of at least $1bn; they are listed on page 223. The extent and quality of the statistics available varies from country to country. Every care has been taken to specify the broad definitions on which the data are based and to indicate cases where data quality or technical difficulties are such that interpretation of the figures is likely to be seriously affected. Nevertheless, figures from individual countries will often differ from standard international statistical definitions.

Statistics do not yet fully reflect the changes that have taken place in the Czech Republic and Slovakia, ex-Yugoslavia and the former Soviet Union. In ex-Yugoslavia, Serbia and Montenegro now constitute the Federal Republic of Yugoslavia, and Macedonia is officially known as the Former Yugoslav Republic of Macedonia. Data for Cyprus normally refer to Greek Cyprus only. For other countries such as Morocco they exclude disputed areas. Data for the EU refer to its 15 members following the enlargement of the Union on January 1 1995.

Statistical basis

The all-important factor in a book of this kind is to be able to make reliable comparisons between countries. Although this is never quite possible for the reasons stated above, the best route, which this book takes, is to compare data for the same year or period and to use actual, not estimated, figures wherever possible. The research for this edition of *The Economist Pocket World in Figures* was carried out in 1997 using the latest available sources that present data on an internationally comparable basis. Data, therefore, unless otherwise indicated, refers to the year ending December 31 1995.

In the country profiles, population density, population under 15 and over 65, and number of men per 100 women refer to 1995; life expectancy, crude birth, death and fertility rates are based on 1995–2000 averages; human development indices are for 1993 and GDP per head in purchasing power parity to 1995; energy data refer to 1994; household data are latest available and marriage and divorce data refer to the latest year with available figures, 1990–95. In a number of cases, data are shown for the latest year within a range.

Other definitions

Data shown on country profiles may not always be consistent with those shown on the world rankings because the definitions or years covered can differ. Data may also differ between two different rankings.

Most countries' national accounts are now compiled on a GDP basis so, for simplicity, the term GDP has been used interchangeably with GNP. GDP figures in this book come from the World Bank. It bases its rouble conversions on purchasing power parities.

Statistics for principal exports and principal imports are normally based on customs statistics. These are generally compiled on different definitions to the visible exports and imports figures shown in the balance of payments section.

Definitions of the statistics shown are given on the relevant page or in the glossary at the end of the book. Figures may not add exactly to totals, or percentages to 100, because of rounding or, in the case of GDP, statistical adjustment. Sums of money have generally been converted to US dollars at the official exchange rate ruling at the time to which the figures refer.

Energy consumption data are not always reliable, particularly for the major oil producing countries. Consumption per head data may therefore be higher than in reality. Energy exports can exceed production and imports can exceed consumption if transit operations distort trade data or oil is imported for refining and re-exported.

Abbreviations

bn	billion (one thousand million)	GNP	Gross national product
CAR	Central African Republic	GRT	Gross tonnage
CIS	Commonwealth of Independent States	m	million
		NDP	Net domestic product
EU	European Union	NMP	Net material product
kg	kilogram	PPP	Purchasing power parity
km	kilometre	UAE	United Arab Emirates
GDP	Gross domestic product	…	not available

Part I
WORLD
RANKINGS

Countries: *natural facts*

Countries: *the largest[a]*
'000 sq km

1	Russia	17,078	31	Nigeria	924
2	Canada	9,922	32	Venezuela	912
3	China	9,597	33	Namibia	824
4	United States	9,363	34	Pakistan	804
5	Brazil	8,512	35	Mozambique	785
6	Australia	7,682	36	Turkey	779
7	India	3,169	37	Zambia	753
8	Kazakhstan	2,717	38	Chile	752
9	Sudan	2,506	39	Myanmar	678
10	Saudi Arabia	2,401	40	Afghanistan	652
11	Algeria	2,382	41	Somalia	630
12	Zaire	2,345	42	Central African Rep	625
13	Argentina	2,278	43	Ukraine	604
14	Mexico	1,973	44	Madagascar	594
15	Indonesia	1,919	45	Kenya	583
16	Libya	1,760	46	Botswana	575
17	Iran	1,648	47	France	544
18	Mongolia	1,565	48	Thailand	514
19	Peru	1,285	49	Spain	505
20	Chad	1,284	50	Turkmenistan	488
21	Angola	1,247	51	Yemen	477
22	Mali	1,240	52	Cameroon	476
23	Niger	1,186	53	Papua New Guinea	463
24	South Africa	1,185	54	Morocco	458
25	Colombia	1,139	55	Sweden	450
26	Bolivia	1,099	56	Uzbekistan	447
27	Mauritania	1,031	57	Iraq	438
28	Egypt	1,023	58	Paraguay	407
29	Ethiopia	1,023	59	Zimbabwe	390
30	Tanzania	940	60	Japan	370

Mountains: *the highest[b]*

	Name	Location	Height (m)
1	Everest	Nepal-China	8,848
2	K2 (Godwin Austen)	Pakistan	8,611
3	Kangchenjunga	Nepal-Sikkim	8,586
4	Lhotse	Nepal-China	8,516
5	Makalu	Nepal-China	8,463
6	Cho Oyu	Nepal-China	8,201
7	Dhaulagiri	Nepal	8,167
8	Manaslu	Nepal	8,163
9	Nanga Parbat	Pakistan	8,125
10	Annapurna I	Nepal	8,091
11	Gasherbrum I	Pakistan-China	8,068
12	Broad Peak	Pakistan-China	8,047
13	Xixabangma (Gosainthan)	China	8,046
14	Gasherbrum II	Pakistan-China	8,035

a Includes freshwater.
b Includes separate peaks which are part of the same massif.

Rivers: *the longest*

	Name	Location	Length (km)
1	Nile	Africa	6,695
2	Amazon	South America	6,516
3	Yangtze	Asia	6,380
4	Mississippi-Missouri	North America	6,019
5	Ob'-Irtysh	Asia	5,570
6	Yenisey-Angara	Asia	5,550
7	Hwang He (Yellow)	Asia	5,464
8	Congo	Africa	4,667
9	Parana	South America	4,500
10	Mekong	Asia	4,425
11	Amur	Asia	4,416
12	Lena	Asia	4,400
13	Mackenzie	North America	4,250
14	Niger	Africa	4,030
15	Missouri	North America	3,969
16	Mississippi	North America	3,779
17	Murray-Darling	Australia	3,750
18	Volga	Europe	3,688
19	Kolyma	Asia	3,513
20	Madeira	South America	3,200
21	Yukon	North America	3,185
22	Indus	Asia	3,180
23	Syrdar'ya	Asia	3,078
24	Salween	Asia	3,060
25	Sao Francisco	South America	2,900
26	Rio Grande	North America	2,870
27	Danube	Europe	2,850
28	Brahmaputra	Asia	2,840
29	Euphrates	Asia	2,815
30	Para-Tocantins	South America	2,750

Waterfalls: *the highest*

	Name	Location	Height (m)
1	Angel	Venezuela	979
2	Tugela	South Africa	948
3	Utigard	Norway	800
4	Mongefossen	Norway	774
5	Yosemite	California, USA	739
6	Mardalsfossen	Norway	656
7	Tyssestrengane	Norway	646
8	Cuquenan	Venezuela	609
9	Ribbon	California, USA	491
10	Della	Canada	440

Notes: Estimates of the lengths of different rivers vary widely according to the rules adopted concerning the selection of tributaries to be followed, the path to take through a delta, where different hydrological systems begin and end etc. The Nile is normally taken as the world's longest river but some estimates put the Amazon as longer if a southerly path through its delta leading to the River Para is followed. Likewise, difficulties in waterfall measurements exist depending on which breaks in the fall are counted. The more famous waterfalls, Niagara and Victoria, are surprisingly small, 50m and 108m respectively; their notoriety evolving from their width and accessibility.

Population: *explosions revealed*

Largest populations, 1995
Millions

1	China	1,220.22	31	Argentina	34.77
2	India	929.01	32	Tanzania	29.69
3	United States	267.12	33	Canada	29.40
4	Indonesia	197.46	34	Algeria	28.11
5	Brazil	159.02	35	Kenya	27.15
6	Russia	148.46	36	Sudan	26.71
7	Pakistan	136.26	37	Morocco	26.52
8	Japan	125.07	38	Peru	23.53
9	Bangladesh	118.23	39	Uzbekistan	22.76
10	Nigeria	111.72	40	Romania	22.73
11	Mexico	91.15	41	North Korea	22.10
12	Germany	81.59	42	Venezuela	21.84
13	Vietnam	73.79	43	Nepal	21.46
14	Iran	68.37	44	Taiwan	21.30
15	Philippines	67.84	45	Malaysia	20.14
16	Egypt	62.10	46	Iraq	20.10
17	Turkey	60.84	47	Uganda	19.69
18	Thailand	58.24	48	Afghanistan	19.66
19	France	58.10	49	Saudi Arabia	18.26
20	United Kingdom	58.08	50	Sri Lanka	17.93
21	Italy	57.20	51	Australia	17.87
22	Ethiopia	56.40	52	Ghana	17.34
23	Ukraine	51.76	53	Mozambique	17.26
24	Zaire	45.45	54	Kazakhstan	16.82
25	Myanmar	45.11	55	Netherlands	15.48
26	South Korea	44.91	56	Yemen	15.03
27	South Africa	41.47	57	Madagascar	14.87
28	Spain	39.63	58	Chile	14.21
29	Poland	38.56	59	Syria	14.20
30	Colombia	35.81	60	Côte d'Ivoire	13.69

Largest populations, 2010
Millions

1	China	1,364.95	13	Vietnam	92.26
2	India	1,152.28	14	Ethiopia	89.52
3	United States	298.89	15	Philippines	88.81
4	Indonesia	239.38	16	Germany	82.48
5	Pakistan	200.62	17	Egypt	80.26
6	Brazil	189.78	18	Turkey	74.62
7	Nigeria	168.37	19	Zaire	69.78
8	Bangladesh	151.89	20	Thailand	64.57
9	Russia	141.06	21	France	59.94
10	Japan	127.04	22	United Kingdom	58.73
11	Mexico	112.89	23	Myanmar	57.46
12	Iran	98.27	24	South Africa	56.61

Fastest growing populations, 1985–95
Average annual growth, %

1	Oman	4.5	11	Macao	3.5
	Yemen	4.5	12	Iran	3.4
3	Qatar	4.3		Jordan	3.4
4	West Bank and Gaza	4.2		Madagascar	3.4
5	Gambia, The	4.1	15	Côte d'Ivoire	3.3
6	Guinea	4.0		Niger	3.3
7	Saudi Arabia	3.7	17	Ethiopia	3.2
	Zaire	3.7		Kenya	3.2
9	Libya	3.6		Mali	3.2
	United Arab Emirates	3.6		Syria	3.2

Slowest growing populations, 1985–95
Average annual growth, %

1	Rwanda	-1.5		Ireland	0.0
2	Bosnia	-1.4		Romania	0.0
3	Bulgaria	-0.5	13	Croatia	0.1
	Hungary	-0.5		Italy	0.1
5	Liberia	-0.4	15	Denmark	0.2
6	Estonia	-0.2		Finland	0.2
	Kuwait	-0.2		Slovenia	0.2
	Latvia	-0.2		Ukraine	0.2
9	Portugal	-0.1	19	Belgium	0.3
10	Czech Republic	0.0		United Kingdom	0.3

Fastest growing populations, 1995–2010
Average annual growth, %

1	Liberia	5.0	11	Angola	3.1
2	Rwanda	4.3		Ethiopia	3.1
3	West Bank and Gaza	4.1		Jordan	3.1
4	Oman	4.0		Madagascar	3.1
5	Yemen	3.6	15	Mali	3.0
6	Afghanistan	3.5	16	Benin	2.9
7	Somalia	3.4		Laos	2.9
8	Libya	3.2		Uganda	2.9
	Niger	3.2		Zaire	2.9
	Saudi Arabia	3.2	20	Burkina Faso	2.8

Slowest growing populations, 1995–2010
Average annual growth, %

1	Latvia	-0.8	7	Belarus	-0.2
2	Estonia	-0.7		Italy	-0.2
3	Hungary	-0.6		Lithuania	-0.2
4	Bulgaria	-0.4		Romania	-0.2
	Ukraine	-0.4		Slovenia	-0.2
6	Russia	-0.3			

Population density

Highest population density
Population per sq km

1	Macau	23,865	21	El Salvador	269
2	Hong Kong	5,859	22	Israel	262
3	Singapore	5,384	23	Réunion	261
4	Bermuda	1,189	24	Haiti	257
5	Malta	1,160	25	Trinidad & Tobago	251
6	Bahrain	821	26	Guadeloupe	249
	Bangladesh	821	27	Netherlands Antilles	242
8	Barbados	606	28	United Kingdom	238
9	Taiwan	592	29	Germany	229
10	Mauritius	547	30	Philippines	226
11	South Korea	454	31	Jamaica	225
12	Puerto Rico	416	32	Vietnam	222
13	Netherlands	379	33	Burundi	218
14	Martinique	345	34	Rwanda	197
15	West Bank and Gaza	344	35	Italy	190
16	Belgium	332	36	North Korea	183
17	Japan	331	37	Switzerland	174
18	Lebanon	289	38	Pakistan	171
19	India	283	39	Dominican Republic	161
20	Sri Lanka	273	40	Luxembourg	158

Lowest population density
Population per sq km

1	Australia	2		Papua New Guinea	9
	Botswana	2		Russia	9
	Mauritania	2	23	Oman	10
	Mongolia	2	24	Sudan	11
	Namibia	2		Zambia	11
6	Canada	3	26	Algeria	12
	Iceland	3		Paraguay	12
	Libya	3	28	Argentina	13
	Suriname	3		New Zealand	13
10	Gabon	4		Norway	13
11	Central African Rep	5	31	Finland	15
	Chad	5		Somalia	15
13	Kazakhstan	6	33	Peru	18
14	Bolivia	7		Uruguay	18
	Niger	7	35	Brazil	19
16	Congo	8		Chile	19
	Saudi Arabia	8		Zaire	19
	Turkmenistan	8	38	Bahamas	20
19	Angola	9		Sweden	20
	Mali	9	40	Mozambique	22

Note: Estimates of population density refer to the total land area of a country. In countries such as Japan and Canada, where much of the land area is virtually uninhabitable, the effective population densities of the habitable areas are much greater than the figures suggest.

Biggest cities
Population millions, latest year

1	Seoul	10.80
2	Mumbai(Bombay)	9.93
3	Sao Paulo	9.84
	Rio de Janeiro	9.84
5	Shanghai	8.76
6	Moscow	8.75
7	Mexico	8.24
8	Jakarta	8.22
9	Tokyo	7.83
10	Istanbul	7.33
11	New York	7.31
12	Delhi	7.21
13	London	6.97
	Cairo	6.80
15	Beijing	6.56
16	Tehran	6.48
17	Lima[a]	6.41
18	Bangkok	5.88
19	Bogota[a]	5.24
20	Karachi[a]	5.18
21	Santiago	5.08
22	Tianjin	4.79
23	St. Petersburg	4.44
24	Calcutta	4.40
25	Ho Chi Minh City	3.92
26	Toronto	3.89
27	Shenyang	3.86
28	Pusan	3.85
29	Madras	3.84
	Baghdad	3.84

Quality of life index[b]
New York=100, November 1996

1	Vancouver	119.37
2	Toronto	118.62
3	Zurich	118.15
4	Geneva	118.10
5	Sydney	118.07
6	Melbourne	117.80
7	Auckland	117.75
8	Helsinki	117.57
9	Perth	117.07
10	Vienna	117.00
11	Copenhagen	116.94
12	Amsterdam	116.88
13	Brussels	116.61
14	Bern	116.17
15	Montreal	115.98
16	Oslo	115.59
17	Stockholm	115.58
18	Dusseldorf	115.33
19	Brisbane	115.29
20	Hamburg	115.12
21	Frankfurt	115.11
22	Munich	115.10
23	Singapore	115.06
24	Atlanta	114.74
25	San Francisco	114.54
26	Calgary	114.19
27	Luxembourg	114.18
28	Washington DC	113.90
29	Honolulu	113.77
30	Paris	113.75

Highest urban pop.
% pop. living in urban areas, latest year

1	Bermuda	100
	Singapore	100
3	Guadeloupe	99
	Macau	99
5	Kuwait	97
6	Hong Kong	95
7	Martinique	93
8	Venezuela	93
9	Iceland	91
10	Qatar	91

Lowest urban pop.
% pop. living in urban areas, latest year

1	Bhutan	6
	Rwanda	6
3	Burundi	8
4	Ethiopia	13
	Oman	13
	Uganda	13
7	Malawi	14
	Nepal	14
9	Papua New Guinea	16
10	Niger	17

a Urban agglomeration.
b Based on 42 factors as diverse as personal security and political stability.
Note: Estimates of cities' populations vary according to where geographical boundaries are defined. As far as possible the data refer to the city proper; urban agglomeration includes adjacent suburbs, eg, the population of the extended agglomeration of Paris (which includes 309 communes) is 10.9m; the population of Paris excluding these communes is 2.17m.

Population: *age and sex*

Youngest populations
% aged under 15, 1995

1	West Bank and Gaza	51.7		Togo	45.9
2	Uganda	48.6	22	Congo	45.7
3	Niger	48.4	23	Nigeria	45.5
	Benin	48.4	24	Libya	45.3
5	Zambia	48.2	25	Mozambique	44.9
6	Angola	47.7	26	Côte d'Ivoire	44.8
7	Somalia	47.5		Ghana	44.8
	Yemen	47.5		Laos	44.8
9	Burkina Faso	47.4		Syria	44.8
	Mali	47.4	30	Senegal	44.5
11	Oman	47.2	31	Iran	44.4
	Zaire	47.2	32	Guatemala	44.3
13	Guinea	47.1		Zimbabwe	44.3
14	Madagascar	46.9	34	Cameroon	44.2
	Malawi	46.9	35	Sierra Leone	44.1
16	Rwanda	46.7	36	Eritrea	44.0
17	Burundi	46.6	37	Honduras	43.8
18	Ethiopia	46.2	38	Chad	43.6
19	Kenya	46.0		Nicaragua	43.6
20	Tanzania	45.9	40	Botswana	43.4

Oldest populations
% aged over 65, 1995

1	Sweden	17.3	22	Estonia	12.9
2	Italy	16.1	23	Croatia	12.8
3	Greece	15.9	24	Czech Republic	12.6
	Norway	15.9		United States	12.6
5	Belgium	15.8	26	Belarus	12.5
	United Kingdom	15.8		Slovenia	12.5
7	France	15.2	28	Uruguay	12.3
	Germany	15.2	29	Lithuania	12.2
9	Denmark	15.1	30	Canada	12.0
10	Spain	15.0		Russia	12.0
11	Portugal	14.8	32	Barbados	11.9
12	Austria	14.7	33	Romania	11.8
13	Bulgaria	14.5	34	Australia	11.7
14	Switzerland	14.3	35	Georgia	11.4
15	Japan	14.2		New Zealand	11.4
16	Finland	14.1		Serbia, Montenegro	11.4
17	Hungary	14.0	38	Ireland	11.3
	Ukraine	14.0	39	Iceland	11.1
19	Luxembourg	13.8	40	Malta	11.0
20	Latvia	13.3		Poland	11.0
21	Netherlands	13.2			

Most male populations
Number of men per 100 women[a], 1995

1	Qatar	197.7	22	Iraq	103.6
2	UAE	179.0	23	Dominican Republic	103.4
3	Bahrain	134.7		Iran	103.4
4	Saudi Arabia	126.8	25	Fiji	103.2
5	Oman	114.4	26	Egypt	103.1
6	Trinidad & Tobago	112.2	27	Tunisia	102.6
7	Brunei	110.8	28	Algeria	102.5
8	Libya	108.7	29	Turkey	102.4
9	Pakistan	107.2	30	Costa Rica	102.3
10	Hong Kong	107.1		Panama	102.3
11	India	106.8		Syria	102.3
12	Kuwait	106.6	33	Nepal	102.2
	Papua New Guinea	106.6	34	Guatemala	102.0
14	China	106.3	35	Malaysia	101.8
15	Taiwan	106.0	36	Honduras	101.6
16	Bangladesh	105.5		Liberia	101.6
17	Afghanistan	105.4		Macedonia, FYR	101.6
18	West Bank and Gaza	105.2		Paraguay	101.6
19	Jordan	105.0	40	Singapore	101.5
20	Albania	104.9		South Korea	101.5
21	Côte d'Ivoire	104.3		Venezuela	101.5

Most female populations
Number of men per 100 women, 1995

1	Latvia	85.1		Kazakhstan	94.6
2	Ukraine	86.7	23	Finland	94.9
3	Russia	88.2		Poland	94.9
4	Belarus	88.7	25	Burundi	95.0
5	Estonia	88.8		France	95.0
6	Lithuania	89.9		Uruguay	95.0
7	Georgia	91.2	28	Lebanon	95.1
8	Moldova	91.5	29	Germany	95.2
9	Hungary	91.8		Slovakia	95.2
10	Swaziland	92.0	31	Czech Republic	95.3
11	Netherlands Antilles	92.4	32	Congo	95.4
12	Portugal	92.9		Macau	95.4
13	Cambodia	93.0	34	Guadeloupe	95.7
14	Barbados	93.1	35	Réunion	95.8
15	Central African Rep	93.7	36	Austria	95.9
	Croatia	93.7		Botswana	95.9
	Puerto Rico	93.7		Bulgaria	95.9
18	Slovenia	94.0	39	Azerbaijan	96.0
19	Martinique	94.0		Belgium	96.0
20	Armenia	94.5		United Kingdom	96.0
21	Italy	94.6			

a Large numbers of immigrant workers, mostly men, result in the high male ratios of several Middle East countries.

Population: *matters of breeding*

Highest crude birth rates
No. of live births per 1,000 population, 1995–2000

1	Afghanistan	53.4	Mozambique	42.5
2	Uganda	51.1	22 Zambia	42.4
3	Niger	50.2	23 Nigeria	42.3
4	Somalia	50.0	24 Benin	42.0
5	Ethiopia	48.2	25 Togo	41.9
	Guinea	48.2	26 Chad	41.6
7	Angola	47.7	27 Bhutan	41.3
	Malawi	47.7	28 Tanzania	41.2
	Yemen	47.7	29 Madagascar	41.1
10	Liberia	47.5	Senegal	41.1
11	Mali	47.4	31 Guinea-Bissau	40.3
12	West Bank and Gaza	46.7	32 Libya	40.0
13	Sierra Leone	46.5	33 Gambia, The	39.9
14	Burkina Faso	45.9	34 Eritrea	39.8
15	Zaire	44.9	35 Cameroon	39.3
16	Laos	44.2	36 Mauritania	38.3
17	Oman	44.1	37 Ghana	38.2
18	Rwanda	42.8	38 Central African Rep	37.6
19	Burundi	42.5	Gabon	37.6
	Congo	42.5	40 Jordan	37.5

Highest fertility rates
Average no. of children per woman, 1995–2000

1	West Bank and Gaza	8.00	21 Rwanda	6.00
2	Yemen	7.60	22 Nigeria	5.97
3	Oman	7.20	23 Libya	5.92
4	Niger	7.10	24 Saudi Arabia	5.90
	Uganda	7.10	25 Bhutan	5.89
6	Ethiopia	7.00	26 Congo	5.87
	Somalia	7.00	27 Benin	5.83
8	Afghanistan	6.90	28 Madagascar	5.65
9	Angola	6.69	29 Senegal	5.62
	Laos	6.69	30 Chad	5.51
	Malawi	6.69	31 Zambia	5.49
12	Guinea	6.61	32 Tanzania	5.48
13	Mali	6.60	33 Guinea-Bissau	5.42
14	Burkina Faso	6.57	34 Gabon	5.40
15	Liberia	6.33	35 Eritrea	5.34
16	Burundi	6.28	36 Cameroon	5.30
17	Zaire	6.24	37 Ghana	5.28
18	Togo	6.08	38 Iraq	5.25
19	Mozambique	6.06	39 Gambia, The	5.20
	Sierra Leone	6.06	40 Jordan	5.13

Lowest crude birth rates

Number of live births per 1,000 population, 1995–2000

1	Estonia	9.0	22	Belgium	11.2
2	Italy	9.1		Portugal	11.2
3	Germany	9.3	24	France	11.6
4	Slovenia	9.5	25	Slovakia	11.7
5	Russia	9.6	26	Canada	11.9
6	Spain	9.7		Netherlands	11.9
	Ukraine	9.7		Poland	11.9
8	Latvia	9.8		Sweden	11.9
9	Belarus	10.0		United Kingdom	11.9
	Greece	10.0	31	Finland	12.0
11	Hungary	10.2	32	Serbia, Montenegro	12.6
12	Austria	10.3	33	Luxembourg	12.7
	Bulgaria	10.3	34	Denmark	13.0
	Japan	10.3		Ireland	13.0
15	Hong Kong	10.6	36	Cuba	13.1
16	Czech Republic	10.7	37	Armenia	13.3
17	Bosnia	10.8	38	Norway	13.4
	Croatia	10.8	39	Moldova	13.6
	Lithuania	10.8	40	Georgia	13.8
20	Switzerland	10.9		United States	13.8
21	Romania	11.0			

Lowest fertility rates

Average number of children per woman, 1995–2000

1	Italy	1.19		Slovakia	1.50
2	Spain	1.22	23	Cuba	1.55
3	Estonia	1.30		Netherlands	1.55
	Germany	1.30	25	Croatia	1.60
	Slovenia	1.30		Macau	1.60
6	Hong Kong	1.32	27	Canada	1.61
7	Russia	1.35	28	Belgium	1.62
8	Greece	1.38	29	France	1.63
	Ukraine	1.38	30	Poland	1.65
10	Belarus	1.40		South Korea	1.65
	Bosnia	1.40	32	Armenia	1.70
	Czech Republic	1.40	33	United Kingdom	1.72
	Hungary	1.40	34	Barbados	1.73
	Latvia	1.40	35	Thailand	1.74
	Romania	1.40	36	Luxembourg	1.76
16	Austria	1.42	37	Singapore	1.79
17	Bulgaria	1.45	38	China	1.80
18	Switzerland	1.46		Ireland	1.80
19	Japan	1.48		Moldova	1.80
	Portugal	1.48		Serbia, Montenegro	1.80
21	Lithuania	1.50		Sweden	1.80

Notes: The crude birth rate is the number of live births in one year per 1,000 population. In addition to the fertility rate (see below) it depends on the population's age structure and will tend to be higher if there is a large proportion of women of childbearing age.

The fertility rate is the average number of children born to a woman who completes her childbearing years.

The world economy

Biggest economies

GDP, $bn

1	United States	7,100	49	Egypt	46
2	Japan	4,964	50	Algeria	45
3	Germany	2,252	51	United Arab Emirates	43
4	France	1,451	52	Hungary	42
5	United Kingdom	1,095	53	Czech Republic	40
6	Italy	1,088		Libya	40
7	China	745	55	Romania	33
8	Brazil	580	56	Morocco	30
9	Canada	574	57	Bangladesh	29
10	Spain	532		Kuwait	29
11	South Korea	435	59	Nigeria	28
12	Netherlands	371		Puerto Rico	28
13	Australia	338	61	Kazakhstan	22
14	Russia	332		North Korea	22
15	India	320		Uzbekistan	22
16	Mexico	305	64	Belarus	21
17	Switzerland	286	65	Vietnam	18
18	Argentina	278	66	Iraq	17
19	Taiwan	260		Luxembourg	17
20	Belgium	251	68	Croatia	16
21	Austria	217		Ecuador	16
22	Sweden	210		Slovakia	16
23	Indonesia	190		Slovenia	16
24	Turkey	169		Syria	16
25	Thailand	160		Tunisia	16
26	Denmark	156		Uruguay	16
27	Hong Kong	142		Serbia, Montenegro	16
28	Norway	136	76	Liberia[a]	15
29	Saudi Arabia	134	77	Cuba	14
30	South Africa	131		Guatemala	14
31	Myanmar	108	79	Sri Lanka	13
32	Poland	108	80	Bulgaria	11
33	Finland	105		Dominican Republic	11
34	Portugal	97		Lebanon	11
35	Israel	88		Oman	11
36	Greece	86	84	Cameroon	9
37	Ukraine	84		Costa Rica	9
38	Singapore	80		Côte d'Ivoire	9
39	Malaysia	78		Cyprus	9
40	Philippines	72		El Salvador	9
41	Colombia	70		Sudan[a]	9
42	Venezuela	65	90	Kenya	8
43	Iran	61		Paraguay	8
44	Pakistan	60	92	Ghana	7
45	Chile	59		Iceland	7
46	Peru	55		Lithuania	7
47	Ireland	53		Panama	7
48	New Zealand	52		Qatar	7

a Estimate.

Regional GDP

$bn, 1995		*growth 1985–95*	
World	27,657	World	3.2
Industrial countries	21,605	Industrial countries	2.5
G7	18,524	G7	2.5
EU12	7,980	EU12	2.4
EU15	7,449		
Asia[a]	2,424	Asia[a]	7.8
Latin America	997	Latin America	2.6
Eastern Europe	756	Eastern Europe	-3.8
Middle East and Europe[b]	699	Middle East and Europe[b]	3.4
Africa	389	Africa	2.3

Regional GDP per head

$, 1995		*growth 1985–95*	
World	4,855		
Industrial countries	24,351	Industrial countries	1.8
G7	27,379	G7	1.8
EU12	21,302	EU12	2.0
EU15	21,475		
Asia[a]	808	Asia[a]	6.0
Latin America	3,162	Latin America	0.6
Eastern Europe	2,022	Eastern Europe	-4.5
Middle East and Europe[b]	2,421	Middle East and Europe[b]	0.3
Africa	612	Africa	-0.5

Regional trade: value

Exports, $bn, 1995		*Imports, $bn 1995*	
World	4,950		
Industrial countries	3,359	Industrial countries	3,261
G7	2,462	G7	2,377
EU12	1,811	EU12	1,701
EU15	2,003	EU15	1,869
Asia[a]	909	Asia[a]	938
Latin America	195	Latin America	198
Middle East and Europe[b]	180	Middle East and Europe[b]	179
Africa	95	Africa	97

Regional trade: volume growth, %

Exports, $bn, 1985–95		*Imports, 1985–95*	
World	6.4		
Industrial countries	5.5	Industrial countries	6.1
G7	5.9	G7	6.1
EU12	5.3	EU12	5.6
Asia[a]	12.9	Asia[a]	12.1
Latin America	5.8	Latin America	8.0
Middle East and Europe[b]	6.1	Middle East and Europe[b]	1.3
Africa	2.9	Africa	1.0

a Excludes Japan.
b Includes Turkey.

Living standards

Highest GDP per head
$

1	Luxembourg	41,464		36	Slovenia	8,482
2	Switzerland	39,913		37	Greece	8,216
3	Japan	39,687		38	Bahrain	8,124
4	Bermuda	32,168		39	Macao[a]	8,037
5	Norway	31,412		40	Argentina	8,008
6	Denmark	29,873		41	Puerto Rico	7,665
7	Germany	27,604		42	Libya	7,425
8	Austria	26,917		43	Saudi Arabia	7,315
9	United States	26,580		44	Liberia[b]	6,995
10	France	24,973		45	Netherlands Antilles[b]	6,807
11	Iceland	24,855		46	Barbados	6,686
12	Belgium	24,757		47	Uruguay	5,166
13	Singapore	23,995		48	Guadeloupe[b]	4,884
14	Netherlands	23,966		49	Oman	4,793
15	Sweden	23,864		50	Hungary	4,169
16	Hong Kong	23,245		51	Chile	4,163
17	Finland	20,594		52	Czech Republic	3,897
18	Canada	19,512		53	Malaysia	3,889
19	United Arab Emirates	19,369		54	Trinidad & Tobago	3,769
20	Italy	19,021		55	Brazil	3,646
21	Australia	18,914		56	Lebanon	3,547
22	United Kingdom	18,849		57	Gabon	3,493
23	Kuwait	17,115		58	Croatia	3,442
24	Israel	15,905		59	Mauritius	3,415
25	Ireland	14,880		60	Mexico	3,342
26	New Zealand	14,506		61	South Africa	3,157
27	Qatar	13,591		62	Botswana	3,021
28	Brunei	13,567		63	Venezuela	2,993
29	Spain	13,434		64	Slovakia	2,969
30	Taiwan	12,214		65	Estonia	2,858
31	Bahamas	11,817		66	Poland	2,797
32	Cyprus	11,517		67	Turkey	2,785
33	Portugal	9,851		68	Panama	2,750
34	South Korea	9,689		69	Thailand	2,741
35	Malta	9,163		70	Costa Rica	2,595

Lowest GDP per head
$

1	Mozambique	78		11	Madagascar	214
2	Ethiopia	101			Niger	214
3	Zaire	117		13	Rwanda	218
4	Tanzania	125		14	Mali	223
5	Burundi	162		15	Burkina Faso	231
6	Bhutan	167		16	Uganda	237
7	Malawi	168		17	Vietnam	239
8	Chad	181		18	Bangladesh	242
9	Sierra Leone	182		19	Guinea-Bissau	248
10	Nepal	205		20	Haiti	249

a 1992.
b Estimate.

Highest purchasing power[a]
GDP per head in PPP (USA = 100)

1	Luxembourg	140.6	36	Chile	35.3
2	United States	100.0	37	Malaysia	33.4
3	Switzerland	95.8	38	Trinidad & Tobago	31.9
4	Kuwait	88.2	39	Argentina	30.8
5	Hong Kong	85.1	40	Oman	30.2
6	Singapore	84.4	41	Venezuela	29.3
7	Japan	81.9	42	Thailand	27.9
8	Norway	81.3	43	Uruguay	24.6
9	Belgium	80.3	44	Hungary	23.8
10	Austria	78.8	45	Mexico	23.7
11	Denmark	78.7	46	Colombia	22.7
12	Canada	78.3	47	Panama	22.2
13	France	77.9	48	Costa Rica	21.7
14	Iceland	75.8	49	Fiji	21.4
15	Germany	74.4	50	Botswana	20.7
16	Netherlands	73.9		Turkey	20.7
17	Italy	73.6	52	Iran	20.3
18	United Kingdom	71.4	53	Brazil	20.0
19	Australia	70.2		Poland	20.0
20	Sweden	68.7	55	Syria	19.7
21	Finland	65.8	56	Algeria	19.6
22	Qatar	65.6	57	South Africa	18.6
23	Israel	61.1	58	Tunisia	18.5
24	United Arab Emirates	61.0	59	Bulgaria	16.6
25	New Zealand	60.6		Russia	16.6
26	Ireland	58.1	61	Romania	16.2
27	Bahamas	54.5	62	Belarus	15.6
28	Spain	53.8		Ecuador	15.6
29	Bahrain	49.7		Estonia	15.6
30	Mauritius	49.0	65	Namibia	15.4
31	Portugal	47.0	66	Lithuania	15.3
32	Greece	43.4	67	Jordan	15.0
33	South Korea	42.4	68	Dominican Republic	14.3
34	Barbados	39.4	69	Egypt	14.2
35	Czech Republic	36.2	70	Indonesia	14.1

Lowest purchasing power[a]
GDP per head in PPP (USA = 100)

1	Ethiopia	1.7		Niger	2.8
2	Zaire	1.8	12	Burkina Faso	2.9
3	Mali	2.0		Guinea-Bissau	2.9
	Rwanda	2.0	14	Mozambique	3.0
5	Sierra Leone	2.1	15	Gambia, The	3.4
6	Burundi	2.3		Haiti	3.4
7	Madagascar	2.4		Tajikistan	3.4
	Tanzania	2.4		Zambia	3.4
9	Chad	2.6	19	Central African Rep	4.0
10	Malawi	2.8	20	Togo	4.2

a See glossary for explanation of purchasing power parity.

The quality of life

Human development index

1	Canada	95.1		United Arab Emirates	86.4
2	United States	94.0	42	Panama	85.9
3	Japan	93.8		Venezuela	85.9
	Netherlands	93.8	44	Hungary	85.5
5	Norway	93.7	45	Fiji	85.3
6	Finland	93.5	46	Mexico	84.5
	France	93.5	47	Colombia	84.0
8	Iceland	93.4	48	Qatar	83.9
9	Spain	93.3	49	Kuwait	83.6
	Sweden	93.3	50	Thailand	83.2
11	Australia	92.9	51	Malaysia	82.6
	Belgium	92.9	52	Mauritius	82.5
13	Austria	92.8	53	Latvia	82.0
14	New Zealand	92.7	54	Poland	81.9
15	Switzerland	92.6	55	Russia	80.4
16	Denmark	92.4	56	Brazil	79.6
	United Kingdom	92.4	57	Libya	79.2
18	Germany	92.0	58	Belarus	78.7
19	Ireland	91.9	59	Bulgaria	77.3
20	Italy	91.4	60	Saudi Arabia	77.1
21	Cyprus	90.9	61	Ecuador	76.4
	Greece	90.9	62	Belize	75.4
	Hong Kong	90.9		Iran	75.4
24	Israel	90.8	64	Estonia	74.9
25	Barbados	90.6	65	Algeria	74.6
26	Bahamas	89.5	66	Botswana	74.1
	Luxembourg	89.5		Jordan	74.1
28	Malta	88.6	68	Kazakhstan	74.0
	South Korea	88.6	69	Romania	73.8
30	Argentina	88.5	70	Suriname	73.7
31	Costa Rica	88.4	71	Tunisia	72.7
32	Uruguay	88.3	72	Cuba	72.6
33	Chile	88.2	73	Lithuania	71.9
34	Singapore	88.1		Ukraine	71.9
35	Portugal	87.8	75	Oman	71.6
36	Brunei	87.2	76	North Korea	71.4
	Czech Republic	87.2	77	Turkey	71.1
	Trinidad & Tobago	87.2	78	Paraguay	70.4
39	Bahrain	86.6	79	Jamaica	70.2
40	Slovakia	86.4	80	Dominican Republic	70.1

Notes: GDP or GDP per head is often taken as a measure of how developed a country is but its usefuless is limited as it refers only to economic welfare. In 1990 the UN Development Programme published its first estimate of a Human Development Index, which combined statistics on two other indicators – adult literacy and life expectancy – with income levels to give a better, though still far from perfect, indicator of human development. In 1991 average years of schooling was combined with adult literacy to give a knowledge variable. The index is shown here scaled from 0 to 100; countries scoring over 80 are considered to have high human development, those scoring from 50 to 79 have medium human development and those under 50 have low human development.

Economic freedom index

1	Hong Kong	1.25	43	Belize	2.70
2	Singapore	1.30		Jordan	2.70
3	Bahrain	1.60		Uruguay	2.70
4	New Zealand	1.75	46	Morocco	2.75
5	Switzerland	1.90		Oman	2.75
	United States	1.90		Paraguay	2.75
7	Taiwan	1.95		Tunisia	2.75
	United Kingdom	1.95	50	Barbados	2.80
9	Bahamas	2.00		Costa Rica	2.80
	Netherlands	2.00		Guatemala	2.80
11	Czech Republic	2.05		Israel	2.80
	Denmark	2.05		Philippines	2.80
	Japan	2.05		Saudi Arabia	2.80
	Luxembourg	2.05		Swaziland	2.80
15	Belgium	2.10		Turkey	2.80
	Canada	2.10	58	Bolivia	2.85
	United Arab Emirates	2.10		Botswana	2.85
18	Australia	2.15		Greece	2.85
	Austria	2.15		Indonesia	2.85
20	Germany	2.20		Zambia	2.85
	Ireland	2.20	63	Hungary	2.90
22	Chile	2.25		Peru	2.90
23	Finland	2.30	65	Uganda	2.90
	Thailand	2.30	66	Benin	2.95
25	Estonia	2.35		Gabon	2.95
26	Kuwait	2.40		Latvia	2.95
27	Norway	2.45		Lebanon	2.95
	South Korea	2.45		Malta	2.95
	Sri Lanka	2.45		Namibia	2.95
	Sweden	2.45	74	Djibouti	3.00
31	France	2.50		South Africa	3.00
	Iceland	2.50	76	Ecuador	3.05
	Panama	2.50		Kenya	3.05
34	El Salvador	2.55		Slovakia	3.05
	Trinidad & Tobago	2.55	79	Colombia	3.10
36	Cyprus	2.60		Ghana	3.10
	Italy	2.60		Lithuania	3.10
	Jamaica	2.60		Mali	3.10
	Malaysia	2.60		Pakistan	3.10
	Portugal	2.60		Papua New Guinea	3.10
	Spain	2.60		Slovenia	3.10
42	Argentina	2.65			

Notes: The index of economic freedom, published by the Heritage Foundation, ranks countries on the basis of ten indicators of how government intervention can restrict the economic relations between individuals. The economic indicators are trade policy, taxation, monetary policy, the banking system, foreign-investment rules, property rights, the amount of economic output consumed by the government, regulation policy, the size of the black market and the extent of wage and price controls. A country can score between 1 and 5 in each category, 1 being the most free and 5 being the least free.

Economic growth

Fastest economic growth, 1985–95
Average annual % increase in real GDP

1	China	9.6	21	Macau[b]	5.5
2	Thailand	9.3	22	Swaziland[c]	5.4
3	South Korea	8.8	23	India	5.3
4	Singapore	8.2		Laos	5.3
5	Malaysia	7.8	25	Israel	5.0
6	Lesotho	7.2		Pakistan	5.0
7	Botswana	7.1	27	Egypt	4.8
8	Chile	7.0		Ireland	4.8
9	Bhutan	6.6	29	Nepal	4.7
	Taiwan	6.6	30	Costa Rica	4.6
11	Hong Kong	6.5		Gambia, The	4.6
	Mauritius	6.5		Ghana	4.6
13	Indonesia	6.4	33	Colombia	4.5
	Vietnam	6.4	34	Sri Lanka	4.4
15	Uganda	6.3		Turkey	4.4
16	Mozambique	6.1	36	Oman	4.3
17	Luxembourg	5.9	37	Tanzania	4.2
18	Malta	5.7	38	Bangladesh	4.1
19	Cambodia[a]	5.6		Nigeria	4.1
	Cyprus	5.6		Papua New Guinea	4.1

Slowest economic growth, 1985–95
Average annual % increase in real GDP

1	Georgia[d]	-18.1	21	Lebanon[c]	-3.2
2	Macedonia[b]	-16.2	22	Libya	-2.9
3	Russia[e]	-14.1		Sierra Leone	-2.9
4	Lithuania[d]	-13.0	24	Slovakia[d]	-2.2
5	Tajikistan[d]	-12.7		Uzbekistan[d]	-2.2
6	Azerbaijan[d]	-12.4	26	Czech Republic[d]	-2.1
7	Ukraine[d]	-11.9		Haiti	-2.1
8	Moldova[d]	-11.8	28	Romania	-2.0
9	Armenia[d]	-11.5	29	Cameroon[c]	-1.8
10	Kazakhstan[d]	-10.9		North Korea	-1.8
11	Iraq	-8.2	31	Bulgaria	-1.5
12	Turkmenistan[d]	-8.1	32	Slovenia[f]	-1.4
13	Latvia[d]	-7.7	33	Kuwait	-1.3
14	Kirgizstan[d]	-7.5	34	Albania	-1.1
15	Estonia[d]	-6.6		Somalia[g]	-1.1
16	Belarus[d]	-5.8	36	Nicaragua	-0.9
17	Cuba[d]	-5.5	37	Afghanistan	-0.8
18	Croatia[d]	-5.0	38	Hungary	-0.7
19	Zaire	-4.3	39	Trinidad & Tobago	-0.3
20	Rwanda[h]	-3.8	40	Congo	-0.2

a	1988–95	e	1991–95
b	1990–95	f	1988–95
c	1987–95	g	1986–93
d	1989–95	h	Estimate.

Fastest economic growth, 1975–84
Average annual % increase in real GDP

1	Botswana	12.4		Malta	7.2
2	Oman	10.3	12	Egypt	7.1
3	Jordan	9.0	13	Malaysia	7.0
4	Hong Kong	8.9		Thailand	7.0
5	Taiwan	8.6	15	Cameroon	6.8
6	Singapore	8.0	16	Paraguay	6.6
	South Korea	8.0	17	Mongolia	6.5
8	Congo	7.6	18	Bahrain	6.2
9	Niger	7.4	19	Vietnam	6.1
10	China	7.2	20	Bhutan	6.0

Slowest economic growth, 1975–84
Average annual % increase in real GDP

1	Kuwait	-1.7	11	Madagascar	-0.2
2	Ghana	-1.5	12	El Salvador	-0.1
3	Nicaragua	-1.4		Zambia	-0.1
4	Nigeria	-1.4	14	Switzerland	0.0
5	Chad	-1.3	15	Argentina	0.1
6	Gabon	-0.9		Mozambique	0.1
7	Zaire	-0.8	17	Uganda	0.2
8	Afghanistan	-0.6	18	Papua New Guinea	0.6
9	Lesotho	-0.5	19	Jamaica	0.7
10	Liberia	-0.4	20	Sierra Leone	0.8

Highest industrial growth, 1980–94
Average annual % increase in real terms

1	China	13.6	6	Lesotho	8.6
2	South Korea	10.7	7	Botswana	8.1
3	Thailand	10.2		Malaysia	8.1
4	Oman	8.9		Mauritius	8.1
	Papua New Guinea	8.9	10	Indonesia	7.9

Highest services growth, 1980–94
Average annual % increase in real terms

1	China	15.9		Singapore	10.3
2	Botswana	12.8	7	Thailand	9.9
3	Oman	11.7	8	Indonesia	9.8
4	South Korea	10.6	9	Chile	9.3
5	Mozambique	10.3	10	Ghana	9.2

Highest agricultural growth, 1980–94
Average annual % increase in real terms

1	Jordan	12.2	6	Tanzania	5.2
2	United Arab Emirates	9.5	7	Chile	5.1
3	Guinea-Bissau	6.0	8	Benin	5.0
4	Oman	5.9	9	Iran	4.9
5	China	5.3	10	Togo	4.8

Trading places

Biggest traders
% of total world exports (visible & invisible)

1	United States	13.47	21	Malaysia	1.15
2	Germany	9.82	22	Australia	1.03
3	Japan	9.55	23	Thailand	1.03
4	France	6.92	24	Hong Kong	0.93
5	United Kingdom	6.37	25	Norway	0.80
6	Italy	4.59	26	Brazil	0.78
7	Belgium/Luxembourg	4.24	27	Saudi Arabia	0.77
8	Netherlands	3.49	28	Ireland	0.74
9	Canada	3.11	29	Indonesia	0.73
10	Switzerland	2.15	30	Finland	0.71
11	China	2.12	31	India	0.56
12	South Korea	2.11	32	Turkey	0.53
13	Spain	2.03	33	Portugal	0.50
14	Taiwan	1.87	34	South Africa	0.47
15	Singapore	1.53	35	Poland	0.46
16	Sweden	1.52	36	Philippines	0.46
17	Austria	1.48	37	Czech Republic	0.41
18	Russia	1.36	38	Israel	0.40
19	Mexico	1.30	39	Argentina	0.39
20	Denmark	1.29	40	Venezuela	0.31

Most trade dependent
Trade as % of GDP[a]

1	Malaysia	96.9
2	Sudan	91.1
3	Singapore	91.0
4	Bahrain	80.7
5	Macedonia FYR	72.9
6	Swaziland	72.4
7	Ireland	69.7
8	Malta	68.8
9	Taiwan	67.8
10	Netherlands Antilles	63.3
11	Belgium/Luxembourg	61.2
12	Czech Republic	58.3
13	Macau	58.1
14	Jamaica	57.8
15	Mongolia	57.2
16	Slovenia	54.0
17	Slovakia	53.9
18	Angola[b]	53.4
19	United Arab Emirates	52.0
20	Estonia	51.9

Least trade dependent
Trade as % of GDP[a]

1	Myanmar	1.0
2	Liberia[b]	1.5
3	Somalia[c]	1.6
4	Iraq	1.9
5	North Korea	4.6
6	Niger[b]	5.6
7	Mali[b]	6.6
8	Argentina	7.1
9	Japan	7.3
10	Zaire	7.9
11	Brazil	8.3
12	United States	9.3
13	Rwanda	9.8
14	India	10.2
15	Sierra Leone	10.5
16	Cuba	11.6
	Malawi[b]	11.6
18	Peru	12.1
19	Paraguay[b]	12.3
20	Ethiopia	13.7

Notes: The figures are drawn from balance of payment statistics and, therefore, have differing technical definitions from trade statistics taken from customs or similar sources. The invisible trade figures do not show some countries, notably ex-Soviet republics, due to unavailable data. For Hong Kong and Singapore, domestic exports and retained imports only are used.

Biggest visible traders
% of world visible exports

1	United States	11.95	21	Thailand	1.15
2	Germany	10.83	22	Australia	1.10
3	Japan	8.88	23	Denmark	1.01
4	France	5.59	24	Brazil	0.96
5	United Kingdom	4.97		Saudi Arabia	0.96
6	Italy	4.79	26	Indonesia	0.94
7	Canada	3.93	27	Ireland	0.90
8	Netherlands	3.59	28	Norway	0.86
9	Belgium/Luxembourg	3.27	29	Finland	0.83
10	China	2.65	30	India	0.64
11	South Korea	2.55	31	Hong Kong	0.62
12	Taiwan	2.29	32	South Africa	0.58
13	Switzerland	2.01	33	Portugal	0.50
14	Spain	1.92	34	Poland	0.49
15	Russia	1.69	35	Turkey	0.45
16	Mexico	1.65	36	United Arab Emirates	0.45
17	Sweden	1.64	37	Czech Republic	0.44
18	Malaysia	1.53	38	Argentina	0.43
19	Austria	1.49	39	Israel	0.39
20	Singapore	1.44		Venezuela	0.39

Biggest invisible traders
% of world invisible exports

1	United States	16.59	22	Russia	0.71
2	Japan	10.93	23	Turkey	0.68
3	France	9.66	24	Norway[b]	0.67
4	United Kingdom	9.25	25	Philippines	0.65
5	Germany	7.77	26	Mexico	0.59
6	Belgium/Luxembourg	6.23	27	Portugal	0.50
7	Italy	4.19	28	Greece	0.46
8	Netherlands	3.29	29	Finland	0.45
9	Switzerland	2.45	30	Egypt	0.43
10	Spain	2.26	31	Ireland	0.42
11	Denmark	1.86	32	Brazil	0.41
12	Singapore	1.71		Israel	0.41
13	Hong Kong	1.58		Poland	0.41
14	Austria	1.46	35	India	0.40
15	Canada	1.45	36	Malaysia[b]	0.38
16	Sweden	1.27	37	Saudi Arabia	0.36
17	South Korea	1.21	38	Czech Republic	0.34
18	China	1.03	39	Argentina	0.30
19	Taiwan	1.01		Indonesia	0.30
20	Australia	0.90	41	Kuwait	0.28
21	Thailand	0.79	42	South Africa	0.24

a   Average of imports and exports of goods as % of GDP.
b   1994
c   1993

Current account

Largest surpluses
$bn

1	Japan	111.25		21	Spain	1.28
2	Italy	25.71		22	Papua New Guinea	0.67
3	Switzerland	21.62		23	Bahrain	0.56
4	Netherlands	17.85		24	Syria	0.44
5	France	16.44		25	Slovakia	0.39
6	Singapore	15.09		26	Armenia	0.35
7	Belgium/Luxembourg	14.25		27	Botswana	0.34
8	Russia	10.64		28	Gabon[a]	0.32
9	Finland	5.33		29	Trinidad & Tobago	0.29
10	Taiwan	5.01		30	Bulgaria	0.28
11	Sweden	4.63		31	Yemen	0.18
12	Kuwait	4.20		32	Chile	0.16
13	Norway[a]	3.65		33	Lesotho[a]	0.11
14	Iran	3.48		34	Netherlands Antilles	0.09
15	Algeria[b]	2.37		35	Barbados[d]	0.06
16	Venezuela	2.26			Suriname	0.06
17	Libya[c]	2.20			Turkmenistan	0.06
18	China	1.62		38	Iceland	0.05
19	Denmark	1.54			Namibia	0.05
20	Ireland	1.38		40	Mongolia	0.04

Largest deficits
$bn

1	United States	-148.23		26	India[d]	-1.88
2	Germany	-20.82		27	Pakistan[a]	-1.80
3	Australia	-19.18		28	Croatia	-1.71
4	Brazil	-18.14		29	Morocco	-1.52
5	Thailand	-13.55		30	Czech Republic	-1.37
6	Canada	-8.69		31	Romania	-1.34
7	South Korea	-8.25		32	Ukraine	-1.15
8	Indonesia	-7.02		33	Oman	-0.98
9	United Kingdom	-6.23		34	Bangladesh	-0.82
10	Saudi Arabia	-5.32			Ecuador	-0.82
11	Israel	-5.28		36	Paraguay[a]	-0.75
12	Austria	-5.11		37	Tunisia	-0.74
13	Hong Kong	-4.90		38	Nicaragua	-0.71
14	Peru	-4.25		39	Kazakhstan	-0.70
	Poland	-4.25		40	Mexico	-0.65
16	Malaysia[a]	-4.15		41	Zaire[c]	-0.64
17	Colombia	-4.12		42	Tanzania	-0.63
18	New Zealand	-3.78		43	Lithuania	-0.61
19	South Africa	-3.50		44	Cameroon[d]	-0.57
20	Greece	-2.86			Congo	-0.57
21	Hungary	-2.54			Guatemala	-0.57
22	Argentina	-2.39		47	Sri Lanka	-0.55
23	Turkey	-2.34		48	Sudan	-0.50
24	Nigeria[a]	-2.13		49	Zimbabwe[e]	-0.43
25	Philippines	-1.98		50	Malta	-0.41

Largest surpluses as % of GDP
%

1	Singapore	18.91	21	Barbados[d]	3.95
2	Suriname	16.39	22	Venezuela	3.45
3	Kuwait	14.51	23	Russia	3.21
4	Papua New Guinea	13.55	24	Norway[a]	3.19
5	Armenia	12.83	25	Syria	2.79
6	Bahrain	12.31	26	Ireland	2.61
7	Libya[c]	8.80	27	Bulgaria	2.50
8	Gabon[a]	8.72	28	Slovakia	2.46
9	Botswana	7.81	29	Italy	2.36
10	Lesotho[a]	7.73	30	Japan	2.24
11	Switzerland	7.56	31	Sweden	2.21
12	Netherlands Antilles	6.59	32	Taiwan	1.92
13	Trinidad & Tobago	6.06	33	Benin[a]	1.84
14	Belgium/Luxembourg	5.69	34	Namibia	1.61
15	Iran	5.66	35	Turkmenistan	1.33
16	Mongolia	5.08	36	France	1.13
17	Finland	5.07	37	Denmark	0.99
18	Netherlands	4.81	38	Iceland	0.76
19	Algeria[b]	4.53	39	Burkina Faso[a]	0.50
20	Yemen	4.53	40	Chile	0.27

Largest deficits as % of GDP
%

1	Nicaragua	-42.56	26	Nigeria[a]	-7.09
2	Congo	-31.95	27	Cambodia	-6.84
3	Mozambique[e]	-28.16	28	Jordan[a]	-6.80
4	Tanzania	-16.99	29	Malia	-6.77
5	Malawia	-16.03	30	Mauritania[a]	-6.59
6	Guinea-Bissau	-15.47	31	Jamaica	-6.44
7	Macedonia, FYR	-14.89	32	Bahamas	-6.43
8	Laos	-13.58	33	Niger[a]	-6.18
9	Sierra Leone[a]	-12.75	34	Malaysia[a]	-6.04
10	Malta	-12.07	35	Hungary	-6.02
11	Croatia	-11.04	36	Israel	-6.01
12	Paraguay[a]	-9.85	37	Uganda	-5.91
13	Oman	-9.26	38	Sudan	-5.88
14	Kirgizstan	-9.21	39	Colombia	-5.86
15	Zambia[b]	-9.02	40	Cameroon[d]	-5.85
16	Lithuania	-8.68	41	Australia	-5.68
	Madagascar	-8.68	42	Honduras	-5.64
18	Rwanda[d]	-8.61	43	Guinea	-5.48
19	Thailand	-8.49	44	Kenya	-5.27
20	Azerbaijan	-8.33	45	Georgia	-5.26
21	Nepal	-8.11	46	Morocco	-5.15
22	Zaire[c]	-7.92	47	Ecuador	-5.14
23	Zimbabwe[a]	-7.84	48	Togo[a]	-4.50
24	Peru	-7.72		Tunisia	-4.50
25	New Zealand	-7.31	50	Swaziland	-4.36

a 1994   b 1991   c 1990   d 1993   e 1992

Inflation

Highest inflation, 1995–96

% consumer price inflation

1	Angola[a]	2,553.7		31	Algeria[a]	32.2
2	Turkmenistan	992.0		32	Kirgizstan	30.0
3	Zaire	659.0		33	Iran[a]	28.9
4	Tajikistan	420.0		34	Myanmar[a]	25.2
5	Bulgaria	123.0		35	Lithuania	25.0
6	Venezuela	99.9		36	Ecuador	24.4
7	Malawi[a]	83.3		37	Hungary	23.6
8	Turkey	81.2		38	Moldova	23.5
9	Ukraine	80.0		39	Sierra Leone	23.2
10	Serbia, Montenegro	79.0		40	Estonia	23.1
11	Ghana[a]	74.3		41	Congo[a]	21.4
12	Nigeria[a]	72.8			Zimbabwe	21.4
13	Uzbekistan	60.0		43	Tanzania[a]	21.0
14	Sudan[a]	57.0		44	Colombia	20.8
15	Mozambique[a]	54.4		45	Armenia	20.0
16	Mongolia[a]	53.1			Azerbaijan	20.0
17	Belarus	52.0		47	Laos[a]	19.6
18	Kazakhstan	51.1		48	Burundi[a]	19.3
19	Iraq[a]	50.0		49	Central African Rep[a]	19.2
20	Madagascar[a]	49.1		50	Poland	19.0
21	Yemen[a]	48.0		51	Honduras[a]	18.5
22	Russia	47.7		52	Costa Rica[a]	18.0
23	Guinea-Bissau[a]	45.4		53	Papua New Guinea[a]	17.3
24	Romania	45.0		54	Latvia	17.0
25	Uruguay[a]	42.2		55	Macedonia, FYR[a]	15.9
26	Rwanda[a]	41.0			Sri Lanka	15.9
27	Georgia	40.0		57	Jamaica	15.7
28	Suriname[a]	37.1			Togo[a]	15.7
29	Mexico	34.4		59	Brazil	15.5
30	Zambia[a]	34.1		60	Haiti[a]	15.0

Highest inflation, 1989–96

% average annual consumer price inflation

1	Serbia, Montenegro	1,643,638.0		16	Uzbekistan	214.9
2	Zaire	1,208.0		17	Moldova[c]	207.1
3	Brazil	746.4		18	Russia	191.9
4	Georgia[c]	516.8		19	Kirgizstan[c]	188.9
5	Nicaragua[d]	489.4		20	Croatia[c]	180.4
6	Turkmenistan	456.3		21	Argentina	173.3
7	Tajikistan[c]	424.6		22	Mongolia[e]	147.9
8	Kazakhstan[c]	355.1		23	Slovenia	141.9
9	Armenia	342.3		24	Lithuania	123.2
10	Angola[d]	338.7		25	Zambia[d]	106.3
11	Ukraine	326.6		26	Estonia	95.3
12	Azerbaijan[c]	316.5		27	Poland	88.5
13	Belarus	308.0		28	Sudan[d]	86.8
14	Peru	288.8		29	Romania	86.0
15	Macedonia, FYR[b]	284.8		30	Bulgaria	83.7

Lowest inflation, 1995–96
% consumer price inflation

1	Japan	0.1	26	Bermuda[a]	2.5
2	Argentina	0.2		Israel	2.5
3	Sweden	0.5	28	Australia	2.6
4	Finland	0.6	29	Kuwait[a]	2.7
5	Switzerland	0.8	30	United States	2.9
6	Panama[a]	0.9	31	Cyprus	3.0
7	Qatar[a]	1.2	32	Bahrain[a]	3.1
8	Norway	1.3		Fiji	3.1
9	Luxembourg	1.4		Portugal	3.1
10	Germany	1.5		Taiwan	3.1
	Oman[a]	1.5	36	Barbados	3.5
12	Canada	1.6		Croatia	3.5
13	Ireland	1.7		Malaysia	3.5
	Singapore	1.7	39	Spain	3.6
15	Austria	1.8		United Arab Emirates[a]	3.6
16	France	2.0	41	Tunisia	3.7
	Netherlands Antilles[a]	2.0	42	Guinea[a]	4.0
	New Zealand	2.0		Italy	4.0
19	Belgium	2.1	44	Saudi Arabia[a]	5.0
	Denmark	2.1		South Korea	5.0
	Netherlands	2.1	46	Trinidad & Tobago[a]	5.5
22	Bahamas[a]	2.2	47	Bangladesh[a]	5.8
23	Iceland	2.3		Egypt[a]	5.8
24	Jordan[a]	2.4		Slovakia	5.8
	United Kingdom	2.4	50	Hong Kong	6.0

Lowest inflation, 1989–96
% average annual consumer price inflation

1	Panama[d]	1.0		Luxembourg	2.8
2	Bahrain[d]	1.3	17	Brunei[d]	2.9
3	Japan	1.5		Germany	2.9
4	Saudi Arabia[d]	2.0	19	Austria	3.0
5	Qatar[d]	2.2		Finland	3.0
6	Denmark	2.4		New Zealand	3.0
7	France	2.5	22	Malta[f]	3.1
	Singapore	2.5		Switzerland	3.1
9	Belgium	2.6	24	Barbados	3.5
	Netherlands	2.6		Bermuda	3.5
	Oman[d]	2.6		Puerto Rico[f]	3.5
12	Ireland	2.7	27	United States	3.6
	Netherlands Antilles[d]	2.7	28	Australia	3.7
	Norway	2.7	29	Malaysia	3.8
15	Canada	2.8		Taiwan	3.8

a	1994–95		d	1989–95
b	1990–95		e	1991–95
c	1990–96		f	1989–94

Notes: Inflation is measured as the % increase in the consumer price index between two dates. The figures shown are based on the average level of the index during the relevant years.

Debt

Highest foreign debt[a]

$m

1	Mexico	165,743	21	Chile	25,562
2	Brazil	159,139	22	Morocco	22,147
3	Russia	120,461	23	Iran	21,935
4	China	118,090	24	Syria	21,318
5	Indonesia	107,831	25	Colombia	20,760
6	India	93,766	26	Côte d'Ivoire	18,952
7	Argentina	89,747	27	Sudan	17,623
8	Turkey	73,592	28	Czech Republic	16,576
9	Thailand	56,789	29	Bangladesh	16,370
10	Poland	42,291	30	Ecuador	13,957
11	Philippines	39,445	31	Ex-Yugoslavia[b]	13,839
12	Venezuela	35,842	32	Zaire	13,137
13	Nigeria	35,005	33	Angola	11,482
14	Malaysia	34,352	34	Bulgaria	10,887
15	Egypt	34,116	35	Tunisia	9,938
16	Algeria	32,610	36	Cameroon	9,350
17	Hungary	31,248	37	Nicaragua	9,287
18	Peru	30,831	38	Ukraine	8,434
19	Pakistan	30,152	39	Sri Lanka	8,230
20	Vietnam	26,495	40	Jordan	7,944

Highest debt service[b]

$m

1	Mexico	23,556	21	Zambia	2,616
2	Brazil	22,328	22	Czech Republic	2,569
3	Indonesia	16,419	23	Egypt	2,395
4	China	15,066	24	Nigeria	1,571
5	India	13,123	25	Tunisia	1,490
6	Turkey	11,476	26	Ecuador	1,416
7	Argentina	9,732	27	Bulgaria	1,256
8	Thailand	7,533	28	Peru	1,182
9	Hungary	7,021	29	Slovakia	1,083
10	Malaysia	6,532	30	Côte d'Ivoire	1,046
11	Russia	6,303	31	Romania	967
12	Philippines	5,328	32	Ukraine	922
13	Chile	5,150	33	Uruguay	865
14	Venezuela	4,867	34	Kenya	765
15	Algeria	4,380	35	Bangladesh	729
16	Iran[d]	4,314	36	Slovenia	723
17	Poland	4,069	37	Jamaica	673
18	Colombia	3,778	38	Zimbabwe	651
19	Morocco	3,541	39	Costa Rica	646
20	Pakistan	3,145	40	Papua New Guinea	626

a   Foreign debt is debt owed to non-residents and repayable in foreign currency; the figures shown include liabilities of government, public and private sectors. Developed countries have been excluded.

b   External debt for the former Yugoslavia had not been entirely allocated to the newly independent republics.

Highest foreign debt burden
Foreign debt as % of GDP

1	Nicaragua	589.7	21	Vietnam	130.2
2	Mozambique	443.6	22	Jordan	126.2
3	Congo	365.8	23	Laos	124.9
4	Guinea-Bissau	353.7	24	Honduras	124.6
5	Somalia[e]	283.9	25	Cameroon	124.4
6	Angola	274.9	26	Gabon	121.6
7	Sudan[f]	262.1	27	Togo	121.2
8	Zaire	255.2	28	Gambia, The[d]	117.9
9	Côte d'Ivoire	251.7	29	Burundi	110.1
10	Mauritania	243.3	30	Central African Rep[d]	103.3
11	Tanzania	207.4	31	Panama	101.4
12	Zambia	191.3	32	Ethiopia	99.9
13	Malawi	166.8	33	Kenya	97.7
14	Sierra Leone	159.7	34	Ghana	95.1
15	Yemen	155.2	35	Bulgaria	92.3
16	Madagascar	141.7	36	Guinea	91.2
17	Nigeria	140.5		Niger	91.2
18	Jamaica	134.9	38	Bolivia	90.6
19	Syria	134.8	39	Rwanda	89.1
20	Mali	131.9	40	Ecuador	84.1

Highest debt service ratios[c]
%

1	Zambia	201.9	21	Chile	25.7
2	Sierra Leone	78.5		Kenya	25.7
3	Somalia[g]	47.6	23	Zimbabwe[d]	25.6
4	Haiti	45.2	24	Guinea	25.3
5	Hungary	39.1		Malawi	25.3
6	Nicaragua	38.7	26	Colombia	25.2
7	Brazil	37.9	27	Mexico	24.2
8	Mozambique	35.7	28	Uruguay	23.5
9	Algeria	35.5	29	Côte d'Ivoire	23.1
10	Argentina	34.7		Ghana	23.1
11	Guinea-Bissau	33.7	31	Venezuela	21.7
12	Morocco	32.1	32	Iran[c]	21.6
13	Honduras	31.0	33	Mauritania	21.5
14	Indonesia	30.9	34	Uganda	21.3
15	Bolivia	28.9	35	Papua New Guinea	20.8
16	India	28.2	36	Niger	20.2
17	Burundi	27.7	37	Bulgaria	18.8
	Turkey	27.7	38	Jamaica	17.9
19	Pakistan	26.9	39	Tanzania	17.4
20	Ecuador	26.7	40	Senegal	17.3

c   Debt service is the sum of interest and principal repayments (amortization) due on
    outstanding foreign debt. The debt service ratio is debt service expressed as a
    percentage of the country's exports of goods and services.
d   1994
e   1990
f   1992
g   1989

Aid

Largest bilateral and multilateral donors
$m

1	Japan	14,489	13	Australia	1,194
2	France	8,443	14	Switzerland	1,084
3	Germany	7,524	15	Belgium	1,034
4	United States	7,367	16	Austria	767
5	Netherlands	3,226	17	Finland	388
6	United Kingdom	3,157	18	Kuwait	371
7	Canada	2,067	19	Portugal	271
8	Sweden	1,704	20	Saudi Arabia	192
9	Denmark	1,623	21	Ireland	153
	Italy	1,623	22	Greece	152
11	Spain	1,348	23	New Zealand	123
12	Norway	1,244	24	South Korea	116

Largest recipients of bilateral and multilateral aid
$m

1	China	3,521	36	Mexico	379
2	Zambia	2,029	37	Brazil	366
3	Egypt	2,017	38	Syria	347
4	India	1,738	39	Iraq	336
5	Ex-Yugoslavia	1,638	40	Iran	326
6	Indonesia	1,389	41	Algeria	310
7	Bangladesh	1,269	42	Turkey	303
8	Côte d'Ivoire	1,200	43	Madagascar	301
9	Mozambique	1,102	44	Burundi	288
10	Philippines	884	45	Kirgizstan	283
11	Ethiopia	876	46	Benin	276
12	Tanzania	875	47	Niger	268
13	Thailand	863	48	Chad	237
14	Vietnam	826	49	Ecuador	235
15	Pakistan	805	50	Colombia	231
16	Uganda	805	51	Sudan	225
17	Rwanda	711	52	Argentina	222
18	Kenya	707	53	Mauritania	220
19	Bolivia	692	54	Afghanistan	214
20	Senegal	663	55	Armenia	213
21	Nicaragua	662	56	Georgia	209
22	Ghana	644	57	Mongolia	208
23	Cambodia	567		Nigeria	208
24	Sri Lanka	553	59	Sierra Leone	205
25	Mali	542	60	Somalia	191
26	Morocco	494	61	Zaire	189
27	Zimbabwe	490	62	Lebanon	188
28	Burkina Faso	483		Namibia	188
29	Cameroon	444	64	Togo	188
30	Nepal	430	65	Albania	179
31	Malawi	429	66	Yemen	173
32	Peru	428	67	Central African Rep	161
33	Angola	423	68	Chile	159
34	Guinea	392	69	Myanmar	152
35	South Africa	384	70	Paraguay	146

Largest bilateral and multilateral donors
% of GDP

1	Denmark	0.96	13	Germany		0.31
2	Norway	0.87	14	Ireland		0.29
3	Netherlands	0.81	15	Japan		0.28
4	Sweden	0.77		United Kingdom		0.28
5	France[a]	0.55	17	Portugal		0.27
6	Belgium	0.38	18	Spain		0.24
	Canada	0.38	19	New Zealand		0.23
8	Australia	0.36	20	Italy		0.15
	Luxembourg	0.36	21	United States		0.10
10	Switzerland	0.34	22	United Arab Emirates		0.03
11	Austria	0.33	23	Kuwait		0.01
12	Finland	0.32		Saudi Arabia		0.01

Largest recipients of bilateral and multilateral aid
$ per head

1	West Bank and Gaza	232	35	Sierra Leone	45
2	Israel	228		Zimbabwe	45
3	Zambia	221	37	Gambia, The	43
4	Suriname	184		Jamaica	43
5	Nicaragua	155		Uganda	43
6	Ex-Yugoslavia	153	40	Liberia	41
7	Gabon	138	41	Angola	40
8	Namibia	125		Malawi	40
9	Guinea-Bissau	113	43	Chad	38
10	Bhutan	108		Georgia	38
11	Mauritania	99		Ghana	38
12	Bolivia	96	46	Egypt	35
13	Rwanda	92	47	Cameroon	34
14	Bahrain	89		Papua New Guinea	34
15	Mongolia	88	49	Sri Lanka	31
16	Côte d'Ivoire	87	50	Cyprus	30
17	Senegal	82		Niger	30
18	Mozambique	66		Paraguay	30
19	Botswana	64		Tanzania	30
20	Kirgizstan	61	54	Oman	28
21	Guinea	60	55	Kenya	27
	Swaziland	60	56	Uruguay	26
23	Cambodia	57	57	Malta	25
	Lesotho	57	58	Syria	24
	Mali	57	59	Madagascar	23
26	Armenia	56	60	Somalia	21
27	Benin	53		Ecuador	21
28	Albania	52		Mauritius	21
29	Central African Rep	50	63	Nepal	20
	Congo	50	64	Morocco	19
31	Burkina Faso	48	65	Peru	18
	Lebanon	48	66	Iraq	17
33	Togo	47	67	Ethiopia	16
34	Burundi	46	68	Azerbaijan	15

a Including overseas territories.

Industry

Largest industrial output
$bn, 1994

1	Japan	1,836	21	Saudi Arabia	59
2	United States	1,496	22	Sweden	59
3	Germany	777	23	Thailand	56
4	France	373	24	Ukraine	46
5	United Kingdom	326	25	Turkey	41
6	Italy	318	26	Denmark	39
7	China	245	27	Norway	38
8	Brazil	216	28	South Africa	38
9	South Korea	162	29	Poland	37
10	Canada	154	30	Finland	31
11	Russia	143	31	Malaysia	30
12	Mexico	106	32	Philippines	26
13	Australia	100	33	Singapore	25
14	Netherlands	92	34	Venezuela	24
15	Argentina	85	35	Greece	24
16	India	82	36	Hong Kong	24
17	Indonesia	72	37	Israel	24
18	Switzerland	68	38	Iran	24
19	Austria	67	39	Colombia	22
20	Belgium	67	40	United Arab Emirates	20

Highest growth in industrial output
Average annual real % growth, 1980–94

1	China	13.2	11	Nepal	7.3
2	South Korea	11.1	12	Pakistan	7.0
3	Thailand	10.2	13	Uganda	6.9
4	Oman	9.1	14	Singapore	6.3
5	Botswana	8.5	15	India	6.0
6	Lesotho	8.4	16	Turkey	5.8
7	Mauritius	8.3	17	Bangladesh	5.5
8	Malaysia	7.9	18	Sri Lanka	5.4
	Papua New Guinea	7.9	19	Tanzania	5.2
10	Indonesia	7.7	20	Chile	4.8

Lowest growth in industrial output
Average annual real % growth, 1980–94

1	Georgia	-12.0	11	Nicaragua	-2.5
2	Latvia	-9.2	12	Hungary	-2.2
3	Armenia	-9.1	13	Slovakia	-2.0
4	Mozambique	-7.7	14	South Africa	-1.1
5	Rwanda	-6.2	15	Togo	-1.0
6	Estonia	-4.9	16	Uruguay	-0.9
7	Albania	-4.7	17	Nigeria	-0.6
8	Trinidad & Tobago	-4.1	18	Philippines	-0.4
9	United Arab Emirates	-3.5	19	Namibia	0.0
10	Niger	-2.7	20	Ethiopia	0.1

Food

Largest exporters, $bn		Largest importers, $bn	
1 United States	58.72	1 Japan	53.94
2 France	40.18	2 Germany	43.64
3 Netherlands	35.20	3 United States	36.78
4 Germany	25.50	4 France	29.39
5 United Kingdom	18.08	5 United Kingdom	26.80
6 Belgium/Luxembourg	17.05	6 Italy	22.89
7 Italy	15.01	7 Netherlands	21.97
8 Canada	14.37	8 Belgium/Luxembourg	16.67
9 Spain	13.79	9 Spain	15.43
10 Brazil	13.26	10 Hpng Kong	10.57

Chemicals

Largest exporters, $bn		Largest importers, $bn	
1 Germany	68.55	1 United States	42.17
2 United States	61.70	2 Germany	41.51
3 France	36.39	3 France	34.29
4 United Kingdom	33.22	4 United Kingdom	28.09
5 Japan	30.12	5 Italy	26.16
6 Netherlands	29.04	6 Japan	24.09
7 Belgium/Luxembourg	26.65	7 Belgium/Luxembourg	20.61
8 Switzerland	21.24	8 Netherlands	20.59
9 Italy	18.28	9 China	17.04
10 Canada	11.16	10 Hong Kong	14.45

Automotive products

Largest exporters, $bn		Largest importers, $bn	
1 Germany	85.05	1 United States	108.02
2 Japan	80.68	2 Germany	44.60
3 United States	52.51	3 Canada	33.47
4 Canada	43.94	4 United Kingdom	29.20
5 France	33.42	5 France	27.66
6 Belgium/Luxembourg	24.34	6 Belgium/Luxembourg	24.94
7 Spain	22.56	7 Italy	18.62
8 United Kingdom	19.97	8 Spain	16.46
9 Italy	18.19	9 Japan	11.93
10 Mexico	14.21	10 Netherlands	11.36

Office machines and telecom equipment

Largest exporters, $bn		Largest importers, $bn	
1 Japan	106.61	1 United States	139.93
2 United States	97.99	2 Singapore	43.77
3 Singapore	60.32	3 Germany	43.12
4 United Kingdom	36.61	4 Hong Kong	40.21
5 Hong Kong	34.05	5 Japan	37.68
6 South Korea	33.22	6 United Kingdom	37.30
7 Malaysia	32.84	7 France	24.83
8 Germany	31.20	8 Malaysia	22.22
9 Taiwan	28.71	9 Netherlands	20.73
10 France	20.93	10 Canada	19.81

Agriculture

Most economically dependent on agriculture
% of GDP from agriculture

1	Somalia	65.5	21	Niger	39.0
2	Albania	55.0	22	Côte d'Ivoire	37.8
3	Afghanistan	52.6		Tanzania	37.8
4	Cambodia	52.2	24	Bangladesh	35.4
5	Burundi	51.9	25	Kirgizstan	35.0
6	Azerbaijan	51.4		Madagascar	35.0
7	Laos	51.0	27	Nicaragua	35.0
8	Ethiopia	50.2	28	Nigeria	34.2
9	Central African Rep	50.0	29	Benin	34.0
10	Uganda	49.0		Georgia	34.0
11	Armenia	48.6	31	Vietnam	33.9
12	Myanmar	46.3	32	West Bank and Gaza	32.9
13	Chad	44.0	33	Zaire	32.3
14	Nepal	43.3	34	Serbia, Montenegro	31.7
15	Ghana	42.9	35	Malawi	30.7
16	Mali	42.4	36	Liberia	30.3
17	Haiti	42.0	37	Sudan	30.1
18	Moldova	41.7	38	Papua New Guinea	29.9
19	Rwanda	41.0	39	Uzbekistan	28.5
	Togo	41.0	40	India	27.8

Least economically dependent on agriculture
% of GDP from agriculture

1	Hong Kong	0.1	21	Canada	2.8
2	Singapore	0.2	22	Taiwan	3.0
3	Kuwait	0.5	23	Sweden	3.1
	Puerto Rico	0.5		Switzerland	3.1
5	Netherlands Antilles	0.9	25	Australia	3.4
6	Germany	1.0		Italy	3.4
7	Bahrain	1.1		Libya	3.4
8	Luxembourg	1.2		Oman	3.4
	Qatar	1.2	29	Trinidad & Tobago	3.5
10	Saudi Arabia	1.6	30	Denmark	3.6
11	United States	1.7		Netherlands	3.6
12	Belgium	1.8	32	Bahamas	4.5
13	United Kingdom	2.0	33	South Africa	4.6
14	Japan	2.1	34	Israel	4.7
15	Brunei	2.2	35	Slovenia	4.8
16	Austria	2.3	36	Botswana	5.0
	United Arab Emirates	2.3		New Zealand	5.0
18	Iceland	2.4		Spain	5.0
19	France	2.6	39	Tajikistan	5.2
20	Norway	2.7	40	Cyprus	5.3

Fastest growth
% average annual growth per head, 1979–95

1	Saudi Arabia	6.1	**8**	Indonesia	1.8
2	Lebanon	3.4		Belgium	1.8
3	China	2.8		Jordan	1.8
	Malaysia	2.8		Vietnam	1.8
5	Nigeria	2.7	**12**	Ghana	1.6
6	Malta	2.2	**13**	Burkina Faso	1.5
7	Denmark	2.0		Martinique	1.5

Slowest growth
% average annual growth per head, 1979–95

1	Liberia	-5.4	**8**	Cuba	-3.1
2	Singapore	-4.9	**9**	Afghanistan	-3.0
3	Lesotho	-4.7		Zambia	-3.0
4	Bulgaria	-3.8	**11**	Bhutan	-2.9
	Libya	-3.8		Botswana	-2.9
6	Barbados	-3.6		Rwanda	-2.9
7	Panama	-3.4		South Africa	-2.9

Biggest producers
'000 tonnes

Cereals

1	China	416,796	**6**	France	53,606
2	United States	276,999	**7**	Canada	49,693
3	India	214,893	**8**	Brazil	49,653
4	Russia	61,795	**9**	Germany	39,870
5	Indonesia	58,083	**10**	Ukraine	32,429

Meat

1	China	53,016	**6**	Germany	5,748
2	United States	33,849	**7**	India	4,272
3	Brazil	10,061	**8**	Italy	3,974
4	France	6,497	**9**	Spain	3,844
5	Russia	5,946	**10**	Argentina	3,577

Fruit

1	China	39,538	**6**	Mexico	11,638
2	India	38,912	**7**	France	11,097
3	Brazil	32,301	**8**	Spain	10,806
4	United States	29,731	**9**	Uganda	10,147
5	Italy	17,494	**10**	Iran	9,775

Vegetables

1	China	128,650	**6**	Italy	13,178
2	India	64,613	**7**	South Korea	10,313
3	United States	33,596	**8**	Spain	10,208
4	Turkey	21,632	**9**	Egypt	10,191
5	Japan	13,540	**10**	Russia	9,975

Commodities

Wheat

Top 10 producers		*Top 10 consumers*	
'000 tonnes		*'000 tonnes*	
1 China	103,000	1 China	117,000
2 EU 15	87,700	2 EU 15	79,000
3 India	65,800	3 India	62,000
4 United States	59,500	4 Russia	35,000
5 Russia	30,100	5 United States	31,000
6 Canada	25,400	6 Pakistan	18,600
7 Australia	17,000	7 Ukraine	18,000
Pakistan	17,000	8 Turkey	15,300
9 Ukraine	16,300	9 Iran	14,500
10 Turkey	15,500	10 Egypt	11,000

Rice

Top 10 producers[a]		*Top 10 consumers*[b]	
'000 tonnes		*'000 tonnes*	
1 China	185,214	1 China	130,000
2 India	119,202	2 India	78,210
3 Indonesia	50,308	3 Indonesia	33,250
4 Vietnam	26,667	4 Bangladesh	18,337
5 Bangladesh	26,533	5 Vietnam	14,500
6 Thailand	21,818	6 Myanmar	9,600
7 Myanmar	17,241	7 Japan	9,300
8 Japan	13,435	8 Thailand	8,500
9 Philippines	11,174	9 Brazil	8,050
10 Brazil	10,050	10 Philippines	7,500

Sugar[c]

Top 10 producers		*Top 10 consumers*	
'000 tonnes		*'000 tonnes*	
1 EU 15	16,932	1 EU 15	14,057
2 India	15,337	2 India	13,900
3 Brazil	13,835	3 United States	8,580
4 United States	7,238	4 Brazil	8,230
5 China	6,148	5 China	8,200
6 Thailand	5,447	6 Russia	5,000
7 Australia	5,129	7 Mexico	4,334
8 Mexico	4,539	8 Pakistan	2,855
9 Ukraine	3,801	9 Indonesia	2,754
10 Cuba	3,259	10 Japan	2,600

Coarse grains[d]

Top 5 producers		*Top 5 consumers*	
'000 tonnes		*'000 tonnes*	
1 United States	209,400	1 United States	180,000
2 China	121,700	2 China	125,000
3 EU 15	88,900	3 EU 15	85,000
4 Brazil	32,400	4 Brazil	35,000
Russia	32,400	Russia	35,000

Tea

Top 10 producers '000 tonnes		*Top 10 consumers* '000 tonnes	
1 India	754	1 India	595
2 China	588	2 China	423
3 Sri Lanka	246	3 Russia	141
4 Kenya	245	4 United Kingdom	136
5 Indonesia	133	5 Japan	130
6 Turkey	105	6 Pakistan	116
7 Japan	85	7 Turkey	102
8 Bangladesh	47	8 United States	83
9 Iran	45	9 Iran	74
10 Malawi	35	10 Egypt	67

Coffee

Top 10 producers '000 tonnes		*Top 10 consumers* '000 tonnes	
1 Brazil	945	1 United States	1,062
2 Colombia	771	2 Brazil	633
3 Indonesia	384	3 Germany	571
4 Mexico	332	4 Japan	357
5 India	274	5 France	327
6 Vietnam	240	6 Italy	279
7 Guatemala	239	7 Spain	168
8 Uganda	196	8 United Kingdom	145
9 Ethiopia	172	9 Netherlands	144
10 Costa Rica	156	10 Indonesia	108

Cocoa

Top 10 producers '000 tonnes		*Top 10 consumers* '000 tonnes	
1 Côte d'Ivoire	850	1 United States	544
2 Ghana	309	2 Germany	245
3 Indonesia	240	3 United Kingdom	184
4 Brazil	225	4 France	157
5 Nigeria	143	5 Russia	144
6 Malaysia	120	6 Japan	113
7 Cameroon	108	7 Brazil	101
8 Ecuador	80	8 Italy	85
9 Dominican Republic	56	9 Belgium	62
10 Colombia	50	10 Spain	60

a Paddy (unmilled rice, in the husk).
b Milled rice.
c Raw.
d Includes: maize (corn), barley, sorghum, rye, oats and millet.

Copper

Top 10 producers[a]		*Top 10 consumers*[b]	
'000 tonnes		*'000 tonnes*	
1 Chile	2,488	**1** United States	2,526
2 United States	1,852	**2** Japan	1,415
3 Canada	726	**3** China	1,148
4 Russia	480	**4** Germany	1,058
5 Indonesia	462	**5** Taiwan	563
6 China	445	**6** France	549
7 Peru	405	**7** South Korea	540
8 Poland	384	**8** Italy	498
9 Australia	379	**9** United Kingdom	398
10 Mexico	360	**10** Belgium	362

Lead

Top 10 producers[a]		*Top 10 consumers*[b]	
'000 tonnes		*'000 tonnes*	
1 China	520	**1** United States	1,472
2 Australia	453	**2** China	448
3 United States	408	**3** Germany	368
4 Peru	233	**4** Japan	334
5 Canada	210	**5** United Kingdom	285
6 Mexico	170	**6** France	265
7 Sweden	100	**7** South Korea	264
8 South Africa	87	**8** Italy	247
9 Morocco	67	**9** Mexico	162
10 North Korea	55	**10** Taiwan	132

Zinc

Top 10 producers[a]		*Top 10 consumers*[c]	
'000 tonnes		*'000 tonnes*	
1 Canada	1,121	**1** United States	1,202
2 China	1,011	**2** China	909
3 Australia	903	**3** Japan	752
4 Peru	688	**4** Germany	503
5 United States	678	**5** Italy	345
6 Mexico	347	**6** South Korea	297
7 Ireland	184	**7** Belgium	250
8 Spain	172	France	250
9 Sweden	168	**9** Taiwan	210
10 India	155	**10** India	200

Tin

Top 5 producers[a]		*Top 5 consumers*[b]	
'000 tonnes		*'000 tonnes*	
1 China	54.0	**1** China	36.3
2 Indonesia	46.1	**2** United States	34.6
3 Peru	22.3	**3** Japan	28.1
4 Brazil	19.4	**4** Germany	19.7
5 Bolivia	14.4	**5** South Korea	12.4

Nickel

Top 10 producers[a]
'000 tonnes

1	Russia	224.0
2	Canada	181.8
3	New Caledonia	133.0
4	Australia	98.5
5	Indonesia	86.6
6	China	31.0
	Cuba	31.0
8	Dominican Republic	30.9
9	South Africa	29.8
10	Colombia	25.7

Top 10 consumers[b]
'000 tonnes

1	Japan	195.9
2	United States	147.8
3	Germany	106.1
4	Russia	68.5
5	France	49.4
6	Italy	49.0
7	South Korea	46.1
8	United Kingdom	41.9
9	China	38.0
10	Finland	36.2

Aluminium

Top 10 producers[d]
'000 tonnes

1	United States	3,375
2	Russia	2,774
3	Canada	2,172
4	China	1,676
5	Australia	1,293
6	Brazil	1,188
7	Norway	847
8	Venezuela	627
9	Germany	575
10	India	528

Top 10 consumers[e]
'000 tonnes

1	United States	5,055
2	Japan	2,336
3	China	1,875
4	Germany	1,504
5	France	747
6	South Korea	693
7	Italy	665
8	Canada	587
9	India	572
10	United Kingdom	540

Precious metals

Gold [a]
Top 10 producers
tonnes

1	South Africa	522.4
2	United States	312.0
3	Australia	253.5
4	China	136.4
5	Russia	129.0
6	Brazil	76.8
7	Uzbekistan	63.6
8	Indonesia	62.9
9	Peru	56.5
10	Papua New Guinea	51.7

Silver [a]
Top 10 producers
tonnes

1	Mexico	2,495
2	Peru	1,908
3	United States	1,450
4	Canada	1,285
5	Chile	1,038
6	Australia	920
7	China	918
8	Poland	800
9	Bolivia	452
10	Kazakhstan	402

a   Mine production.
b   Refined consumption.
c   Slab consumption.
d   Primary refined production.
e   Primary refined consumption.

Rubber (natural and synthetic)

Top 10 producers		*Top 10 consumers*	
'000 tonnes		*'000 tonnes*	
1 United States	2,540	1 United States	3,176
2 Thailand	1,784	2 Japan	1,777
3 Japan	1,498	3 China	1,480
4 Indonesia	1,467	4 South Korea	687
5 Malaysia	1,089	5 India	649
6 China	917	6 Germany	628
7 Russia	830	7 France	599
8 France	618	8 Brazil	451
9 India	565	9 Russia	437
10 Germany	488	10 Italy	408

Raw wool

Top 10 producers [a]		*Top 10 consumers* [b]	
'000 tonnes		*'000 tonnes*	
1 Australia	697	1 China	409
2 China	275	2 Italy	170
3 New Zealand	269	3 United Kingdom	72
4 Ex-Soviet Union	249	4 Japan	71
5 Argentina	81	5 Turkey	68
6 Uruguay	79	6 South Korea	57
7 Turkey	74	7 United States	57
8 South Africa	67	8 India	53
9 Britain	66	9 Germany	47
10 Pakistan	54	10 Ex-Soviet Union	26

Cotton

Top 10 producers		*Top 10 consumers*	
'000 tonnes		*'000 tonnes*	
1 China	4,767	1 China	4,251
2 United States	3,897	2 India	2,517
3 India	2,734	3 United States	2,309
4 Pakistan	1,799	4 Pakistan	1,563
5 Uzbekistan	1,254	5 Turkey	950
6 Turkey	851	6 Brazil	845
7 Greece	444	7 Indonesia	461
8 Australia	429	8 Italy	341
9 Argentina	420	9 Japan	333
10 Brazil	415	10 South Korea	328

Major oil seeds[c]

Top 5 producers		*Top 5 consumers*	
'000 tonnes		*'000 tonnes*	
1 United States	68,023	1 United States	41,712
2 China	39,410	2 China	26,855
3 Brazil	24,002	3 EU 15	26,775
4 India	21,320	4 Brazil	21,534
5 Argentina	19,596	5 India	21,124

Oil[d]

Top 15 producers		*Top 15 consumers*	
'000 barrels per day		*'000 barrels per day*	
1 Saudi Arabia[e]	8,885	1 United States	16,935
2 United States	8,290	2 Japan	5,780
3 Russia	6,200	3 China	3,310
4 Iran[e]	3,705	4 Russia	2,935
5 Mexico	3,065	5 Germany	2,880
6 Norway	2,995	6 South Korea	2,010
7 China	2,990	7 Italy	1,975
8 Venezuela[e]	2,840	8 France	1,895
United Kingdom	2,755	9 Canada	1,750
10 United Arab Emirates[e]	2,485	10 United Kingdom	1,750
11 Canada	2,390	11 Mexico	1,560
12 Kuwait[e]	2,105	12 Brazil	1,510
13 Nigeria[e]	1,890	India	1,510
14 Indonesia[e]	1,575	14 Iran	1,190
15 Libya[e]	1,415	15 Spain	1,170

Natural gas

Top 10 producers		*Top 10 consumers*	
Billion cubic metres		*Billion cubic metres*	
1 Russia	555.4	1 United States	621.6
2 United States	538.5	2 Russia	353.2
3 Canada	145.8	3 Ukraine	76.2
4 United Kingdom	71.5	4 Germany	74.4
5 Netherlands	66.3	5 Canada	74.2
6 Algeria	60.6	6 United Kingdom	73.1
7 Indonesia	58.5	7 Japan	61.2
8 Uzbekistan	45.3	8 Italy	47.8
9 Saudi Arabia	39.6	9 Uzbekistan	42.4
10 Iran	35.3	10 Saudi Arabia	39.6

Coal

Top 10 producers		*Top 10 consumers*	
Million tonnes		*Million tonnes*	
1 China	655.5	1 China	640.3
2 United States	547.8	2 United States	494.4
3 India	131.0	3 India	128.3
4 Australia	125.9	4 Russia	119.4
5 Russia	116.9	5 Germany	92.5
6 South Africa	107.8	6 Japan	85.9
7 Poland	86.8	7 South Africa	80.3
8 Germany	74.6	8 Poland	70.0
9 Kazakhstan	42.9	9 United Kingdom	47.8
10 Ukraine	42.8	10 Ukraine	42.1

a Greasy basis.
b Clean basis.
c Soybeans, sunflower seed, cottonseed, groundnuts and rapeseed.
d Includes crude oil, shale oil, oil sands and natural gas liquids.
e Opec members.

Energy

Largest producers
Million tonnnes coal equivalent, 1994

1	United States	2,447.5	16	France	159.4
2	Russia	1,384.0	17	Kuwait	156.6
3	China	1,142.6	18	Algeria	153.0
4	Saudi Arabia	656.1	19	Ukraine	146.6
5	Canada	482.3	20	South Africa	145.5
6	United Kingdom	347.7	21	Nigeria	143.9
7	Iran	317.5	22	Poland	134.6
8	India	296.5	23	Kazakhstan	127.5
9	Mexico	283.1	24	Japan	121.8
10	Venezuela	261.3	25	Libya	106.4
11	Indonesia	255.3	26	Netherlands	102.6
12	Norway	241.3	27	Argentina	90.7
13	Australia	237.0	28	North Korea	90.3
14	Germany	200.7	29	Brazil	88.4
15	United Arab Emirates	190.6	30	Egypt	82.1

Largest consumers
Million tonnes coal equivalent, 1994

1	United States	2,968.7	16	Poland	134.4
2	China	1,092.5	17	South Africa	126.3
3	Russia	883.6	18	Iran	123.6
4	Japan	621.3	19	Spain	119.2
5	Germany	445.0	20	Netherlands	111.1
6	India	343.7	21	Kazakhstan	100.9
7	Canada	326.7	22	Saudi Arabia	100.7
8	United Kingdom	311.0	23	North Korea	98.8
9	France	297.6	24	Indonesia	90.4
10	Ukraine	226.1	25	Venezuela	80.1
11	Italy	225.8	26	Argentina	73.5
12	Mexico	186.6	27	Turkey	70.3
13	South Korea	168.1	28	Belgium	69.2
14	Australia	135.9	29	Uzbekistan	65.6
15	Brazil	135.2	30	Thailand	62.4

Energy efficiency

Most efficient
GDP per kg of energy, 1994, $

1	Uganda	22.6
2	Benin	18
3	Bhutan	16.9
4	Burkina Faso	16
5	Central African Rep	12.1
6	Sudan	12.1
7	Mali	11.5
8	Chad	10.9
9	Macau	9.2
10	Laos	9.1

Least efficient
GDP per kg of energy, 1994, $

1	Azerbaijan	0.2
2	Kazakhstan	0.3
3	Uzbekistan	0.3
4	Ukraine	0.4
5	Russia	0.5
	Tajikistan	0.5
7	China	0.7
	Estonia	0.7
	Georgia	0.7
	Poland	0.7

Largest exporters
Million tonnes coal equivalent, 1994

1	Saudi Arabia	507.7	14	Netherlands	111.6
2	Russia	475.6	15	Algeria	106.6
3	Canada	218.5	16	Mexico	104.6
4	Norway	210.3	17	Libya	87.2
5	Iran	194.5	18	Singapore	59.8
6	Kuwait	176.3	19	Oman	55.6
7	Venezuela	171.5	20	China	53.4
8	Indonesia	150.6	21	Kazakhstan	48.3
9	United Arab Emirates	150.2	22	Malaysia	47.1
10	United Kingdom	145.1	23	South Africa	43.3
11	Australia	139.3	24	Egypt	37.4
12	United States	114.7	25	Angola	33.9
13	Nigeria	114.6			

Largest importers
Million tonnes coal equivalent, 1994

1	United States	737.0	14	Brazil	67.3
2	Japan	558.8	15	Canada	61.1
3	Germany	303.9	16	Turkey	48.6
4	Italy	211.3	17	Sweden	41.5
5	France	188.7	18	China	41.2
6	South Korea	181.6	19	Thailand	40.4
7	Netherlands	133.3	20	Russia	38.6
8	Spain	108.7	21	Belarus	36.2
9	United Kingdom	107.8	22	Finland	32.2
10	Singapore	104.7	23	Poland	30.0
11	Ukraine	95.4	24	Greece	28.5
12	Belgium	90.9	25	Hong Kong	28.0
13	India	68.1			

Largest consumption per head
Kg coal equivalent, 1994

1	Qatar	35,204	16	Sweden	6,794
2	United Arab Emirates	21,025	17	Iceland	6,699
3	Bahrain	17,058	18	Netherlands Antilles	6,259
4	Brunei	15,225	19	Russia	5,996
5	Luxembourg	12,823	20	Kazakhstan	5,929
6	United States	11,391	21	Saudi Arabia	5,769
7	Canada	11,209	22	Germany	5,475
8	Kuwait	9,846	23	New Zealand	5,467
9	Singapore	9,674	24	Oman	5,405
10	Australia	7,614	25	United Kingdom	5,333
11	Trinidad & Tobago	7,530	26	Denmark	5,151
12	Norway	7,441	27	France	5,151
13	Finland	7,401	28	Japan	4,978
14	Netherlands	7,401	29	Czech Republic	4,974
15	Belgium	6,861	30	Estonia	4,895

Note: Consumption data for small countries, especially oil producers, can be unreliable, often leading to unrealistically high consumption per head rates.

Workers of the world

Highest % of population in labour force
1995–96 or latest

1	Singapore	57.0	26	Central African Rep	48.2
2	Denmark	55.8	27	Brazil	47.9
3	Iceland	55.6		Slovenia	47.9
4	Latvia	55.1	29	New Zealand	47.8
5	Switzerland	55.0	30	Australia	47.7
6	Romania	53.4	31	Burkina Faso	47.6
7	Japan	53.2	32	Moldova	47.5
8	Burundi	52.9		Panama	47.5
9	Czech Republic	52.6	34	Cyprus	47.0
	Thailand	52.6		Russia	47.0
11	Belarus	52.5	36	Uruguay	46.8
12	United States	51.3	37	Bulgaria	46.3
13	Hong Kong	50.8		Rwanda	46.3
	Lithuania	50.8	39	Slovakia	46.2
	Ukraine	50.8	40	Colombia	45.4
16	Bahamas	50.7	41	Poland	45.2
17	Canada	50.1		Suriname	45.2
18	Sweden	49.6	43	Bangladesh	45.0
19	Finland	49.4		France	45.0
	Norway	49.4	45	Bahrain	44.6
	United Kingdom	49.4		Indonesia	44.6
22	Germany	49.1		Paraguay	44.6
23	Estonia	48.9	48	South Korea	44.4
24	Portugal	48.8	49	Macao	44.1
25	Austria	48.3		Mauritius	44.1

Most male workforce
% male workers, 1995–96 or latest

1	Iran	90.4	21	Chile	67.6
2	Pakistan	84.6	22	Nigeria	66.7
3	Bahrain	82.0		Sri Lanka	66.7
	Syria	82.0	24	Venezuela	66.4
5	Tunisia	79.1	25	Mauritius	65.9
6	Egypt	77.0		Nicaragua	65.9
7	Kuwait	75.7	27	Malaysia	65.7
8	Saudi Arabia	74.4	28	Peru	65.3
9	Guatemala	74.2	29	Suriname	64.9
10	Morocco	73.9	30	Luxembourg	63.5
11	Ecuador	73.6	31	Italy	63.1
12	Malta	73.2	32	Trinidad & Tobago	63.0
13	Argentina	72.1	33	El Salvador	62.9
14	India	71.4	34	Philippines	62.6
15	Panama	70.8	35	Ireland	62.2
16	Honduras	70.1	36	Hong Kong	62.1
17	Costa Rica	69.9	37	Greece	61.9
18	Turkey	69.6	38	Spain	61.7
19	Mexico	67.9	39	Botswana	61.5
20	Côte d'Ivoire	67.7	40	Cyprus	61.4

Lowest % of population in labour force
1995–96 or latest

1	Iran	26.0	26	Malaysia	39.2
2	Syria	27.8	27	Côte d'Ivoire	39.4
3	Pakistan	27.9		Mexico	39.4
4	Tunisia	29.8		Venezuela	39.4
5	Egypt	30.4	30	Hungary	40.1
6	Nigeria	31.1		Italy	40.1
7	Puerto Rico	32.4	32	Spain	40.2
8	Morocco	32.5	33	Ireland	40.3
9	Botswana	33.3	34	Sri Lanka	40.5
10	Guatemala	33.5		Trinidad & Tobago	40.5
11	Saudi Arabia	34.0	36	Barbados	40.6
12	Zimbabwe	34.6	37	Philippines	40.8
13	Nicaragua	34.7	38	Bolivia	41.3
14	Ecuador	34.8	39	Argentina	41.5
15	Honduras	35.0		Greece	41.5
16	Fiji	35.2	41	Netherlands	41.9
17	Malta	36.1	42	Belgium	42.1
18	Israel	36.9	43	Taiwan	42.6
19	India	37.5	44	Netherlands Antilles	42.7
	South Africa	37.5	45	Cambodia	43.1
21	Chile	37.8		Macedonia, FYR	43.1
	Peru	37.8	47	Malawi	43.3
23	Costa Rica	38.7	48	Ethiopia	43.4
24	Kuwait	38.9	49	Luxembourg	43.5
25	El Salvador	39.1	50	Jamaica	43.6

Most female workforce
% female workers, 1995–96 or latest

1	Cambodia	55.7		Russia	46.7
2	Lithuania	53.8	22	Romania	46.3
3	Rwanda	53.5	23	Slovenia	46.2
4	Burundi	52.3	24	United States	46.0
5	Malawi	51.0	25	Poland	45.9
6	Latvia	50.0	26	Norway	45.7
7	Ukraine	49.2	27	Denmark	45.3
8	Belarus	49.0	28	Canada	45.2
9	Burkina Faso	48.7		France	45.2
10	Barbados	48.4	30	Netherlands Antilles	45.1
	Bulgaria	48.4	31	Slovakia	44.9
12	Sweden	47.9	32	Portugal	44.6
13	Zimbabwe	47.8	33	Thailand	44.5
14	Czech Republic	47.6	34	New Zealand	44.1
	Estonia	47.6	35	Bolivia	43.9
16	Bahamas	47.5	36	United Kingdom	43.8
17	Jamaica	47.4	37	Hungary	43.6
18	Finland	47.0	38	Colombia	43.4
19	Central African Rep	46.8	39	Macau	43.2
20	Iceland	46.7		Switzerland	43.2

The business world

Global competitiveness

	Overall	Market growth	Executive opinion
1	Singapore	United States	United States
2	Hong Kong	China	Japan
3	United States	India	Singapore
4	Canada	Japan	Germany
5	New Zealand	Indonesia	South Korea
6	Switzerland	United Kingdom	Taiwan
7	United Kingdom	Brazil	Hong Kong
8	Taiwan	Mexico	United Kingdom
9	Malaysia	Canada	China
10	Norway	Thailand	France
11	Luxembourg	Germany	Malaysia
12	Netherlands	South Korea	Canada
13	Chile	France	Switzerland
14	Japan	Taiwan	Italy
15	Indonesia	Turkey	Chile
16	Ireland	Malaysia	Netherlands
17	Australia	Egypt	New Zealand
18	Thailand	Australia	Thailand
19	Finland	Philippines	Indomesia
20	Denmark	Spain	Australia
21	South Korea	Netherlands	Brazil
22	Sweden	Chile	Sweden
23	France	South Africa	Mexico
24	Israel	Hong Kong	India
25	Germany	Argentina	Denmark
26	Spain	Colombia	Israel
27	Austria	Switzerland	Spain
28	Egypt	Peru	Norway
29	China	Singapore	Luxembourg
30	Portugal	Venezuela	Philippines
31	Belgium	Israel	Czech Republic
32	Czech Republic	Sweden	Austria
33	Mexico	Norway	Ireland
34	Philippines	Austria	Belgium
35	Slovakia	New Zealand	Vietnam
36	Turkey	Poland	Poland
37	Argentina	Finland	Russia
38	Iceland	Denmark	South Africa
39	Italy	Portugal	Argentina
40	Peru	Belgium	Finland
41	Colombia	Ireland	Hungary
42	Brazil	Czech Republic	Venezuela
43	Jordan	Vietnam	Colombia

Notes: Rankings reflect assessments for the ability of a country to achieve sustained high rates of GDP growth per head. Column 1 is based on 155 criteria covering: the openness of an economy, the role of the government, the development of financial markets, the quality of infrastructure, technology, business management and judicial and political institutions and labour-market flexibility.
Column 2 looks at the growth prospects and takes into account the economic size of each country. Column 3 is based on business respondents' subjective judgments.

The business environment

		1996 score	1995 score	Ranking
1	Hong Kong	8.69	8.15	14
2	United Kingdom	8.72	0.18	2
3	Netherlands	8.45	8.78	1
4	Singapore	8.40	8.49	4
5	Canada	8.25	8.53	3
6	United States	8.23	8.45	5
7	Denmark	8.14	8.40	6
8	New Zealand	8.00	8.19	13
9	Switzerland	7.94	8.31	9
10	Germany	7.92	8.39	7
11	Ireland	7.89	8.04	18
12	Australia	7.77	8.11	16
13	France	7.74	8.37	8
14	Austria	7.72	8.11	15
15	Belgium	7.68	8.20	12
16	Norway	7.66	8.04	17
17	Finland	7.65	8.23	11
18	Sweden	7.63	8.31	10
19	Chile	7.39	7.85	20
20	Malaysia	7.28	7.80	22
21	Taiwan	7.07	7.57	25
22	Spain	6.71	7.81	21
23	Portugal	6.67	7.58	24
24	Thailand	6.64	6.86	29
25	Japan	6.63	7.69	23
26	Argnetina	6.51	6.61	31
27	Israel	6.50	6.83	30
28	South Korea	6.35	7.33	26
29	Italy	6.33	7.89	19
30	Indonesia	6.26	6.55	33
31	Czech Republic	6.07	6.94	27
32	Philippines	5.80	6.43	35
33	Greece	5.77	6.60	32
34	Colombia	5.70	5.59	47
35	Saudi Arabia	5.57	5.82	40
36	Hungary	5.44	6.91	28
37	Poland	5.40	6.54	34
38	Turkey	5.35	5.82	41
39	Mexico	5.31	6.02	39
40	South Africa	5.25	6.26	37
41	Sri Lanka	5.24	5.79	42
42	Slovakia	5.23	6.07	38
43	Egypt	5.23	5.69	45
44	India	5.17	5.68	46
45	Peru	5.05	5.72	43
46	Brazil	5.04	6.31	36
47	China	4.71	5.49	50

Note: Scores reflect the opportunities for, and hindrances to, the conduct of business, measured by countries' rankings in ten categories including market potential, tax and labour-market policies, infrastructure, skills and the political environment.

Businesses and banks

Largest businesses
By sales, $bn

1	Mitsubishi[a]	Japan	184.4
2	Mitsui[a]	Japan	181.5
3	Itochu[a]	Japan	169.2
4	General Motors	United States	168.8
5	Sumitomo[a]	Japan	167.5
6	Marubeni[a]	Japan	161.1
7	Ford Motor	United States	137.1
8	Toyota Motor[a]	Japan	111.1
9	Exxon	United States	110.0
10	Royal Dutch/Shell Group	United Kingdom/Netherlands	109.8
11	Nissho Iwai[a]	Japan	97.9
12	Wal-Mart Stores[b]	United States	93.6
13	Hitachi[a]	Japan	84.2
14	Nippon Life Insurance[a]	Japan	83.2
15	Nippon Telegraph and Telephone[a]	Japan	81.9
16	AT&T	United States	79.6
17	Daimler-Benz	Germany	72.3
18	Intl. Business Machines	United States	71.9
19	Matsushita Electric Industrial[a]	Japan	70.4
20	General Electric	United States	70.0
21	Tomen[a]	Japan	67.8
22	Mobil	United States	66.7
23	Nissan Motor[a]	Japan	62.6
24	Volkswagen	Germany	61.5
25	Siemens	Germany	60.7
26	Dai-Ichi Mutual Life Insurance[a]	Japan	58.1
27	British Petroleum	United Kingdom	57.0
28	Metro Holding	Switzerland	56.5
29	U.S. Postal Service[cd]	United States	54.3
30	Chrysler	United States	53.2
31	Philip Morris	United States	53.1
32	Toshiba[a]	Japan	53.0
33	Tokyo Electric Power[a]	Japan	52.4
34	Daewoo	South Korea	51.2
35	Nichimen[a]	Japan	50.8
36	Sumitomo Life Insurance[a]	Japan	50.7
37	Kanematsu[a]	Japan	49.8
38	Unilever	United Kingdom/Netherlands	49.7
39	Nestlé	Switzerland	47.8
40	Sony[a]	Japan	47.6

a   Year ended March 31, 1996.   c   Year ended September 30, 1995.
b   Year ended January 31, 1996.   d   Government owned.

Notes: Industrial and service corporations. Figures refer to the year ended December 31, 1995, except where specified. They include sales of consolidated subsidiaries but exclude excise taxes, thus differing, in some instances, from figures published by the companies themselves.

Largest banks
By capital, $m

1	HSBC Holdings	United Kingdom	21,445
2	Crédit Agricole	France	20,386
3	Union Bank of Switzerland	Switzerland	19,903
4	Citicorp	United States	19,239
5	Dai-Ichi Kangyo Bank	Japan	19,172
6	Deutsche Bank	Germany	18,937
7	Sumitomo Bank	Japan	18,605
8	Sanwa Bank	Japan	17,676
9	Mitsubishi Bank	Japan	16,667
10	Sakura Bank	Japan	15,961
11	Fuji Bank	Japan	15,443
12	BankAmerica Corp	United States	14,820
13	C.S. Holding	Switzerland	13,751
14	ABN-Amro Bank	Netherlands	13,372
15	Groupe Caisse d'Epargne	France	12,667
16	Industrial Bank of Japan	Japan	12,497
17	Swiss Bank Corp	Switzerland	11,733
18	National Westminster Bank	United Kingdom	11,501
19	Banque Nationale de Paris	France	11,453
20	Chemical Banking Corp	United States	11,436
21	Rabobank Nederland	Netherlands	11,310
22	Bank of Tokyo	Japan	11,169
23	NationsBank	United States	11,074
24	Barclays Bank	United Kingdom	11,068
25	Compagnie Financière de Paribas	France	10,980
26	Bank of China	China	10,869
27	Société Générale	France	10,474
28	Industrial & Commercial Bank of China	China	10,060
29	Long-Term Credit Bank of Japan	Japan	9,929
30	J.P. Morgan & Co.	United States	9,636
31	Dresdner Bank	Germany	9,203
32	Asahi Bank	Japan	9,187
33	Tokai Bank	Japan	8,996
34	Westdeutsche Landesbank Girozentrale	Germany	8,717
35	Chase Manhattan Corp	United States	8,444
36	Commerzbank	Germany	8,210
37	First Chicago NBD Corporation	United States	7,890
38	Crédit Lyonnais	France	7,835
39	Banc One Corp	United States	7,824
40	Crédit Mutuel Confédération Nationale	France	7,775

Notes: Capital is essentially equity and reserves.
Figures for Japanese banks refer to the year ended March 31, 1996. Figures for all other countries refer to the year ended December 31, 1995.

Stockmarkets

Largest market capitalisation
$m, end 1995

1	United States	6,857,622		26	Philippines	58,859
2	Japan	3,667,292		27	Denmark	56,223
3	United Kingdom	1,407,737		28	Norway	44,587
4	Germany	577,365		29	Finland	44,138
5	France	522,053		30	China	42,055
6	Switzerland	433,621		31	Saudi Arabia	40,961
7	Canada	366,344		32	Argentina	37,783
8	Netherlands	356,481		33	Israel	36,399
9	Hong Kong	303,705		34	Austria	32,513
10	South Africa	280,526		35	New Zealand	31,950
11	Australia	245,218		36	Luxembourg	30,443
12	Malaysia	222,729		37	Ireland	25,817
13	Italy	209,522		38	Turkey	20,772
14	Spain	197,788		39	Portugal	18,362
15	Taiwan	187,206		40	Colombia	17,893
16	South Korea	181,955		41	Greece	17,060
17	Sweden	178,049		42	Russia	15,863
18	Singapore	148,004		43	Czech Republic	15,664
19	Brazil	147,636		44	Kuwait	13,623
20	Thailand	141,507		45	Peru	11,795
21	India	127,199		46	Pakistan	9,286
22	Belgium	104,960		47	Egypt	8,088
23	Mexico	90,694		48	Iran	6,561
24	Chile	73,860		49	Morocco	5,951
25	Indonesia	66,585		50	Jordan	4,670

Highest growth in market capitalisation, $ terms
% increase, 1986–95

1	Indonesia	82,104		21	Pakistan	443
2	Thailand	4,817		22	Uruguay	423
3	Philippines	2,831		23	Peru	408
4	Argentina	2,275		24	Zimbabwe	397
5	Turkey	2,122		25	Austria	388
6	Colombia	2,077		26	Sri Lanka	375
7	Morocco	2,033		27	Egypt	371
8	Chile	1,718		28	Norway	340
9	Mexico	1,424		29	Netherlands	326
10	Greece	1,411		30	Spain	304
11	Malaysia	1,378		31	Finland	278
12	South Korea	1,207		32	Israel	268
13	Taiwan	1,118		33	Brazil	251
14	Portugal	1,100		34	France	249
15	India	836		35	Denmark	245
16	Singapore	791		36	Switzerland	228
17	Bangladesh	611		37	United Kingdom	220
18	Tunisia	573		38	Trinidad and Tobago	204
19	Kenya	502		39	Belgium	181
20	Hong Kong	465			Sweden	181

Highest growth in value traded, $ terms
% increase, 1986–95

1	Indonesia	1,440,200	24	Denmark	1,290
2	Turkey	395,223	25	Zimbabwe	1,150
3	Morocco	26,856	26	Finland	917
4	Greece	18,934	27	Venezuela	881
5	Tunisia	10,950	28	Mexico	795
6	Bangladesh	7,800	29	Germany	745
7	Portugal	6,955	30	Netherlands	699
8	Malaysia	6,410	31	United Kingdom	668
9	Thailand	4,931	32	Egypt	652
10	Sri Lanka	4,320	33	Hong Kong	599
11	Chile	3,615	34	Israel	529
12	Philippines	2,516	35	Trinidad and Tobago	427
13	Colombia	2,459	36	Jamaica	401
14	Singapore	2,157	37	Sweden	370
15	Pakistan	1,971	38	Cote d'Ivoire	367
16	Taiwan	1,924	39	Kuwait	352
17	Austria	1,749	40	Spain	300
18	South Korea	1,601	41	Australia	264
19	Peru	1,546	42	Belgium	251
20	Costa Rica[a]	1,500	43	South Africa	242
21	Argentina	1,387	44	New Zealand	233
22	Norway	1,335	45	Canada	223
23	France	1,314	46	United States	184

Highest growth in number of listed companies
% increase, 1986–95

1	Indonesia	892	21	Philippines	58
2	Turkey	413	22	Finland	49
3	Thailand	324	23	Austria	47
4	Portugal	168	24	Sweden	45
5	Taiwan	167	25	Peru	39
6	Israel	156	26	Germany	38
7	Malaysia	137	27	Italy	36
8	Bangladesh	135	28	Sri Lanka	32
9	Pakistan	112	29	Jamaica	28
10	Hong Kong	109	30	Cote d'Ivoire	24
11	South Korea	103	31	Chile	23
12	Costa Rica	93	32	Japan	21
	Egypt	93		Zimbabwe	21
14	Colombia	92	34	Mexico	19
15	Greece	86		South Africa	19
16	Nigeria	83	36	Canada	16
17	Netherlands	77		Spain	16
18	Singapore	74	38	Kenya	6
19	India	68	39	Australia	4
20	Switzerland	61	40	Norway	1

a 1987–95

Transport: *roads and cars*

Longest road networks
Km, 1995 or latest

1	United States	6,238,500	21	Austria	200,000
2	India	2,009,600	22	South Africa	182,580
3	Brazil	1,939,000	23	Ukraine	172,257
4	Japan	1,144,360	24	Bangladesh	168,513
5	China	1,110,000	25	Saudi Arabia	159,000
6	Canada	1,021,000	26	Kazakhstan	158,655
7	Russia	949,000	27	Hungary	158,633
8	Australia	895,030	28	Iran	158,000
9	France	812,700	29	Romania	153,170
10	Germany	650,700	30	Belgium	142,563
11	Turkey	381,300	31	Sweden	136,233
12	Indonesia	378,000	32	Czech Republic	124,770
13	Poland	372,479	33	Netherlands	120,800
14	United Kingdom	367,000	34	Greece	116,440
15	Spain	343,197	35	Colombia	106,600
16	Italy	314,360	36	Vietnam	106,048
17	Mexico	249,520	37	Sri Lanka	102,600
18	Pakistan	216,564	38	Algeria	102,424
19	Argentina	216,100	39	Malaysia	93,975
20	Philippines	204,200	40	Ireland	92,430

Densest road networks
Km of road per km² land area, 1995 or latest

1	Belgium	4.80	21	Malawi	1.51
2	Singapore	4.70	22	France	1.47
3	Bahrain	4.54	23	Ireland	1.31
4	Barbados	3.72	24	Poland	1.19
5	Japan	3.03	25	Bangladesh	1.14
6	Netherlands	2.93	26	Cyprus	1.10
7	Macau	2.69	27	Italy	1.04
8	Austria	2.38	28	Mauritius	1.01
9	Luxembourg	1.99	29	Lithuania	0.94
10	Germany	1.82	30	Latvia	0.93
11	Switzerland	1.72	31	Greece	0.88
12	Hungary	1.71	32	Portugal	0.80
13	Jamaica	1.69	33	South Korea	0.75
14	Denmark	1.66	34	Slovenia	0.73
15	Hong Kong	1.60	35	Israel	0.71
	United Kingdom	1.60	36	Costa Rica	0.70
17	Trinidad & Tobago	1.59	37	Philippines	0.68
18	Czech Republic	1.58		Spain	0.68
19	Sri Lanka	1.56	39	Azerbaijan	0.67
20	Puerto Rico	1.54	40	Romania	0.64

Most crowded road networks
Number of vehicles per km of road network, 1995 or latest

1	Hong Kong	280	26	Mauritius	49
2	Taiwan	229	27	Luxembourg	48
3	Lebanon	202	28	Togo	45
4	Kuwait	166	29	Peru	43
5	Singapore	163	30	Jordan	39
6	Qatar	161	31	France	37
7	Brunei	145		Portugal	37
8	Italy	116		Macedonia, FYR	37
9	South Korea	114	34	Belgium	33
10	Israel	95		Malaysia	33
11	Thailand	90	36	Cyprus	32
12	Puerto Rico	79	37	United States	31
13	Germany	66	38	South Africa	30
	Slovakia	66	39	Egypt	29
15	United Kingdom	63		Argentina	29
16	Bahrain	61		Croatia	29
17	Czech Republic	59		Sweden	29
	Japan	59		Barbados	29
19	United Arab Emirates	52		Dominican Republic	29
	Netherlands	52	45	Finland	28
21	Bulgaria	51	46	Estonia	27
	Mexico	51		Sudan	27
23	Spain	50	48	Ukraine	26
	Slovenia	50	49	Greece	25
	Switzerland	50		Russia	25

Most used road networks
'000 vehicle-km per year per km of road network, 1995 or latest

1	Hong Kong	6,036.1	16	Saudi Arabia	592.1
2	Israel	2,044.4	17	Denmark	567.1
3	Thailand	1,442.9	18	France	560.5
4	Bahrain	1,418.3	19	Finland	542.6
5	Italy	1,383.4	20	Slovenia	500.5
6	Portugal	1,184.4	21	Macedonia, FYR	491.4
7	United Kingdom	1,162.9	22	Sweden	470.1
8	Germany	874.4	23	Spain	375.7
9	Netherlands	870.9	24	China	365.8
10	Luxembourg	820.7	25	Oman	358.3
11	South Korea	707.9	26	Poland	303.2
12	Switzerland	698.3	27	Ecuador	297.1
13	Belgium	649.0	28	Ireland	276.2
14	United States	606.1	29	Norway	250.0
15	Japan	600.2	30	Czech Republic	224.3

Highest car ownership
Number of cars per 1,000 people, 1995 or latest

1	Luxembourg	563.3	26	Ireland	270.3
2	United States	562.8	27	Bahrain	251.0
3	Italy	552.4	28	Puerto Rico	244.7
4	Germany	494.8	29	Portugal	242.2
5	Canada	467.0	30	Qatar	233.7
6	Australia	464.7	31	Estonia	226.4
7	New Zealand	462.6	32	Hungary	220.0
8	Switzerland	457.0	33	Greece	210.5
9	Austria	447.0	34	Israel	200.0
10	Iceland	445.0	35	Bulgaria	196.5
11	France	433.0	36	Poland	194.7
12	Belgium	418.0	37	Lithuania	193.6
13	Sweden	410.9	38	Slovakia	189.2
14	Norway	385.6	39	Taiwan	184.8
15	Finland	371.0	40	Bahamas	172.5
16	United Kingdom	365.8	41	Croatia	149.0
17	Netherlands	363.4	42	Macedonia, FYR	147.6
18	Japan	360.3	43	Barbados	142.8
19	Kuwait	358.7	44	Argentina	134.9
20	Spain	351.3	45	South Korea	133.9
21	Slovenia	351.0	46	Latvia	132.7
22	Cyprus	340.5	47	Malaysia	130.2
23	Denmark	340.0	48	Brunei	128.0
24	Lebanon	304.7	49	Singapore	115.7
25	Czech Republic	302.0	50	Libya	110.1

Lowest car ownership
Number of cars per 1,000 people, 1995 or latest

1	Cambodia	0.1	16	Burundi	2.6
2	Central African Rep	0.2	17	Mali	2.8
	Somalia	0.2	18	China	2.9
	Tajikistan	0.2	19	Chad	3.0
5	Armenia	0.4		India	3.0
	Bangladesh	0.4	21	Liberia	3.1
7	Ethiopia	0.8	22	Laos	3.6
8	Tanzania	0.9	23	Madagascar	4.0
9	Uganda	1.2		Niger	4.0
10	Rwanda	1.3	25	Mozambique	4.2
11	Afghanistan	1.5	26	Pakistan	4.3
	Eritrea	1.5	27	Haiti	4.7
13	Cuba	1.9		Sierra Leone	4.7
14	Guinea	2.0	29	Ghana	4.9
15	Malawi	2.2	30	Lesotho	5.3

Most accidents
Number of people injured per 100m vehicle-km, 1995 or latest

1	Malawi	2,730	26	Slovakia	71
2	Rwanda	1,764	27	Mexico	66
3	South Korea	725	28	Bahrain	65
4	Costa Rica	406	29	Hungary	63
5	Kenya	363		Italy	63
6	Turkey	328	31	Senegal	56
7	Honduras	317	32	Switzerland	55
8	Egypt	222	33	New Zealand	54
9	Sri Lanka	209		Yemen	54
10	Portugal	194	35	Colombia	53
11	Hong Kong	185		Iran	53
12	Morocco	180		Oman	53
13	Belgium	143	38	Thailand	40
14	United States	137	39	Ireland	38
15	Kirgizstan	134	40	France	36
16	Japan	129	41	Ecuador	35
	South Africa	129	42	Sweden	33
18	Israel	127	43	Zimbabwe	32
19	Latvia	125	44	Denmark	26
20	Czech Republic	113	45	Finland	24
21	Spain	112	46	Netherlands	11
22	Germany	87	47	Albania	9
23	Slovenia	83	48	Zambia	6
24	Macedonia, FYR	81	49	Taiwan	2
25	United Kingdom	72		Vietnam	2

Most deaths
Number of people killed per 100m vehicle-km, 1995 or latest

1	Malawi	1,117	16	Albania	8
2	Egypt	44	17	Ecuador	7
3	Kenya	41	18	Portugal	6
4	Latvia	25		Slovenia	6
5	Kirgizstan	24	20	Colombia	5
6	South Korea	21		Czech Republic	5
7	Sri Lanka	19		Hungary	5
8	Morocco	18		Iran	5
9	Turkey	17		Slovakia	5
10	Honduras	16		Spain	5
11	Thailand	13	26	Macedonia, FYR	4
12	Costa Rica	11		Oman	4
	Yemen	11		Senegal	4
14	Mexico	10	29	Belgium	3
	South Africa	10		Zambia	3

Transport: *planes and trains*

Most air passenger-km
Million passenger-km[a] per year

1	United States	853,389	21	Mexico	19,403
2	United Kingdom	152,453	22	Saudi Arabia	18,501
3	Japan	129,981	23	New Zealand	18,008
4	Australia	67,145	24	South Africa	14,496
5	France	66,932	25	Philippines	14,374
6	China	64,204	26	Argentina	11,976
7	Germany	62,158	27	Israel	11,412
8	Russia	61,035	28	Pakistan	10,384
9	Canada	49,288	29	United Arab Emirates	9,958
10	Netherlands	48,474	30	Turkey	9,475
11	South Korea	48,441	31	Belgium	8,620
12	Singapore	48,400	32	Sweden	8,615
13	Brazil	34,370	33	Finland	8,562
14	Italy	33,289	34	Portugal	8,057
15	Spain	29,003	35	Norway	7,996
16	Thailand	27,053	36	Greece	7,945
17	Indonesia	24,028	37	Egypt	7,678
18	Malaysia	23,431	38	Austria	6,752
19	India	20,960	39	Chile	6,333
20	Switzerland	20,359	40	Venezuela	6,180

Busiest airports
Number of passengers '000

1	Chicago	O'Hare	67,253
2	Altanta	Hartsfield	57,735
3	Dallas	Dallas/Ft. Worth	56,491
4	London	Heathrow	54,453
5	Los Angeles	Los Angeles Intl.	53,909
6	Tokyo	Haneda	45,823
7	Frankfurt	Frankfurt/Main	38,180
8	San Francisco	San Francisco Intl.	36,263
9	Miami	Miami Intl.	33,236
10	Denver	Denver Intl.	31,037

Busiest international airports
Number of international passengers '000

1	London	Heathrow	46,806
2	Frankfurt	Frankfurt/Main	30,257
3	Hong Kong	Hong Kong Intl.	27,424
4	Paris	Charles de Gaulle	25,534
5	Amsterdam	Schipol	24,710
6	Singapore	Changi	21,743
7	Tokyo	New Tokyo Intl. (Narita)	21,488
8	London	Gatwick	20,600
9	New York	Kennedy	17,051
10	Bangkok	Bangkok Intl.	15,119

a   Air passenger–km data refer to the distance travelled by each aircraft of national
origin.

Longest railway networks
'000 km

1	United States	235.7		21	Czech Republic	9.4
2	Russia	87.4		22	Pakistan[d]	8.8
3	India	62.7		23	Turkey	8.5
4	China	54.6		24	Hungary	7.8
5	Germany	41.7		25	Finland	5.9
6	Australia[a]	35.8		26	Austria	5.7
7	Argentina[b]	34.2		27	Belarus	5.5
8	France	31.9		28	Iran	5.3
9	Mexico[c]	26.5		29	Philippines[a]	4.9
10	South Africa	26.3		30	Egypt	4.8
11	Poland	24.0		31	Zaire[e]	4.1
12	Ukraine	22.6		32	Cuba[c]	4.8
13	Brazil[c]	22.1		33	Sudan	4.6
14	Japan	20.1		34	Tanzania	4.5
15	United Kingdom	16.6			North Korea[a]	4.5
16	Italy	16.0		36	Bulgaria	4.3
17	Canada	13.5			New Zealand[f]	4.3
18	Spain	12.3			Serbia[e]	4.3
19	Romania	11.4		39	Indonesia	4.2
20	Sweden	9.8		40	Norway	4.0

Most rail passengers
Km per year per person

1	Japan	1,983		11	Italy	867
2	Switzerland	1,659		12	Romania	830
3	Russia	1,299		13	Slovakia	784
4	Ukraine	1,243		14	Czech Republic	777
5	Belarus	1,219		15	Germany	744
6	Austria	1,198		16	Sweden	703
7	France	952		17	Luxembourg	698
8	Denmark	916		18	Belgium	665
9	Netherlands	906		19	South Korea	657
10	Egypt	873		20	Hong Kong	640

Most rail freight
Million tonnes-km per year

1	United States	1,906,268		11	Poland	68,206
2	China	1,283,601		12	Uzbekistan[g]	51,696
3	Russia	1,213,711		13	France	47,924
4	Kazakhstan[g]	281,076		14	Mexico[g]	33,600
5	Canada[d]	250,117		15	Australia	26,492
6	India	249,564		16	Belarus	25,510
7	Ukraine	195,762		17	Japan	24,747
8	Brazil[d]	120,108		18	Romania	24,041
9	South Africa	99,850		19	Czech Republic	22,634
10	Germany	68,742		20	Italy	22,243

a 1989   e 1994
b 1987   f 1985
c 1988   g 1992
d 1990

Transport: *sail away*

Largest merchant fleets
Number of vessels over 100 GRT [a], mid-1996

1	Japan	9,399		21	Netherlands	1,115
2	Panama	6,105		22	Turkey	1,114
3	United States	5,289		23	Germany	1,101
4	Russia	4,866		24	Ukraine	1,061
5	China	3,121		25	India	920
6	Indonesia	2,348		26	Canada	872
7	South Korea	2,327		27	Georgia	844
8	Norway	2,227		28	France	827
9	Greece	1,743		29	Malaysia	755
10	Spain	1,713		30	Peru	695
11	Liberia	1,684		31	Taiwan	681
12	Cyprus	1,652		32	Mexico	630
13	United Kingdom	1,619		33	Australia	625
14	Philippines	1,617		34	Sweden	618
15	Singapore	1,480		35	Vietnam	604
16	Honduras	1,408		36	Thailand	540
17	Italy	1,348		37	Brazil	539
18	Malta	1,247		38	Poland	507
19	Bahamas	1,186		39	Morocco	481
20	Denmark	1,137		40	Argentina	480

Largest ports[b]
Total cargo traffic, '000 tonnes[c]

1	Singapore	305,484		21	Yokkaichi	58,534
2	Rotterdam	290,000		22	Le Havre	53,783
3	Chiba	173,688		23	Tampa	51,359
4	Kobe	170,970		24	London	51,332
5	Houston	128,820		25	New York	47,299
6	Hong Kong	127,175		26	Forth	47,083
7	Nagoya	124,500		27	Genoa	45,594
8	Yokohama	108,100		28	Grimsby-Immingham	44,746
9	Antwerp	108,073		29	Tees and Hartlepool	44,562
10	Kawasaki	100,694		30	Kelang	40,034
11	Long Beach	87,065		31	Sydney	40,000
12	Marseilles	86,599		32	Dunkirk	39,380
13	Bergen	78,726		33	Sullom Voe	38,335
14	Hamburg	72,189		34	Arzew	38,308
15	Corpus Christi	70,439		35	Augusta	37,860
16	Richard's Bay	68,735		36	Trieste	37,732
17	Vancouver	67,633		37	Warri	37,167
18	Port Hedland	64,263		38	Gladstone	35,752
19	Newcastle	60,302		39	Algeciras	35,436
20	Virginia	59,649		40	Santos	35,111

a   Gross Tonnage (GRT) = total volume within the hull and above deck. 1 GRT=100 cu ft.
b   Recent figures for some Asian and American ports are not available.
c   Total cargo loaded and discharged.

Tourism

Most tourist arrivals
Number of arrivals, '000

1	France	61,500	21	Thailand	7,517
2	United States	44,791	22	Netherlands	6,692
3	Spain	41,425	23	Singapore	6,608
4	Italy	35,500	24	Belgium	5,627
5	China	26,055	25	Ireland	4,749
6	United Kingdom	25,800	26	South Africa	4,640
7	Mexico	21,732	27	Indonesia	4,475
8	Hungary	20,670	28	Argentina	4,285
9	Poland	19,420	29	Macau	4,275
10	Canada	17,345	30	Australia	4,167
11	Czech Republic	17,205	31	Tunisia	3,884
12	Austria	16,641	32	South Korea	3,815
13	Germany	15,070	33	Egypt	3,675
14	Hong Kong	11,700	34	Saudi Arabia	3,458
15	Switzerland	11,097	35	Bulgaria	3,420
16	Portugal	9,900	36	Puerto Rico	3,200
17	Greece	9,725	37	Norway	2,909
18	Russia	9,678	38	Morocco	2,701
19	Turkey	7,935	39	Bahrain	2,669
20	Malaysia	7,742	40	Sweden	2,595

Biggest tourist spending
$m

1	Germany	48,054	11	Belgium	9,215
2	United States	45,855	12	Taiwan	8,457
3	Japan	36,792	13	Switzerland	7,714
4	United Kingdom	24,815	14	South Korea	5,919
5	France	16,341	15	Poland	5,500
6	Italy	12,419	16	Sweden	5,422
7	Austria	11,689	17	Singapore	5,134
8	Russia	11,599	18	Australia	4,604
9	Netherlands	11,455	19	Spain	4,450
10	Canada	10,220	20	Denmark	4,280

Largest tourist receipts
$m

1	United States	64,373	11	Singapore	9,410
2	Spain	28,428	12	Thailand	8,829
3	France	28,241	13	Canada	8,727
4	Italy	27,439	14	Australia	8,264
5	United Kingdom	20,415	15	Poland	7,000
6	Austria	15,095	16	Mexico	6,898
7	Germany	13,168	17	Turkey	6,536
8	Hong Kong	11,200	18	South Korea	6,315
9	China	10,500	19	Belgium	5,893
10	Switzerland	9,892	20	Netherlands	5,877

Education

Highest primary enrolment
Number enrolled as % of relevant age group, 1993

1	Namibia	136	17	South Africa	111
2	Gabon	134	18	United Arab Emirates	110
3	Ecuador	123	19	Jamaica	109
4	Portugal	120		Philippines[a]	109
5	Colombia	119		Syria[b]	109
	Peru[a]	119		Uruguay	109
	Zimbabwe	119	23	Argentina	108
8	China	118		Australia	108
	Tunisia	118		Hong Kong[a]	108
10	Bangladesh	117		Laos	108
	Botswana	117		Vietnam[a]	108
12	Indonesia	114	28	Mauritius	107
13	United Kingdom	113		Nepal	107
14	Honduras	112		Russia	107
	Mexico	112		Singapore[a]	107
	Paraguay	112		United States	107

Lowest primary enrolment
Number enrolled as % of relevant age group, 1993

1	Ethiopia	23	14	Mozambique	60
2	Afghanistan[c]	24	15	Kuwait	65
3	Bhutan[d]	26		Pakistan	65
4	Niger	28	17	Benin	66
5	Mali	31	18	Côte d'Ivoire	69
6	Liberia[e]	35		Mauritania	69
7	Burkina Faso	39	20	Burundi	70
8	Guinea	46		Tanzania	70
9	Sierra Leone[a]	48	22	Central African Rep	72
10	Sudan[d]	49	23	Gambia, The	73
11	Rwanda	50		Morocco	73
12	Chad	59	25	Madagascar	74
	Senegal	59		Papua New Guinea	74

Highest tertiary enrolment[f]
Number enrolled as % of relevant age group, 1993

1	Canada	103	12	Belarus	44
2	United States	81	13	Austria	43
3	Finland	63	14	Australia	42
4	New Zealand	58		Kazakhstan	42
5	Norway	54	16	Argentina	41
6	France	50		Denmark	41
7	Armenia	49		Spain	41
8	South Korea	48	19	Peru	40
9	Ukraine	46	20	Latvia	39
10	Netherlands	45		Lithuania	39
	Russia	45			

Notes: The gross enrolment ratios shown are the actual number enrolled as a percentage of the number of children in the official primary age group. They may exceed 100 when children outside the primary age group are receiving primary education either because they have not moved on to secondary education or because they have started primary education early.

Least literate
% adult literacy rate, 1993

1	Niger	12.8	**14**	Oman	35.0
2	Burkina Faso	18.0	**15**	Liberia	36.4
3	Somalia	24.9	**16**	Pakistan	36.4
4	Nepal	26.3	**17**	Gambia, The	36.6
5	Mali	28.4	**18**	Mauritania	36.7
6	Sierra Leone	29.6	**19**	Bangladesh	37.0
7	Afghanistan	29.8	**20**	Côte d'Ivoire	37.8
8	Senegal	31.4	**21**	Mozambique	37.9
9	Ethiopia	33.6	**22**	Namibia	40.0
10	Burundi	33.7	**23**	Bhutan	40.2
11	Guinea	33.9	**24**	Yemen	41.1
12	Benin	34.3	**25**	Morocco	41.7
13	Cambodia	35.0			

Highest education spending[g]
% of GNP

1	Uzbekistan	11.0	**14**	Barbados	7.5
2	Tajikistan	9.5	**15**	Armenia	7.4
3	Norway	9.2	**16**	New Zealand	7.3
4	Namibia	8.7		Peru	7.3
5	Botswana	8.5	**18**	Côte d'Ivoire	7.2
	Denmark	8.5	**19**	Libya	7.1
7	Finland	8.4		South Africa	7.1
	Sweden	8.4	**21**	Jamaica	7.0
9	Congo	8.3	**22**	Kenya	6.8
	Zimbabwe	8.3		Swaziland	6.8
11	Ukraine	8.2		Kirgizstan	6.8
12	Turkmenistan	7.9	**25**	Kenya	6.7
13	Canada	7.6		Hungary	6.7

Lowest education spending[g]
% of GNP

1	Somalia	0.5	**14**	Afghanistan	2.0
2	Zaire	1.0		Lebanon	2.0
3	Nigeria	1.3		United Arab Emirates	2.0
	Indonesia	1.3	**17**	Mali	2.1
5	Sierra Leone	1.4	**18**	Chad	2.2
	Haiti	1.4		Romania	2.2
7	El Salvador	1.6	**20**	Bangladesh	2.3
	Guatemala	1.6		Laos	2.3
	Brazil	1.6	**22**	Myanmar	2.4
10	Madagascar	1.9		Philippines	2.4
	Uganda	1.9	**24**	Uruguay	2.5
	Dominican Republic	1.9	**25**	Zambia	2.6
	Georgia	1.9		China	2.6

a 1992   b 1991   c 1989   d 1990   e 1988
f   Tertiary education includes all levels of post-secondary education including courses
    leading to awards not equivalent to a university degree, courses leading to a first
    university degree and postgraduate courses.
g   Latest available year up to 1994.

Life: *the chances*

Highest life expectancy
Years, 1995–2000

1	Japan	80.0		Netherlands Antilles	76.4
2	Iceland	79.3	32	Cuba	76.0
3	Canada	78.9		Kuwait	76.0
4	France	78.8	34	Denmark	75.6
	Hong Kong	78.8	35	Brunei	75.5
6	Switzerland	78.6		Guadeloupe	75.5
7	Sweden	78.5	37	Portugal	75.4
8	Australia	78.3	38	Chile	75.3
	Italy	78.3		Réunion	75.3
10	Greece	78.1	40	United Arab Emirates	74.8
11	Spain	78.0	41	Jamaica	74.6
12	Netherlands	77.9	42	Panama	73.9
13	Israel	77.7	43	Bahamas	73.8
14	Cyprus	77.6	44	Trinidad & Tobago	73.7
	Norway	77.6	45	Slovenia	73.5
16	Belgium	77.3	46	Argentina	73.2
	Singapore	77.3		Bosnia	73.2
18	New Zealand	77.2	48	Sri Lanka	73.1
19	Martinique	77.1	49	Bahrain	72.9
	United Kingdom	77.1		Czech Republic	72.9
21	Austria	77.0		Uruguay	72.9
22	Malta	76.9	52	Venezuela	72.8
23	Costa Rica	76.8	53	Georgia	72.7
24	Germany	76.7	54	Fiji	72.6
	United States	76.7	55	Macedonia, FYR	72.5
26	Finland	76.6		Mexico	72.5
	Ireland	76.6		Serbia, Montenegro	72.5
28	Puerto Rico	76.5	58	South Korea	72.4
29	Barbados	76.4	59	Croatia	72.2
	Luxembourg	76.4		North Korea	72.2

Highest male life expectancy
Years, 1995–2000

1	Iceland	77.4	6	Israel	75.7
2	Japan	76.9	7	Greece	75.5
3	Sweden	76.2	8	Australia	75.4
4	Canada	76.1		Cyprus	75.4
	Hong Kong	76.1	10	Switzerland	75.3

Highest female life expectancy
Years, 1995–2000

1	France	82.9	6	Spain	81.5
	Japan	82.9	7	Italy	81.4
3	Canada	81.8	8	Australia	81.2
	Hong Kong	81.8		Iceland	81.2
	Switzerland	81.8	10	Sweden	80.8

Lowest life expectancy
Years, 1995–2000

1	Sierra Leone	37.5	31	Laos	53.5
2	Malawi	40.7		Mauritania	53.5
3	Uganda	41.4	33	Cambodia	54.1
4	Rwanda	42.1	34	Haiti	54.4
5	Zambia	43.0	35	Kenya	54.5
6	Guinea-Bissau	43.8	36	Benin	54.8
7	Afghanistan	45.5	37	Sudan	55.0
8	Burkina Faso	46.0	38	Gabon	55.5
9	Angola	46.5		Namibia	55.5
	Guinea	46.5	40	Cameroon	55.9
11	Mozambique	46.9	41	Nepal	57.3
12	Gambia, The	47.0	42	Papua New Guinea	57.9
13	Burundi	47.2	43	Ghana	58.0
14	Chad	47.7		Yemen	58.0
15	Mali	48.0	45	Bangladesh	58.1
16	Niger	48.5	46	Madagascar	58.5
	Zimbabwe	48.5	47	Lesotho	58.6
18	Central African Rep	48.6	48	Swaziland	60.0
19	Somalia	49.0	49	Myanmar	60.1
20	Togo	50.1	50	Bolivia	61.5
21	Botswana	50.4	51	India	62.4
22	Ethiopia	50.6		Iraq	62.4
23	Congo	50.9	53	Pakistan	63.9
24	Côte d'Ivoire	51.0	54	Russia	64.4
25	Senegal	51.3	55	Turkmenistan	64.6
26	Tanzania	51.4	56	Indonesia	65.1
27	Liberia	51.5	57	South Africa	65.2
28	Nigeria	52.4	58	Libya	65.5
29	Zaire	52.9	59	Mongolia	65.8
30	Bhutan	53.2	60	Egypt	66.0

Lowest male life expectancy
Years, 1995–2000

1	Sierra Leone	36.0	6	Guinea-Bissau	42.4
2	Malawi	40.3	7	Angola	44.9
3	Uganda	40.4	8	Afghanistan	45.0
4	Rwanda	40.8	9	Burkina Faso	45.1
5	Zambia	42.2	10	Gambia, The	45.4

Lowest female life expectancy
Years, 1995–2000

1	Sierra Leone	39.1	6	Guinea-Bissau	45.2
2	Malawi	41.1	7	Afghanistan	46.0
3	Uganda	42.3	8	Burkina Faso	47.0
4	Rwanda	43.4		Guinea	47.0
5	Zambia	43.7	10	Angola	48.1

Death: *the chances*

Highest death rates[a]

Number of deaths per 1,000 population

1	Sierra Leone	25.7	**51**	Lithuania	11.6
2	Malawi	22.4		Romania	11.6
3	Uganda	21.0	**53**	Kenya	11.3
4	Afghanistan	20.8	**54**	Sweden	11.2
5	Guinea-Bissau	20.6	**55**	United Kingdom	11.1
6	Rwanda	19.7	**56**	Nepal	11.0
7	Angola	18.7	**57**	Germany	10.9
8	Guinea	18.4		Portugal	10.9
9	Zambia	18.0	**59**	Moldova	10.8
10	Burkina Faso	17.7	**60**	Norway	10.7
11	Mozambique	17.5		Poland	10.7
12	Gambia, The	17.4		Slovenia	10.7
13	Chad	17.3	**63**	Lesotho	10.6
14	Mali	17.1	**64**	Belgium	10.5
	Niger	17.1		Slovakia	10.5
16	Burundi	17.0	**66**	Ghana	10.4
17	Somalia	16.9		Uruguay	10.4
18	Central African Rep	16.4		Yemen	10.4
19	Ethiopia	16.2	**69**	Finland	10.2
20	Liberia	15.3	**70**	Austria	10.0
21	Togo	14.9	**71**	Greece	9.9
22	Eritrea	14.7		Italy	9.9
23	Congo	14.6		Luxembourg	9.9
	Hungary	14.6		Madagascar	9.9
	Zimbabwe	14.6		Papua New Guinea	9.9
26	Russia	14.5	**76**	Myanmar	9.8
	Senegal	14.5	**77**	Bangladesh	9.7
28	Gabon	14.3		Serbia, Montenegro	9.7
29	Nigeria	13.9	**79**	Georgia	9.5
30	Côte d'Ivoire	13.8	**80**	Spain	9.4
	Latvia	13.8	**81**	Swaziland	9.2
	Ukraine	13.8	**82**	Bolivia	9.1
33	Bhutan	13.7		France	9.1
34	Laos	13.5		Switzerland	9.1
	Tanzania	13.5	**85**	India	9.0
	Zaire	13.5	**86**	Barbados	8.9
37	Bulgaria	13.3	**87**	Netherlands	8.8
38	Estonia	13.1	**88**	United States	8.7
	Mauritania	13.1	**89**	Ireland	8.6
40	Botswana	13.0	**90**	Iraq	8.5
41	Haiti	12.8		Kazakhstan	8.5
42	Benin	12.4	**92**	Japan	8.2
43	Cambodia	12.2	**93**	Argentina	7.9
44	Belarus	12.1		Malta	7.9
45	Czech Republic	12.0		New Zealand	7.9
46	Cameroon	11.9		South Africa	7.9
47	Denmark	11.8	**97**	Pakistan	7.8
	Namibia	11.8	**98**	Cyprus	7.6
49	Croatia	11.7		Indonesia	7.6
	Sudan	11.7		Turkmenistan	7.6

Highest infant mortality[a]
Number of deaths per 1,000 live births

1	Sierra Leone	169	26	Congo	90
2	Afghanistan	154	27	Zaire	89
3	Liberia	153	28	Côte d'Ivoire	86
4	Mali	149		Laos	86
5	Malawi	142		Togo	86
6	Guinea-Bissau	132	31	Gabon	85
7	Rwanda	125	32	Benin	84
8	Angola	124	33	Haiti	82
	Guinea	124		Nepal	82
10	Gambia, The	122	35	Tanzania	80
11	Chad	115		Yemen	80
12	Burundi	114	37	Bangladesh	78
	Niger	114		Myanmar	78
14	Uganda	113	39	Madagascar	77
15	Somalia	112		Nigeria	77
16	Mozambique	110	41	Pakistan	74
17	Ethiopia	107	42	Ghana	73
18	Bhutan	104	43	India	72
19	Zambia	103		Lesotho	72
20	Cambodia	102	45	Sudan	71
21	Eritrea	98	46	Zimbabwe	68
22	Burkina Faso	97	47	Bolivia	66
23	Central African Rep	96	48	Kenya	65
24	Iraq	95		Swaziland	65
25	Mauritania	92	50	Senegal	62

Lowest death rates[a]
Number of deaths per 1,000 pop.

1	Kuwait	2.2
2	United Arab Emirates	2.9
3	Brunei	3.0
4	Bahrain	3.6
5	Qatar	3.7
6	Costa Rica	3.8
7	Saudi Arabia	4.2
8	Oman	4.3
9	Fiji	4.6
	Macao	4.6

Lowest infant mortality[a]
Number of deaths per 1,000 pop

1	Japan	4
2	Finland	5
	Hong Kong	5
	Iceland	5
	Norway	5
	Singapore	5
	Sweden	5
	Switzerland	5
9	Australia	6
	Austria	6
	Canada	6
	Germany	6
	Ireland	6
	Luxembourg	6
	Netherlands	6
	United Kingdom	6

Notes: The data for the number of deaths per 1,000 population are crude rates, i.e. not adjusted for differences in age structure. Thus a country with a high proportion of older people will have a higher rate than one with a younger population. This explains why a number of developed countries have apparently high death rates.

Both death and, in particular, infant mortality rates can be underestimated in certain countries where not all deaths are officially recorded.

a   1995-2000

Death: *the causes*

Cancer[a]
%

1	Netherlands	25.7
2	France	25.3
3	Hong Kong	25.0
4	Switzerland	24.9
5	Canada	24.8
6	Denmark	24.7
7	United Kingdom	24.6
8	Italy	24.5
	New Zealand	24.5
10	Australia	24.2
11	Ireland	23.4
12	Germany	23.3
13	Austria	23.0
	Czech Republic	23.0
15	Japan	22.9
16	United States	22.7
17	Singapore	21.8
	Uruguay	21.8
19	Hungary	21.7
20	Norway	21.6

Heart attack[a]
%

1	Georgia	45.4
2	Armenia	43.8
3	Uzbekistan	42.7
4	Azerbaijan	41.9
5	Lithuania	39.0
	Turkmenistan	39.0
7	Estonia	36.9
8	Austria	36.6
9	Belarus	35.0
10	Latvia	34.7
11	Sweden	34.6
12	United States	34.4
13	Finland	33.4
14	Australia	32.6
	Israel	32.6
16	Argentina	32.5
	Germany	32.5
18	Ireland	32.2
19	Bulgaria	31.8
	Cuba	31.8
	Kazakhstan	31.8

Infectious disease[a]
%

1	Hong Kong	4.7
2	Mexico	4.1
3	Kuwait	3.6
4	Tajikistan	3.4
5	Argentina	3.3
	Turkmenistan	3.3
7	Chile	2.7
8	Singapore	2.6
9	Puerto Rico	2.5
10	China	2.3
11	Kirgizstan	2.2
12	Costa Rica	2.1
	South Korea	2.1
	Uzbekistan	2.1
15	Azerbaijan	2.0
16	Kazakhstan	1.9
17	Mauritius	1.8
	Trinidad & Tobago	1.8
19	Israel	1.6
	Japan	1.6

Motor accident[a]
%

1	South Korea	3.1
2	Latvia	2.2
3	Kuwait	1.9
4	Slovenia	1.8
5	Estonia	1.7
6	Greece	1.6
	Mexico	1.6
	Portugal	1.6
9	Costa Rica	1.5
	Lithuania	1.5
11	Mauritius	1.4
	Poland	1.4
	Puerto Rico	1.4
	Russia	1.4
15	Italy	1.3
	New Zealand	1.3
	Spain	1.3
	Tajikistan	1.3
19	Austria	1.2
	Ukraine	1.2
	United States	1.2

a   Latest available.

Notes: Data refer to the chances a newborn baby has of eventually dying from one of the causes shown. Statistics are available for only a limited number of countries and many less developed countries are excluded.

Stroke[a]

%

1	Ukraine	28.6
2	Georgia	26.2
3	Portugal	24.7
4	Bulgaria	21.0
5	Greece	20.5
6	China	20.3
7	Russia	19.9
8	Latvia	19.3
9	Kirgizstan	19.2
10	South Korea	18.3
11	Tajikistan	17.9
12	Kazakhstan	17.5
13	Estonia	17.4
14	Czech Republic	17.2
15	Croatia	16.9
16	Romania	16.4
	Uzbekistan	16.4
18	Armenia	16.1
19	Mauritius	15.9
20	Albania	15.2

Injury and poisoning[a]

%

1	Estonia	14.5
2	Russia	14.4
3	Latvia	14.0
4	Lithuania	12.5
5	Kazakhstan	9.5
6	Belarus	8.9
7	Ukraine	8.3
8	Kirgizstan	8.2
	Slovenia	8.2
10	Moldova	8.0
11	Cuba	7.9
	Hungary	7.9
13	France	7.5
14	Finland	7.0
15	Mexico	6.9
	South Korea	6.9
17	Czech Republic	6.5
	Switzerland	6.5
19	Azerbaijan	6.3
	Chile	6.3
	China	6.3

AIDS

Cases per 100,000 inhabitants[a]

1	Bahamas	790.3	21	Gabon	127.9
2	Bermuda	527.0	22	Netherlands Antilles	126.3
3	Zimbabwe	514.0	23	Swaziland	109.1
4	Malawi	475.8	24	Ghana	108.0
5	Zambia	456.6	25	Spain	105.0
6	Congo	394.3	26	Honduras	96.4
7	Namibia	314.5	27	Martinique	90.5
8	Tanzania	273.7	28	Eritrea	83.6
9	Botswana	260.1	29	Guinea-Bissau	77.0
10	Kenya	254.2	30	Thailand	76.4
11	Uganda	245.4	31	Burkina Faso	75.9
12	Barbados	242.1	32	Switzerland	75.3
13	Côte d'Ivoire	233.4	33	France	74.8
14	United States	211.6	34	Jamaica	71.6
15	Rwanda	206.5	35	Haiti	69.7
16	Togo	177.6	36	Zaire	64.8
17	Trinidad & Tobago	161.8	37	Lesotho	63.5
18	Central African Rep	156.2	38	Italy	62.8
19	Guadeloupe	146.9	39	Cameroon	61.7
20	Burundi	138.2	40	Chad	54.6

a AIDS data refer to the total number of cases reported to the World Health
Organisation up to the 20th November 1996. The number of cases diagnosed and
reported depends on the quality of medical practice and administration and is likely
to be under-recorded in a number of countries.

Health

Highest health spending
As % of GDPª

1	United States	14.3
2	Canada	9.8
3	Austria	9.7
	France	9.7
5	Switzerland	9.6
6	Germany	9.5
7	Netherlands	8.8
8	Australia	8.5
9	Finland	8.3
	Italy	8.3
11	Belgium	8.2
12	Iceland	8.1
13	Ireland	7.9
14	Sweden	7.7
15	Czech Republic	7.6
	Portugal	7.6
17	New Zealand	7.5
18	Norway	7.3
	Spain	7.3
20	Burkina Faso	7.0
	Hungary	7.0
22	Japan	6.9
	United Kingdom	6.9
24	Nicaragua	6.7
25	Denmark	6.6
26	Tajikistan	6.0
27	Uzbekistan	5.9
28	Luxembourg	5.8
29	Algeria	5.4
	Bulgaria	5.4

Lowest health spending
As % of GDPª

1	Syria	0.4
2	Sudan	0.5
3	Indonesia	0.7
4	Zaire	0.8
5	Morocco	0.9
	Somalia	0.9
7	Cameroon	1.0
	Egypt	1.0
	Laos	1.0
	Philippines	1.0
11	Hong Kong	1.1
	Singapore	1.1
	Thailand	1.1
	Vietnam	1.1
15	Nigeria	1.2
	Paraguay	1.2
17	India	1.3
	Madagascar	1.3
	Malaysia	1.3
20	Bangladesh	1.4
21	Iran	1.5
	Yemen	1.5
23	Uganda	1.6
24	Burundi	1.7
	Côte d'Ivoire	1.7
	Ghana	1.7
	Sierra Leone	1.7
28	Colombia	1.8
	Jordan	1.8
	Pakistan	1.8
	Sri Lanka	1.8

Highest population per doctor
1988–91

1	Malawi	50,000
2	Burkina Faso	33,330
	Chad	33,330
	Ethiopia	33,330
	Mozambique	33,330
	Tanzania	33,330
7	Angola	25,000
	Cambodia	25,000
	Central African Rep	25,000
	Ghana	25,000
	Lesotho	25,000
	Rwanda	25,000
	Uganda	25,000
14	Kenya	20,000
	Mali	20,000

16	Burundi	16,667
	Mauritania	16,667
	Nepal	16,667
	Senegal	16,667
20	Sierra Leone	14,290
	Somalia	14,290
22	Benin	14,286
	Zaire	14,286
24	Bangladesh	12,500
	Cameroon	12,500
	Myanmar	12,500
	Papua New Guinea	12,500
28	Gambia, The	11,690
29	Bhutan	11,110
	Côte d'Ivoire	11,110

Highest calorie intake
Calories per person, per day, latest available year

1	Ireland	3,847	31	Mexico	3,181
2	Greece	3,815	32	Australia	3,179
3	Cyprus	3,782	33	Syria	3,175
4	United States	3,732	34	Czech Republic	3,156
5	Spain	3,708	35	Hong Kong	3,144
6	Belgium	3,681	36	Canada	3,094
	Luxembourg	3,681	37	Fiji	3,092
8	New Zealand	3,669	38	Iceland	3,058
9	Denmark	3,664	39	Romania	3,051
10	Portugal	3,634	40	Israel	3,050
11	France	3,633	41	Taiwan	3,048
	Germany	3,633	42	Jordan	3,031
13	Italy	3,561	43	Finland	3,018
14	Serbia, Montenegro	3,551	44	Morocco	2,985
15	Hungary	3,503	45	Sweden	2,972
16	Austria	3,497	46	Japan	2,903
17	Malta	3,486	47	Algeria	2,897
18	Turkey	3,429	48	Costa Rica	2,889
19	Switzerland	3,379	49	Malaysia	2,884
20	Egypt	3,336	50	Argentina	2,880
21	Tunisia	3,333	51	Iran	2,861
22	Lebanon	3,319	52	North Korea	2,834
23	United Kingdom	3,317	53	Cuba	2,833
24	Libya	3,310	54	Bulgaria	2,831
25	Poland	3,301	55	Martinique	2,829
26	South Korea	3,298	56	Brazil	2,824
27	Norway	3,244	57	Indonesia	2,755
28	Barbados	3,223	58	Saudi Arabia	2,751
29	Netherlands	3,222	59	Uruguay	2,750
30	Belarus	3,207	60	Brunei	2,745

Lowest population per doctor
1988–91

1	Georgia	170		Uzbekistan	280
2	Latvia	200	17	Belarus	282
3	Estonia	210	18	Turkmenistan	290
	Russia	210	19	Belgium	298
5	Italy	211	20	Norway	309
6	Lithuania	220	21	Hungary	312
7	Austria	230	22	Greece	313
8	Vietnam	247	23	Bulgaria	315
9	Armenia	250	24	Argentina	329
	Azerbaijan	250	25	Cuba	332
	Kazakhstan	250	26	France	333
	Moldova	250	27	Israel	350
13	Ukraine	259		Tajikistan	350
14	Spain	262		Uruguay	350
15	Kirgizstan	280	30	Portugal	352

a   Latest available year to 1995.

Till death us do part

Highest marriage rates[a]
Number of marriages per 1,000 population

1	Cuba	17.7		Russia	7.3
2	Bermuda	14.2	32	Tunisia	7.2
3	Uzbekistan	11.0	33	Brunei	7.1
4	Bangladesh	10.9		Macedonia, FYR	7.1
5	Mauritius	10.3	35	Canada	7.0
6	Azerbaijan	10.1		Georgia	7.0
7	Turkmenistan	9.8	37	Malta	6.9
8	Puerto Rico	9.6	38	Cyprus	6.8
9	Tajikistan	9.2		Romania	6.8
10	Bahamas	9.1	40	Denmark	6.7
	Kirgizstan	9.1		Portugal	6.7
	United States	9.1	42	Chile	6.6
13	Moldova	9.0		Uruguay	6.6
	Sri Lanka	9.0	44	Costa Rica	6.4
15	Singapore	8.8		Ecuador	6.4
16	Kazakhstan	8.6		Netherlands Antilles	6.4
17	Egypt	8.4		Slovakia	6.4
	Thailand	8.4	48	Hong Kong	6.3
19	Syria	8.2		Japan	6.3
	Ukraine	8.2		Lithuania	6.3
21	Jordan	8.1		New Zealand	6.3
22	Turkey	8.0	52	Australia	6.2
23	Barbados	7.9		Greece	6.2
	Taiwan	7.9		Israel	6.2
25	Belarus	7.7		Réunion	6.2
	Kuwait	7.7	56	Philippines	6.0
27	Albania	7.6	57	Bahrain	5.9
28	South Korea	7.5		United Kingdom	5.9
29	Iran	7.4	59	Armenia	5.8
30	Mexico	7.3		Switzerland	5.8

Lowest marriage rates[a]
Number of marriages per 1,000 population

1	Qatar	3.0	12	Croatia	4.6
2	Paraguay	3.7		Finland	4.6
3	Sweden	3.8		Ireland	4.6
4	El Salvador	4.2	15	Guadeloupe	4.7
5	Slovenia	4.3	16	Norway	4.8
6	France	4.4	17	Italy	4.9
	Latvia	4.4		Suriname	4.9
	Martinique	4.4	19	Spain	5.0
9	Bulgaria	4.5	20	Belgium	5.1
	Estonia	4.5		Libya	5.1
	Iceland	4.5		Luxembourg	5.1

a Latest available year.

Note: Marriage rates refer to registered marriages only and, therefore, reflect the customs surrounding registry and efficiency of administration. The data are based on latest available figures and hence will be affected by the population age structure at the time.

Highest divorce rates[a]
Number of divorces per 1,000 population

1	United States	4.6		Spain	2.0
2	Russia	4.3	33	Iceland	1.9
3	Cuba	4.2	34	Kirgizstan	1.8
	Ukraine	4.2		Kuwait	1.8
5	Puerto Rico	4.0		Luxembourg	1.8
6	Belarus	3.9	37	Azerbaijan	1.6
7	Estonia	3.7	38	Slovakia	1.5
	Lithuania	3.7		Tajikistan	1.5
9	Latvia	3.4		Uzbekistan	1.5
	Moldova	3.4	41	Barbados	1.4
11	Bermuda	3.2		Egypt	1.4
	Uruguay	3.2		Georgia	1.4
13	United Kingdom	3.0		Japan	1.4
14	Canada	2.9		Portugal	1.4
	Czech Republic	2.9		Romania	1.4
16	Finland	2.7		Turkmenistan	1.4
	Kazakhstan	2.7	48	Bahrain	1.3
	New Zealand	2.7		Bulgaria	1.3
19	Australia	2.6		Israel	1.3
20	Denmark	2.5		Réunion	1.3
	Norway	2.5		Singapore	1.3
	Suriname	2.5	53	Bahamas	1.2
	Sweden	2.5		Jordan	1.2
24	Austria	2.3	55	Brunei	1.1
25	Belgium	2.2		Costa Rica	1.1
	Netherlands	2.2		Guadeloupe	1.1
	Netherlands Antilles	2.2	58	Hong Kong	1.0
	Switzerland	2.2		Martinique	1.0
29	Hungary	2.1		South Korea	1.0
30	France	2.0		Venezuela	1.0
	Germany	2.0			

Lowest divorce rates[a]
Number of divorces per 1,000 population

1	Guatemala	0.2		Mexico	0.6
	Nicaragua	0.2		Serbia, Montenegro	0.6
3	Macedonia, FYR	0.3	15	Albania	0.7
4	Chile	0.4		Greece	0.7
5	Brazil	0.5		Iran	0.7
	El Salvador	0.5		Mauritius	0.7
	Italy	0.5		Poland	0.7
	Libya	0.5		Slovenia	0.7
	Turkey	0.5		Syria	0.7
10	Cyprus	0.6	22	Panama	0.8
	Ecuador	0.6		Qatar	0.8
	Jamaica	0.6	24	Trinidad & Tobago	0.9

Households and prices

Biggest households[a]
Population per dwelling

1	Gabon	8.3		25	Mali	5.6
2	Bosnia	7.3			Qatar	5.6
3	Iraq	7.1			Sudan	5.6
4	Algeria	7.0			Venezuela	5.6
5	Yemen	6.8		29	Mauritania	5.5
6	Guinea	6.7			Sri Lanka	5.5
	Jordan	6.7			Tunisia	5.5
	Pakistan	6.7		32	Benin	5.4
9	Bahrain	6.6			Philippines	5.4
10	Kuwait	6.5			Zaire	5.4
11	Niger	6.4		35	Congo	5.3
12	Syria	6.3			Tanzania	5.3
13	Burkina Faso	6.2		37	Cambodia	5.2
	Liberia	6.2			Cameroon	5.2
15	Afghanistan	5.9			Guatemala	5.2
	Morocco	5.9			Iran	5.2
17	Brunei	5.8			Myanmar	5.2
	Côte d'Ivoire	5.8			Paraguay	5.2
	Croatia	5.8		43	Kenya	5.1
	Fiji	5.8			Nigeria	5.1
	Nepal	5.8		45	India	5.0
22	Bangladesh	5.7			Mexico	5.0
	Togo	5.7			South Africa	5.0
	Ukraine	5.7				

Highest cost of living[b]
December 1996=100 USA=100

1	Libya[c]	184		17	Congo	110
2	Japan	171			Finland	110
3	Norway	140			South Korea	110
4	Switzerland	133		20	Côte d'Ivoire	107
5	France	129			Israel	107
	Gabon	129		22	Luxembourg	105
7	Austria	123			United Kingdom	105
	Denmark	123		24	China	103
	Sweden	123		25	Australia	100
10	Hong Kong	120			Ireland	100
	Russia	120			United States	100
12	Singapore	115		28	Spain	99
13	Germany	114		29	Greece	97
14	Belgium	113		30	Brazil	96
15	Taiwan	112			Italy	96
16	Netherlands	111				

a Latest available year.
b The cost of living index shown is compiled by The Economist Intelligence Unit for use by companies in determining expatriate compensation: it is a comparison of the cost of maintaining a typical international lifestyle in the country rather than a comparison of the purchasing power of a citizen of the country. The index is based on typical urban prices an international executive and family will face abroad. The

Smallest households[a]
Population per dwelling

1	Denmark	2.3	24	Greece	2.9
	Germany	2.3		Luxembourg	2.9
	Sweden	2.3		New Zealand	2.9
4	Finland	2.4		Slovakia	2.9
	Iceland	2.4	28	Cyprus	3.0
	Latvia	2.4		Portugal	3.0
	Netherlands	2.4		Romania	3.0
	Norway	2.4	31	Czech Republic	3.1
	Switzerland	2.4		Japan	3.1
10	Austria	2.5	33	Malta	3.2
11	Bermuda	2.6	34	Belarus	3.3
	France	2.6		Poland	3.3
	Hungary	2.6		Puerto Rico	3.3
	Italy	2.6		Uruguay	3.3
	Spain	2.6	38	Albania	3.4
	United States	2.6		China	3.4
17	Australia	2.7		Gambia, The	3.4
	Belgium	2.7		Hong Kong	3.4
	Canada	2.7		South Korea	3.4
	United Kingdom	2.7	43	Barbados	3.6
21	Argentina	2.8		Estonia	3.6
	Bulgaria	2.8		Macao	3.6
	Russia	2.8		Serbia	3.6

Lowest cost of living[b]
December 1996=100 USA=100

1	India	45	17	Vietnam	66
2	Iran	47	18	Czech Republic	67
3	Zimbabwe	53	19	Philippines	68
4	Pakistan	54	20	Paraguay	69
5	Hungary	57		Poland	69
	Venezuela	57	22	Kuwait	70
7	Kenya	58	23	Colombia	71
8	Algeria	59	24	Turkey	72
9	Ecuador	60	25	Panama	73
	South Africa	60		Peru	73
11	Romania	62		Tunisia	73
	Sri Lanka	62	28	Chile	74
13	Mexico	64		Saudi Arabia	74
	Serbia	64	30	Nigeria	76
15	Bangladesh	65		Uruguay	76
	Costa Rica	65			

prices are for products of international comparable quality found in a supermarket
or department store. Prices found in local markets and bazaars are not used unless
the available merchandise is of the specified quality and the shopping area itself is
safe for executive and family members. New York City prices are used as the base,
so USA = 100.

c   December 1995

Consumer goods: *ownership*

TV
Number of people per receiver

1	Bermuda	0.9		Greece		2.3
2	United States	1.3		Hungary		2.3
3	Australia	1.6		Italy		2.3
	Brunei	1.6	29	Estonia		2.4
	Canada	1.6	30	Czech Republic		2.5
	Japan	1.6		Poland		2.5
	United Kingdom	1.6	32	Ireland		2.6
8	France	1.7		Russia		2.6
	Luxembourg	1.7	34	Kuwait		2.7
10	Germany	1.8		Slovenia		2.7
	Norway	1.8	36	Bulgaria		2.8
12	Denmark	1.9		Hong Kong		2.8
	Finland	1.9		Lithuania		2.8
14	Austria	2.0		Singapore		2.8
	Netherlands	2.0	40	Argentina		2.9
	New Zealand	2.0	41	Portugal		3.0
	Spain	2.0	42	Netherlands Antilles		3.1
18	Latvia	2.1		Puerto Rico		3.1
	Sweden	2.1		South Korea		3.1
20	Belgium	2.2	45	Taiwan		3.2
	Iceland	2.2		Trinidad & Tobago		3.2
	Malta	2.2	47	Israel		3.3
	Qatar	2.2		Jamaica		3.3
	Switzerland	2.2		Moldova		3.3
25	Bahrain	2.3		Uruguay		3.3

Telephone
Number of people per telephone line

1	Bermuda	1.4		Belgium		2.2
2	Sweden	1.5		Malta		2.2
3	Denmark	1.6	25	Italy		2.3
	Switzerland	1.6		Taiwan		2.3
	United States	1.6	27	Israel		2.4
6	Canada	1.7		Martinique		2.4
7	Finland	1.8		South Korea		2.4
	France	1.8	30	Spain		2.6
	Iceland	1.8	31	Guadeloupe		2.7
	Luxembourg	1.8		Ireland		2.7
	Norway	1.8		Netherlands Antilles		2.7
12	Hong Kong	1.9	34	Macau		2.8
	Netherlands	1.9		Portugal		2.8
14	Australia	2.0	36	Barbados		2.9
	Germany	2.0	37	Puerto Rico		3.0
	Greece	2.0		Réunion		3.0
	United Kingdom	2.0	39	Slovenia		3.2
18	Cyprus	2.1	40	Bulgaria		3.3
	Japan	2.1	41	Bahamas		3.5
	New Zealand	2.1		United Arab Emirates		3.5
	Singapore	2.1	43	Croatia		3.6
22	Austria	2.2		Estonia		3.6

Home computer
Computers per 100 people

1	United States	35		Singapore	18
2	Australia	27		Sweden[a]	18
3	Canada	25	13	Germany	17
	Norway	25	14	France	16
5	Finland	23		Switzerland[a]	16
	New Zealand	23	16	Belgium	15
7	Denmark	22		Hong Kong	15
8	Netherlands	20	18	Japan	14
	United Kingdom	20	19	Austria	12
10	Ireland	18		Israel	12

Video cassette recorder[b]
% of households owning

1	United Kingdom	86		Sweden	69
2	United States	79	11	France	68
3	Japan	76		Ireland	68
4	Belgium	73		Netherlands	68
5	Italy	72	14	Germany	67
6	Denmark	71	15	Austria	66
	Luxembourg	71	16	Spain	62
8	Canada	69		Switzerland	62
	Finland	69	18	Norway	60

Dishwasher[b]
% of households owning

1	Luxembourg	55	11	Portugal	27
2	Sweden	50	12	Belgium	26
3	Norway	48	13	Slovenia	23
4	Switzerland	46	14	Turkey	21
5	United States	45	15	Ireland	20
6	France	43		Spain	20
7	Denmark	42	17	United Kingdom	19
	Finland	42	18	Italy	18
9	Germany	41		Netherlands	18
10	Austria	36	19	Greece	15

Microwave[b]
% of households owning

1	United States	84	11	Netherlands	35
2	Japan	81	12	Austria	34
3	Finland	71	13	Luxembourg	33
4	Sweden	68	14	Spain	27
5	United Kingdom	66		Switzerland	27
6	Germany	52	16	Hungary	24
7	Ireland	51		Portugal	24
8	France	50	17	Belgium	21
9	Norway	43		Slovenia	14
10	Denmark	37	19	Czech Republic	12

a 1994   b Latest available year up to 1995.
Note: A number of difficulties arise when dealing with household penetration data. Definitions of articles may vary.

Books

Book sales

$m			Per head, $		
1	United States	25,490	1	Norway	137
2	Japan	10,467	2	Germany	122
3	Germany	9,962	3	Belgium	117
4	United Kingdom	3,651	4	Switzerland	112
5	France	3,380	5	Austria	101
6	Spain	2,992	6	United States	95
7	South Korea	2,805	7	Japan	84
8	Brazil	2,526	8	Denmark	81
9	Italy	2,246	9	New Zealand	79
10	China	1,760	9	Singapore	79
11	Canada	1,274	11	Netherlands	78
12	Netherlands	1,200	12	Spain	76
13	Belgium	1,189	13	Australia	66
14	Australia	1,187	14	United Kingdom	63
15	Mexico	822	15	South Korea	62
16	Austria	809	16	France	58
17	Switzerland	805	17	Ireland	56
18	Taiwan	665		Sweden	56
19	Russia	634	19	Finland	52
20	Argentina	614	20	Canada	43
21	Norway	602	21	Italy	39
22	South Africa	506	22	Taiwan	31
23	Sweden	491	23	Portugal	22

Fiction book sales

Per head, $

1	Norway	46
2	United States	38
3	Germany	34
	Switzerland	34
5	Belgium	33
6	Japan	30
7	Austria	27
8	New Zealand	25
9	Denmark	24
10	Netherlands	22
11	Australia	20
	Singapore	20
13	United Kingdom	19
14	Sweden	18
15	Spain	17
	France	17
17	Ireland	16
18	Canada	15
	Finland	15
20	South Korea	12
21	Slovenia	8
22	Portugal	7
	Italy	7

Non-fiction book sales

Per head, $

1	Norway	93
2	Germany	88
3	Belgium	85
4	Switzerland	79
5	Austria	73
6	Singapore	60
7	Spain	58
8	United States	57
	Denmark	57
10	Netherlands	55
	New Zealand	55
12	Japan	54
13	South Korea	51
14	Australia	47
15	United Kingdom	44
16	France	42
17	Ireland	40
18	Finland	38
19	Sweden	37
20	Italy	32
21	Canada	28
	Taiwan	28
23	Portugal	15

Music and the Internet

Music sales[a]

$m			$ per head	
1	United States	12,102	1 Norway	67
2	Japan	7,552	2 Switzerland	63
3	Germany	3,270	3 Japan	60
4	United Kingdom	2,572	4 Denmark	59
5	France	2,392	5 Austria	51
6	Canada	1,113	6 Belgium	47
7	Brazil	1,053	7 Netherlands	46
8	Netherlands	717	8 United States	45
9	Australia	681	9 United Kingdom	44
10	Italy	583	10 Sweden	43
11	Spain	557	11 France	41
12	South Korea	505	12 Germany	40
13	Belgium	475	13 Australia	38
14	Switzerland	449	Canada	38
15	Austria	409	15 New Zealand	31
16	Sweden	382	16 Hong Kong	30
17	Taiwan	336	17 Finland	28
18	Denmark	306	18 Singapore	23
19	Mexico	299	19 Ireland	22
20	Norway	291	20 United Arab Emirates	19
21	Argentina	290	21 Taiwan	16
22	India	275	22 Israel	15

Internet hosts[b]

By country, Jan. 1997			Per 1,000 pop., Jan. 1997	
1	United States	10,267,901	1 Finland	55.5
2	Britain	733,538	2 Norway	39.4
3	Japan	732,898	3 United States	38.4
4	Germany	721,291	4 Australia	28.5
5	Canada	599,213	5 Sweden	26.4
6	Australia	509,360	6 New Zealand	23.6
7	Finland	283,490	7 Canada	20.4
8	Netherlands	270,935	Denmark	20.4
9	France	245,199	9 Switzerland	18.2
10	Sweden	231,915	10 Netherlands	17.5
11	Norway	170,594	11 Britain	12.6
12	Italy	148,158	12 Austria	11.4
13	Switzerland	130,636	13 Singapore	10.0
14	Spain	111,352	14 Hong Kong	8.9
15	Denmark	106,393	15 Germany	8.8
16	Austria	91,954	16 Ireland	7.6
17	South Africa	91,223	17 Israel	7.1
18	New Zealand	84,075	18 Belgium	6.4
19	Belgium	64,509	19 Japan	5.9
20	Hong Kong	54,311	20 France	4.2
21	Czech Republic	40,539	21 Czech Republic	4.0
22	Israel	39,172	22 Hungary	2.9

a Includes vinyl, tape and compact disc sales.
b Includes all hosts ending ".com", ".net" and ".org", which exaggerates the numbers.

Drinking and smoking

Beer drinkers
Litres consumed per head

1	Czech Republic	160.0
2	Ireland	141.3
3	Germany	137.7
4	Denmark	120.1
5	Austria	115.6
6	Belgium	104.0
7	United Kingdom	102.7
8	Hungary	102.4
9	Luxembourg	99.4
10	New Zealand	98.8
11	Australia	95.4
12	United States	87.9
13	Netherlands	85.8
14	Slovakia	81.0
15	Finland	80.2
16	Venezuela	71.9
17	Canada	70.0
18	Spain	66.6
19	Sweden	64.5
20	Portugal	64.2

Wine drinkers
Litres consumed per head

1	France	63.5
2	Italy	60.4
3	Portugal	58.4
4	Luxembourg	58.2
5	Argentina	43.8
6	Switzerland	43.6
7	Spain	36.3
8	Hungary	34.7
9	Greece	34.5
10	Austria	32.0
11	Uruguay	30.8
12	Denmark	27.6
13	Romania	25.3
14	Belgium	25.0
15	Germany	22.2
16	Bulgaria	21.8
17	Chile	21.7
18	Australia	18.2
19	Czech Republic	16.9
20	New Zealand	16.8

Pure alcohol
Litres consumed per head

1	Luxembourg	11.6
2	France	11.5
3	Portugal	11.0
4	Hungary	10.2
	Spain	10.2
6	Czech Republic	10.1
7	Denmark	10.0
8	Germany	9.9
9	Austria	9.8
10	Switzerland	9.4
11	Ireland	9.2
12	Belgium	9.1
13	Greece	9.0
	Romania	9.0
15	Italy	8.8
16	Bulgaria	8.1
17	Netherlands	8.0
18	Cyprus	7.9
19	Slovakia	7.8
20	Australia	7.6

Smokers
Av. ann. consumption of cigarettes per head per day

1	Greece	7.4
	Japan	7.4
3	Hungary	7.3
4	Poland	6.5
5	Estonia[a]	6.4
6	South Korea	6.1
	Switzerland	6.1
8	Lativa[a]	5.6
9	Czech Republic	5.4
	Spain	5.4
11	Bulgaria	5.3
12	Romania	5.2
13	Belarus[a]	5.0
14	Austria	4.9
	Russia	4.9
	United States	4.9
17	New Zealand	4.8
18	Australia	4.7
	Luxembourg	4.7
20	Ireland	4.6
	Slovakia	4.6

a 1994

Crime and punishment

Serious assault[a]
No. per 100,000 pop., 1992

1	Swaziland	630.59
2	Botswana	519.21
3	United States	441.81
4	United Kingdom[b]	331.82
5	New Zealand	313.61
6	Israel	229.37
7	Bermuda	221.69
8	Zimbabwe[b]	203.33
9	Netherlands	191.75
10	Trinidad & Tobago	177.37
11	Venezuela	175.23
12	Lesotho	170.55
13	Denmark	169.23
14	Canada[b]	159.66
15	Barbados[b]	159.14
16	Luxembourg	131.05
17	Belgium	117.91
18	Hong Kong	116.80
19	Colombia[b]	110.46
20	Germany	104.77

Theft[a]
No. per 100,000 pop., 1992

1	New Zealand	9035.24
2	Denmark	8494.91
3	Sweden	8419.05
4	United Kingdom[b]	7805.28
5	Netherlands	7527.44
6	United States	5166.33
7	Germany	4976.60
8	Bermuda	4681.11
9	Switzerland	4527.60
10	France	4487.28
11	Canada[b]	4289.77
12	Norway	3884.18
13	Luxembourg	3728.68
14	Austria	3027.00
15	Finland	2971.84
16	Belgium	2873.10
17	Barbados[b]	2686.77
18	Hungary	2668.95
19	Swaziland	2629.60
20	Italy	2574.87

Prisoners[c]
Total prison pop.

1	United States	1,585,400
2	Russia	1,017,372
3	Ukraine	201,852
4	Germany	68,396
5	Poland	65,819
6	United Kingdom	58,662
7	France	53,697
8	Belarus	52,278
9	Turkey	49,895
10	Italy	47,323
11	Romania	45,309
12	Spain	40,157
13	Japan	37,520
14	Canada	34,988
15	Czech Republic	19,508
16	Australia	16,132
17	Lithuania	13,228
18	Hungary	12,455
19	Portugal	12,150
20	Netherlands	10,143

Per 100,000 pop.

1	Russia	690
2	United States	600
3	Belarus	505
4	Ukraine	390
5	Latvia	375
6	Lithuania	360
7	Estonia	270
8	Romania	200
9	Czech Republic	190
10	Poland	170
11	Slovakia	150
12	Portugal	125
13	Hungary	120
14	Canada	119
15	New Zealand	114
16	Spain	105
17	United Kingdom	101
18	Bulgaria[d]	99
19	France	95
20	Australia	90

---

a Crime statistics are based on offences recorded by the police. The number will
   therefore depend partly on the efficiency of police administration systems, the
   definition of offences, and the proportion of crimes reported, and therefore may not
   be strictly comparable.
b 1991
c Only developed countries and other countries in Europe considered.
d 1993

Environment: *trees and disasters*

Top deforesters
Average annual rate, km² 1981–90

1	Brazil	-36,710		21	Ghana	-1,380
2	Indonesia	-12,120		22	Vietnam	-1,370
3	Zaire	-7,320		23	Madagascar	-1,350
4	Mexico	-6,780			Mozambique	-1,350
5	Bolivia	-6,250		25	Cambodia	-1,310
6	Venezuela	-5,990		26	Central African Rep	-1,290
7	Thailand	-5,150			Laos	-1,290
8	Sudan	-4,820		27	Nicaragua	-1,240
9	Tanzania	-4,380		28	Cameroon	-1,220
10	Paraguay	-4,030		29	Côte d'Ivoire	-1,190
11	Myanmar	-4,010			Nigeria	-1,190
12	Malaysia	-3,960		31	Gabon	-1,160
13	Columbia	-3,670		32	Papua New Guinea	-1,130
14	Zambia	-3,630		33	Honduras	-1,120
15	India	-3,390		34	Mali	-1,060
16	United States	-3,170		35	Chad	-890
17	Philippines	-3,160		36	Guinea	-870
18	Peru	-2,710		37	Guatemala	-810
19	Ecuador	-2,380		38	Botswana	-770
20	Angola	-1,740			Pakistan	-770
				40	Benin	-700

Top reafforesters
Average annual rate, km² 1980s

1	China	45,520		6	Japan	2,400
2	Ex-Soviet Union	45,400		7	Sweden	2,070
3	United States	17,750		8	North Korea	2,000
4	Canada	7,200		9	Finland	1,580
5	Brazil	4,490		10	India	1,380

Fastest forest depletion
% average annual decrease in forested area, 1981–90

1	Jamaica	7.2		15	Ecuador	1.8
2	Haiti	4.8		16	Guatemala	1.7
3	Bangladesh	3.9			Paraguay	1.7
4	Pakistan	3.4		18	Togo	1.5
5	Philippines	3.3			Vietnam	1.5
	Thailand	3.3		20	Malawi	1.4
7	Costa Rica	2.9			Sri Lanka	1.4
8	Dominican Rep	2.8		22	Benin	1.3
9	El Salvador	2.2			Ghana	1.3
10	Bahamas	2.1			Mexico	1.3
	Honduras	2.1			Myanmar	1.3
12	Malaysia	2.0		26	Bolivia	1.2
13	Nicaragua	1.9			Guinea	1.2
	Panama	1.9			Tanzania	1.2

Most forested countries
% of total area covered with forest, 1992

1	Suriname	90.6	13	Guinea	58.8
2	Papua New Guinea	82.5	14	Malaysia	58.7
3	North Korea	74.4	15	Central African Rep	57.4
4	Gabon	74.2	16	Brazil	57.3
5	Zaire	74.1	17	Indonesia	57.0
6	Finland	68.7	18	Bhutan	54.5
7	Japan	66.8	19	Senegal	53.1
8	South Korea	65.3	20	Peru	52.9
9	Fiji	64.9	21	Laos	52.8
10	Cambodia	64.1	22	Cameroon	51.2
11	Sweden	62.3	23	Bolivia	50.5
12	Congo	61.8	24	Slovenia	50.2

Oil tanker spills

	Country affected	Oil spilled ('000 tonnes)	Name	Flag	Year
1	Trinidad & Tobago	276	Atlantic Express	Greece	1979
2	South Africa	256	Castello de Belvar	Spain	1983
3	France	228	Amoco Cadiz	Liberia	1978
4	Canada	140	Odyssey	Liberia	1988
5	United Kingdom	121	Torrey Canyon	Liberia	1967
6	Oman	120	Sea Star	South Korea	1972
7	Greece	102	Irenes Serenade	Greece	1980
8	Spain	101	Urquiola	Spain	1976
9	United States	99	Hawaiian Patriot	Liberia	1977
10	Turkey	95	Independenta	Romania	1979
11	United Kingdom	85	Braer	Liberia	1993

Industrial disasters, 1984–96[a]

	Location	Origin of accident	Deaths
1984	St J Ixhuatepec	gas explosion	503
	Bhopal, India	chemical leakage	2,800
	Cubatao, Brazil	pipeline explosion	508
1986	Chernobyl, Ukraine	reactor explosion	31
1988	Islamabad, Pakistan	explosives	100
	Arzamas, Russia	explosives	73
	North Sea, UK	oil explosion	167
	Sverdlosk, Russia	explosives	5
1989	Ionava, Russia	chemical explosion	6
	Acha Ufa, Russia	gas explosion	575
1990	Ufa, Russia	chemical explosion	...
	Bangkok, Thailand	explosion (lorry)	54
	Patna, India	explosion (train)	100
1991	Thailand	explosives	171
	Livorno, Italy	oil explosion	140
	Sterlington, USA	gas explosion	8
1992	Kozlu, Turkey	gas explosion	270
1993	Shenzhen, China	fire (toy factory)	84
	Thailand	fire (toy factory)	189

a Not ranked due to difficulties in comparing the effects of each.

Environment: *pollution and waste*

Carbon dioxide emissions
Kg per head

1	Qatar[a]	44,700	21	Netherlands	9,160
2	United Arab Emirates	42,280	22	Poland	8,900
3	United States	19,130	23	Ireland	8,870
4	Singapore	17,990	24	Japan	8,790
5	Kazakhstan	17,480	25	Azerbaijan	8,760
6	Trinidad & Tobago	16,300	26	Finland	8,210
7	Australia	15,240	27	Israel	8,100
8	Canada	14,990		Kuwait	8,100
9	Russia	14,110		Libya	8,100
10	Norway	14,030	30	New Zealand	7,580
11	Saudi Arabia	13,850	31	Austria	7,290
12	Estonia	13,190		South Africa	7,290
13	Czech Republic	13,040	33	Greece	7,250
14	Ukraine	11,720	34	Italy	7,030
15	Germany	10,960	35	Slovakia	7,000
16	Turkmenistan	10,960	36	Iceland	6,850
17	Denmark	10,440	37	Sweden	6,560
18	Belgium	10,190	38	Switzerland	6,380
19	Belarus	9,890	39	France	6,340
20	United Kingdom	9,780	40	Oman	6,120

Nitrogen oxide emissions
Kg per head

1	Belgium	116.4	11	New Zealand	41.3
2	Iceland	86.5	12	United Kingdom	40.4
3	United States	80.6	13	Ex-Yugoslavia	39.2
4	Czech Republic	67.8	14	Luxembourg	37.4
5	Canada	66.6	15	Greece	37.3
6	Norway	53.0	16	Ireland	36.1
7	Finland	52.7	17	Germany	35.8
8	Denmark	51.6	18	Italy	35.7
9	Sweden	45.7	19	Netherlands	35.4
10	Slovakia	42.0	20	Spain	31.5

Sulphur dioxide emissions
Kg per head

1	Czech Republic	149.4	11	Spain	55.8
2	Ex-Yugoslavia	138.2	12	United Kingdom	54.9
3	Bulgaria	116.8	13	Ukraine	54.1
4	Canada	104.0	14	Ireland	52.8
5	Hungary	81.4	15	Greece	49.0
6	Romania	79.2	16	Germany	48.0
7	United States	79.2	17	Iceland	33.8
8	Poland	71.1	18	Denmark	30.5
9	Slovakia	70.1	19	Italy	29.4
10	Belarus	57.5	20	Portugal	29.1

Solid hazardous waste generated
Kg per head

1	Belgium	2,731	11	Poland	90
2	United States	1,059	12	Austria	84
3	Czech Republic	808		Mexico	84
4	Slovenia	507	14	Germany	82
5	Canada	267	15	Hungary	78
6	Luxembourg	214	16	France	69
7	Portugal	139	17	Italy	59
8	Switzerland	117	18	Sweden	57
9	Finland	110	19	Greece	43
10	Netherlands	93	20	Spain	43

Industrial waste generated
Kg per head

1	United States	485.4	11	Austria	16.1
2	Canada	138.0	12	Finland	14.9
3	Hungary	61.6		France	12.3
4	Japan	52.6	14	France	12.3
5	Switzerland	42.6		Greece	10.0
6	Germany	32.5	16	Australia	8.4
7	Luxembourg	31.4	17	Spain	8.3
8	Netherlands	30.3	18	Mexico	6.1
9	Iceland	21.4	19	Poland	4.6
10	Norway	16.6			

Solid municipal waste generated
Kg per head

1	United States	730	11	Austria	430
2	Australia	690	12	Japan	410
3	Canada	660	13	Belgium	400
4	Finland	620		Switzerland	400
5	Iceland	560	15	Turkey	390
6	Norway	510		Hungary	390
7	Netherlands	500	17	Sweden	370
8	Luxembourg	490	18	Germany	360
9	France	470		Slovakia	360
10	Denmark	460		Spain	360

a Excluding emissions from industrial processes.

The statistics for all tables (including those on page 86) except carbon dioxide emissions, fresh water resources and water use cover OECD and emerging Eastern European countries only. They normally refer to various years in the late 1980s to early 1990s, though some refer to an earlier period.

Environment: *recycling and water*

Glass recycling
Recovery rates, %, 1994

1	Switzerland	84		Sweden	56
2	Netherlands	77	12	Italy	54
3	Austria	76	13	Finland	50
4	Canada[a]	75	14	France	48
5	Germany	75	15	Australia[a]	36
	Iceland[a]	75	16	Portugal	32
7	Norway	72	17	Ireland	31
8	Belgium	67		Spain	31
	Denmark	67	19	Greece	29
10	Japan[a]	56	20	United Kingdom	28

Paper recycling
Recovery rates, %, 1993

1	Austria[b]	78	11	France	42
	Spain	78	12	Portugal[a]	41
3	Switzerland	54	13	Turkey[a]	39
4	Netherlands[c]	53	14	Denmark[a]	36
5	Japan[a]	51	15	United States	34
6	Australia[c]	50	16	Canada[a]	32
	Sweden	50		Norway	32
8	Italy[c]	47		United Kingdom	32
9	Germany	46	19	Greece	30
10	Finland[a]	45		Iceland[c]	30

Freshwater resources
Cubic metres per head, '000

1	Iceland	624.5	11	Venezuela	60.3
2	Suriname	472.8	12	Bhutan	58.0
3	Congo	321.2	13	Malaysia	55.6
4	Papua New Guinea	186.2	14	Laos	55.3
5	Gabon	124.2	15	Panama	54.7
6	Canada	98.5	16	Cambodia	48.6
7	New Zealand	91.5	17	Brazil	43.0
8	Norway	90.4	18	Central African Rep	42.5
9	Liberia	76.3	19	Bolivia	40.5
10	Paraguay	63.3	20	Nicaragua	39.5

Water use
Cubic metres per head, latest year

1	Turkmenistan	6,390	11	Afghanistan	1,830
2	Iraq	4,575	12	Chile	1,626
3	Uzbekistan	4,121	13	Canada	1,602
4	Kirgizstan	2,729	14	Madagascar	1,584
5	Tajikistan	2,455	15	Bulgaria	1,544
6	Kazakhstan	2,294	16	Iran	1,362
7	Azerbaijan	2,248	17	Lithuania	1,190
8	Estonia	2,097	18	Suriname	1,189
9	Pakistan	2,053	19	Armenia	1,145
10	United States	1,870	20	Romania	1,134

a 1992   c 1991
b 1990

Part II
COUNTRY PROFILES

ALGERIA

Area	2,381,741 sq km	Currency	Algerian dinar (AD)
Capital	Algiers		

People

Population	28.1m	Life expectancy: men	67.5 yrs
Pop. per sq km	12	women	70.3 yrs
Av. ann. growth	.	Adult literacy	58.8%
in pop. 1985–95	2.5%	Fertility rate (per woman)	3.8
Pop. under 15	39.2%		
Pop. over 65	3.6%		*per 1,000 pop.*
No. of men per 100 women	102.5	Crude birth rate	29.2
Human Development Index	74.6	Crude death rate	5.6

The economy

GDP	AD2,145bn	GDP per head	$1,587
GDP	$45bn	GDP per head in purchasing	
Av. ann. growth in real		power parity (USA=100)	20
GDP 1985–95	nil		

Origins of GDP		Components of GDP	
	% of total		*% of total*
Agriculture	9.6	Private consumption	55.5
Industry, of which:	66.6	Public consumption	15.7
manufacturing	...	Investment	32.0
Services	23.8	Exports	26.7
		Imports	-29.9

Structure of employment

	% of total		*% of labour force*
Agriculture	26	Unemployed 1992	23.8
Industry	31	Av. ann. rate 1990–92	21.5
Services	43		

Energy

	'000 TCE		
Total output	153.015	% output exported	69.7
Total consumption	43,262	% consumption imported	2.9
Consumption per head,			
kg coal equivalent	1,583		

Inflation and finance

Consumer price		*av. ann. increase 1989–95*	
inflation 1995	32.2%	Narrow money (M1)	10.9%
Av. ann. inflation 1989–95	27.9%	Broad money	15.4%

Exchange rates

	end 1996		*June 1996*
AD per $	56.19	Effective rates	*1990 = 100*
AD per SDR	80.79	– nominal	...
AD per Ecu	70.24	– real	...

Principal exports

	$bn fob		$bn fob
Energy & products	9.3	Total including others	**10.3**

Main export destinations

	% of total		% of total
Italy	18.8	Spain	8.0
United States	14.8	Germany	7.9
France	11.8	Netherlands	7.5

Principal imports

	$bn cif		$bn cif
Food	3.5		
Hydrocarbon sector	2.0	Total incl. others	**10.2**

Main origins of imports

	% of total		% of total
France	29.6	United States	8.0
Spain	10.5	Germany	5.6
Italy	8.2	Austria	3.0

Balance of payments[b], reserves and debt, $bn

Visible exports fob	12.3	Overall balance	1.0
Visible imports fob	-6.9	Change in reserves	-0.6
Trade balance	5.5	Level of reserves	
Invisibles inflows	0.5	end Dec.	4.2
Invisibles outflows	-3.8	No. months of import cover	3.7
Net transfers	0.2	Foreign debt	32.6
Current account balance	2.4	– as % of GDP	83.1
– as % of GDP	5.3	Debt service paid	4.4
Capital balance	-1.0	Debt service ratio	35.5

Family life

No. of households	3.3m	Divorces per 1,000 pop.	...
Av. no. per household	7.0	Cost of living, Dec. 1996	
Marriages per 1,000 pop.	5.7	New York = 100	59

a   1990
b   1991

ARGENTINA

Area	2,766,889 sq km	Currency	Peso (P)
Capital	Buenos Aires		

People

Population	34.8m	Life expectancy: men		69.6 yrs
Pop. per sq km	13	women		76.8 yrs
Av. ann. growth		Adult literacy		98.8%
in pop. 1985–95	1.4%	Fertility rate (per woman)		2.6
Pop. under 15	28.9%			
Pop. over 65	9.4%			*per 1,000 pop.*
No. of men per 100 women	96.3	Crude birth rate		19.9
Human Development Index	88.5	Crude death rate		7.9

The economy

GDP	P278bn	GDP per head	$8,008
GDP	$278bn	GDP per head in purchasing	
Av. ann. growth in real		power parity (USA=100)	31
GDP 1985–95	3.5%		

Origins of GDP		Components of GDP	
	% of total		*% of total*
Agriculture	5.9	Private consumption[a]	81.8
Industry, of which:	30.7	Public consumption	...
manufacturing	20.2	Investment	18.1
Services	63.4	Exports	8.5
		Imports	-8.3

Structure of employment

	m		*% of labour force*
Total	4.16	Unemployed 1995	18.8
		Av. ann. rate 1990–94	8.8

Energy

	'000 TCE		
Total output	90,748	% output exported	21.7
Total consumption	73,506	% consumption imported	10.0
Consumption per head			
kg coal equivalent	2,150		

Inflation and finance

Consumer price		*av. ann. increase 1989–95*	
inflation 1996	0.2%	Narrow money (M1)	210.4%
Av. ann. inflation 1989–95	173.3%	Broad money	193%

Exchange rates

	end 1996		*June 1996*
P per $	1.00	Effective rates	*1990 = 100*
P per SDR	1.44	– nominal	...
P per Ecu	1.25	– real	...

Principal exports

	$bn fob		$bn fob
Vegetable products	3.6	Live animals	2.1
Processed foods	2.6	Oils	2.1
Minerals	2.2	Total incl. others	**21.0**

Main export destinations

	% of total		% of total
Brazil	26.1	Netherlands	5.7
United States	8.5	Italy	3.5
Chile	7.0		

Principal imports

	$bn cif		$bn cif
Machinery & industrial		Metals	1.3
equipment	6.4	Plastics	1.3
Chemicals	3.0	Total incl. others	**20.1**
Transport equipment	2.5		

Main origins of imports

	% of total		% of total
United States	20.8	Germany	6.2
Brazil	20.7	France	5.2
Italy	6.3		

Balance of payments, reserves and debt, $bn

Visible exports fob	21.0	Overall balance	-2.2
Visible imports fob	-18.7	Change in reserves	0.0
Trade balance	2.2	Level of reserves	
Invisibles inflows	7.1	end Dec.	16.0
Invisibles outflows	-12.1	No. months of import cover	6.2
Net transfers	0.4	Foreign debt	89.7
Current account balance	-2.4	– as % of GDP	33.1
– as % of GDP	-0.9	Debt service paid	9.7
Capital balance	0.2	Debt service ratio	34.7

Family life

No. of households	12.6m	Divorces per 1,000 pop.	...
Av. no. per household	2.8	Cost of living, Dec. 1996	
Marriages per 1,000 pop.	5.7	New York = 100	91

a Including public consumption.
b 1993

AUSTRALIA

Area	7,682,300 sq km	Currency	Australian dollar (A$)
Capital	Canberra		

People

Population	17.9m	Life expectancy: men	75.4 yrs
Pop. per sq km	2	women	81.2 yrs
Av. ann. growth		Adult literacy	99.0%
in pop. 1985–95	1.3%	Fertility rate (per woman)	1.9
Pop. under 15	21.5%		
Pop. over 65	11.7%		*per 1,000 pop.*
No. of men per 100 women	99.7	Crude birth rate	14.3
Human Development Index	92.9	Crude death rate	7.5

The economy

GDP	A$456bn	GDP per head	$18,914
GDP	$338bn	GDP per head in purchasing	
Av. ann. growth in real		power parity (USA=100)	70
GDP 1985–95	2.9%		

Origins of GDP[a]		**Components of GDP**[a]	
	% of total		*% of total*
Agriculture & mining	8.0	Private consumption	62.4
Industry, of which:	23.4	Public consumption	17.2
manufacturing	17.2	Investment	20.9
Services	68.6	Exports	20.1
		Imports	-20.5

Structure of employment

	% of total		*% of labour force*
Agriculture	5	Unemployed 1995	8.5
Industry	23	Av. ann. rate 1990–94	9.5
Services	72		

Energy

	'000 TCE		
Total output	236,996	% output exported	58.8
Total consumption	135,928	% consumption imported	20.3
Consumption per head,			
kg coal equivalent	7,614		

Inflation and finance

Consumer price		*av. ann. increase 1989–95*	
inflation 1996	2.6%	Narrow money (M1)	11.0%
Av. ann. inflation 1989–96	3.7%	Broad money	1.5%

Exchange rates

	end 1996		*June 1996*
A$ per $	1.26	Effective rates	*1990 = 100*
A$ per SDR	1.81	– nominal	113.4
A$ per Ecu	1.58	– real	94.9

Principal exports[a]

	$bn fob		$bn fob
Ores & minerals	12.1	Gold	4.3
Coal & oil	6.0		
Machinery	5.4	Total incl. others	**57.1**

Main export destinations

	% of total		% of total
Japan	21.6	United States	6.0
Asean[b]	15.4	Developing countries	45.9
EU	11.1		

Principal imports[a]

	$bn cif		$bn cif
Machinery	16.8	Energy & products	3.2
Consumer goods	11.7	Chemicals	2.1
Motor vehicles & other transport equipment	9.1	Total incl. others	**58.6**

Main origins of imports

	% of total		% of total
United States	25.0	Asean[b]	9.4
EU	22.6	Developing countries	29.1
Japan	13.9		

Balance of payments, reserves and aid, $bn

Visible exports fob	53.1	Capital balance	13.7
Visible imports fob	-57.1	Overall balance	0.4
Trade balance	-4.0	Change in reserves	0.6
Invisibles inflows	21.3	Level of reserves	
Invisibles outflows	-36.4	end Dec.	15.0
Net transfers	-0.1	No. months of import cover	1.9
Current account balance	-19.2	Aid given	1.2
– as % of GDP	-5.7	– as % of GDP	0.36

Family life

No. of households	6.8m	Divorces per 1,000 pop.	2.6
Av. no. per household	2.7	Cost of living, Dec. 1996	
Marriages per 1,000 pop.	6.2	New York = 100	100

a Year ending June 30, 1996.
b Brunei, Indonesia, Malaysia, Philippines, Singapore, Thailand.

AUSTRIA

Area	83,855 sq km	Currency	Schilling (ASch)
Capital	Vienna		

People

Population	8.0m	Life expectancy: men	73.7 yrs
Pop. per sq km	96	women	80.1 yrs
Av. ann. growth		Adult literacy	99.0%
in pop. 1985–95	0.6%	Fertility rate (per woman)	1.4
Pop. under 15	17.7%		
Pop. over 65	14.7%		*per 1,000 pop.*
No. of men per 100 women	95.9	Crude birth rate	10.3
Human Development Index	92.8	Crude death rate	10.0

The economy

GDP	ASch2,188bn	GDP per head	$26,917
GDP	$217bn	GDP per head in purchasing	
Av. ann. growth in real		power parity (USA=100)	79
GDP 1985–95	2.6%		

Origins of GDP		Components of GDP	
	% of total		*% of total*
Agriculture	2.2	Private consumption	55.2
Industry, of which:	34.4	Public consumption	18.9
manufacturing	...	Investment	27.0
Services	63.4	Exports	37.5
		Imports	-38.7

Structure of employment[a]

	% of total		*% of labour force*
Agriculture	7	Unemployed 1994	6.6
Industry	33	Av. ann. rate 1990–94	6.1
Services	60		

Energy

	'000 TCE		
Total output	8,462	% output exported	27.7
Total consumption	32,953	% consumption imported	81.3
Consumption per head,			
kg coal equivalent	4,162		

Inflation and finance

Consumer price		*av. ann. increase 1989–95*	
inflation 1996	1.8%	Narrow money (M1)	7.6%
Av. ann. inflation 1989–96	3.0%	Broad money	6.7%

Exchange rates

	end 1996		*June 1996*
ASch per $	10.95	Effective rates	*1990 = 100*
ASch per SDR	15.75	– nominal	104.8
ASch per Ecu	13.69	– real	86.6

Principal exports[a]

	$bn fob		$bn fob
Machinery & transport		Chemicals	4.1
equipment	17.6	Raw materials	1.9
Manufactured goods	13.0	Food, drink & tobacco	1.3
Consumer goods	6.6	Total incl. others	**45.0**

Main export destinations[a]

	% of total		% of total
Germany	38.1	France	4.6
Italy	8.1	Hungary	3.9
Switzerland	6.4	United States	3.5

Principal imports[a]

	$bn cif		$bn cif
Machinery & transport		Chemicals	5.8
equipment	21.0	Food, drink & tobacco	2.7
Manufactured products	10.6	Fuel & energy	2.4
Consumer goods	10.2	Total incl. others	**55.3**

Main origins of imports[a]

	% of total		% of total
Germany	40.0	United States	4.4
Italy	8.8	Japan	4.3
France	4.7	Switzerland	4.1

Balance of payments, reserves and aid, $bn

Visible exports fob	72.1	Capital balance	4.7
Visible imports fob	-77.6	Overall balance	1.7
Trade balance	-5.4	Change in reserves	-0.5
Invisibles inflows	34.4	Level of reserves	
Invisibles outflows	-32.5	end Dec.	23.4
Net transfers	-1.5	No. months of import cover	2.5
Current account balance	-5.1	Aid given	0.8
– as % of GDP	-2.4	– as % of GDP	0.33

Family life

No. of households	3.3m	Divorces per 1,000 pop.	2.3
Av. no. per household	2.5	Cost of living, Dec. 1996	
Marriages per 1,000 pop.	5.3	New York = 100	123

a 1994

BANGLADESH

Area	143,998 sq km	Currency	Taka (Tk)
Capital	Dhaka		

People

Population	118.2m	Life expectancy: men		58.1 yrs
Pop. per sq km	821	women		58.2 yrs
Av. ann. growth		Adult literacy		37.0%
in pop. 1985–94	1.8%	Fertility rate (per woman)		3.1
Pop. under 15	41.6%			
Pop. over 65	3.3%			*per 1,000 pop.*
No. of men per 100 women	105.5	Crude birth rate		26.8
Human Development Index	36.5	Crude death rate		9.7

The economy

GDP	Tk1,168bn	GDP per head	$242
GDP	$29bn	GDP per head in purchasing	
Av. ann. growth in real		power parity (USA=100)	5
GDP 1985–95	4.1%		

Origins of GDP[a]		**Components of GDP**[a]	
	% of total		*% of total*
Agriculture	30.7	Private consumption	78.6
Industry, of which:	14.9	Public consumption	13.7
manufacturing	9.6	Investment	17.8
Services	54.4	Exports	14.2
		Imports	-24.3

Structure of employment[b]

	% of total		*% of labour force*
Agriculture	65	Unemployed 1995	...
Industry	16	Av. ann. rate 1990–94	...
Services	19		

Energy

	'000 TCE		
Total output	8,222	% output exported	0.0
Total consumption	10,394	% consumption imported	29.8
Consumption per head,			
kg coal equivalent	93		

Inflation and finance

		av. ann. increase 1989–95	
Consumer price			
inflation 1995	5.8%	Narrow money (M1)	14.3%
Av. ann. inflation 1989–95	5.5%	Broad money	13.7%

Exchange rates

	end 1996		*June 1996*
Tk per $	42.45	Effective rates	*1990 = 100*
Tk per SDR	61.04	– nominal	...
Tk per Ecu	53.06	– real	...

Principal exports[a]

	$m fob		$m fob
Clothing	1,961	Leather	215
Fish & fish products	314		
Jute goods	297	Total incl. others	**3,114**

Main export destinations[a]

	% of total		% of total
United States	30.0	France	6.8
United Kingdom	11.1	Italy	5.5
Germany	10.1	Netherlands	4.9

Principal imports[a]

	$m cif		$m cif
Textiles	1,532	Chemicals	364
Machinery & transport		Fuels	314
equipment	948		
Foods	487	Total incl. others	**6,616**

Main origins of imports[a]

	% of total		% of total
India	15.9	South Korea	7.2
China	9.7	Japan	7.0
Singapore	8.7	Hong Kong	6.2

Balance of payments, reserves and debt, $bn

Visible exports fob	3.7	Overall balance	-0.5
Visible imports fob	-6.1	Change in reserves	-0.8
Trade balance	-2.3	Level of reserves	
Invisibles inflows	1.0	end Dec.	2.4
Invisibles outflows	-1.7	No. months of import cover	3.7
Net transfers	2.3	Foreign debt	16.4
Current account balance	-0.8	– as % of GDP	56.3
– as % of GDP	-2.9	Debt service paid	0.7
Capital balance	0.2	Debt service ratio	13.3

Family life

No. households	14.8m	Divorces per 1,000 pop.	…
Av. no. per household	5.7	Cost of living, Dec. 1996	
Marriages per 1,000 pop.	10.9	New York = 100	65

a Fiscal year ending June 30 1996.
b 1990

BELGIUM

Area	30,520 sq km	Currency	Belgian franc (BFr)
Capital	Brussels		

People

Population	10.1m	Life expectancy: men	73.9 yrs
Pop. per sq km	332	women	80.6 yrs
Av. ann. growth		Adult literacy	99.0%
in pop. 1985–95	0.3%	Fertility rate (per woman)	1.6
Pop. under 15	17.8%		
Pop. over 65	15.8%		*per 1,000 pop.*
No. of men per 100 women	96.0	Crude birth rate	11.2
Human Development Index	92.9	Crude death rate	10.5

The economy

GDP	BFr7,399bn	GDP per head	$24,757
GDP	$251bn	GDP per head in purchasing	
Av. ann. growth in real		power parity (USA=100)	80
GDP 1985–95	2.2%		

Origins of GDP		**Components of GDP**	
	% of total		*% of total*
Agriculture	1.5	Private consumption	62.3
Industry, of which:	32.0	Public consumption	14.8
manufacturing	23.9	Investment	18.0
Services	66.5	Exports	72.6
		Imports	-67.8

Structure of employment

	% of total		*% of labour force*
Agriculture	3	Unemployed 1995	9.4
Industry	31	Av. ann. rate 1990–94	8.1
Services	66		

Energy

	'000 TCE		
Total output	15,530	% output exported[b]	172.2
Total consumption	69,161	% consumption imported[b]	131.4
Consumption per head,			
kg coal equivalent	6,711		

Inflation and finance

Consumer price		*av. ann. increase 1989–95*	
inflation 1996	2.1%	Narrow money (M1)	2.9%
Av. ann. inflation 1989–96	2.6%	Broad money	5.7%

Exchange rates

	end 1996		*June 1996*
BFr per $	32.01	Effective rates	*1990 = 100*
BFr per SDR	46.02	– nominal	106.6
BFr per Ecu	40.01	– real	101.6

Principal exports[a]

	$bn fob		$bn fob
Vehicles	25.4	Rubber & plastic goods	13.8
Chemicals	22.0	Precious stones & jewellery	11.8
Machinery & electrical goods	20.8		
Metals & products	18.9	Total incl. others	**168.3**

Main export destinations[a]

	% of total		% of total
Germany	21.5	United Kingdom	8.1
France	18.3	United States	4.0
Netherlands	13.3		

Principal imports[a]

	$bn cif		$bn cif
Machinery & electrical		Metals & products	13.2
products	24.9	Mineral products	11.7
Vehicles	20.3	Precious stones & jewellery	11.4
Chemicals	16.6	Total incl. others	**154.2**

Main origins of imports[a]

	% of total		% of total
Germany	21.0	United Kingdom	8.8
Netherlands	17.6	United States	5.7
France	15.7		

Balance of payments[a], reserves and aid, $bn

Visible exports fob	157.9	Capital balance[c]	-10.5
Visible imports fob	-149.1	Overall balance[c]	0.2
Trade balance	8.8	Change in reserves	0.6
Invisibles inflows	147.1	Level of reserves	
Invisibles outflows	-137.7	end Dec.	24.1
Net transfers	-3.2	No. months of import cover	1.2
Current account balance	15.0	Aid given	1.0
– as % of GDP	5.7	– as % of GDP	0.38

Family life

No. of households	3.7m	Divorces per 1,000 pop.	2.2
Av. no. per household	2.7	Cost of living, Dec. 1996	
Marriages per 1,000 pop.	5.1	New York = 100	113

---

a Including Luxembourg.
b Energy trade data are distorted by transitory and oil refining activities.
c 1994

BRAZIL

Area	8,511,965 sq km	Currency	Real (R)
Capital	Brasilia		

People

Population	159.0m	Life expectancy: men	63.4 yrs
Pop. per sq km	19	women	71.2 yrs
Av. ann. growth		Adult literacy	82.1%
in pop. 1985–95	1.6%	Fertility rate (per woman)	2.2
Pop. under 15	31.6%		
Pop. over 65	4.8%		*per 1,000 pop.*
No. of men per 100 women	98.1	Crude birth rate	19.6
Human Development Index	79.6	Crude death rate	7.1

The economy

GDP	R532bn	GDP per head	$3,646
GDP	$580bn	GDP per head in purchasing	
Av. ann. growth in real		power parity (USA=100)	20
GDP 1985–95	2.2%		

Origins of GDP		**Components of GDP**	
	% of total		*% of total*
Agriculture	10.7	Private consumption	65.1
Industry, of which:	42.0	Public consumption	15.2
manufacturing	28.3	Investment	22.1
Services	47.3	Exports	11.7
		Imports	-13.6

Structure of employment[a]

	% of total		*% of labour force*
Agriculture	27	Unemployed 1993	6.2
Industry	21	Av. ann. rate 1992–93	6.4
Services	52		

Energy

	'000 TCE		
Total output	88,407	% output exported	8.4
Total consumption	135,209	% consumption imported	49.8
Consumption per head,			
kg coal equivalent	850		

Inflation and finance

Consumer price		*av. ann. increase 1989–95*	
inflation 1996	15.5%	Narrow money (M1)	929.2
Av. ann. inflation 1989–96	746%	Broad money	952.3

Exchange rates

	end 1996		*June 1996*
R per $	1.04	Effective rates	*1990 = 100*
R per SDR	1.50	– Nominal	...
R per Ecu	1.59	– Real	...

Principal exports

	$bn fob		$bn fob
Manufactures	29.7	Soybeans etc.	2.1
Iron ore	3.8		
Coffee	2.4	Total incl. others	**46.5**

Main export destinations

	% of total		% of total
United States	18.9	Japan	6.7
Argentina	8.7	Germany	4.6

Principal imports

	$bn cif		$bn cif
Machines & electrical		Transport equipment & parts	5.9
materials	13.7	Chemical products	4.6
Fuels & lubricants	7.3	Total incl. others	**49.7**

Main origins of imports

	% of total		% of total
United States	23.9	Argentina	10.3
Germany	11.0	Japan	5.1

Balance of payments, reserves and debt, $bn

Visible exports fob	46.5	Overall balance	13.0
Visible imports fob	-49.7	Change in reserves	13.0
Trade balance	-3.2	Level of reserves	
Invisibles inflows	9.6	end Dec.	51.5
Invisibles outflows	-28.2	No. months of import cover	7.9
Net transfers	3.6	Foreign debt	159.1
Current account balance	-18.1	– as % of GDP	24.0
– as % of GDP	-3.1	Debt service paid	22.3
Capital balance	29.7	Debt service ratio	37.9

Family life

No. of households	38.4m	Divorces per 1,000 pop.	0.5
Av. no. per household	4.1	Cost of living, Dec. 1996	
Marriages per 1,000 pop.	5.2	New York = 100	96

a 1993

BULGARIA

Area	110,994 sq km	Currency	Lev (BGL)
Capital	Sofia		

People

Population	8.5m	Life expectancy: men	67.8 yrs
Pop. per sq km	77	women	74.9 yrs
Av. ann. growth		Adult literacy	94.0%
in pop. 1985–94	-0.4%	Fertility rate (per woman)	1.5
Pop. under 15	18.4%		
Pop. over 65	14.5%		*per 1,000 pop.*
No. of men per 100 women	95.9	Crude birth rate	10.3
Human Development Index	77.3	Crude death rate	13.3

The economy

GDP	BGL752bn	GDP per head	$1,319
GDP	$11.2bn	GDP per head in purchasing	
Av. ann. growth in real		power parity (USA=100)	17
GDP 1985–95	-1.9%		

Origins of GDP		Components of GDP	
	% of total		*% of total*
Agriculture	14.1	Private consumption	78.2
Industry, of which:	34.8	Public consumption	6.7
manufacturing	...	Investment	14.6
Services	51.1	Net exports	0.5

Structure of employment[a]

	% of total		*% of labour force*
Agriculture	13	Unemployed 1995	11.1
Industry	48	Av. ann. rate 1990–94	11.4
Services	39		

Energy

	'000 TCE		
Total output	13,108	% output exported	22.2
Total consumption	28,721	% consumption imported	68.5
Consumption per head,			
kg coal equivalent	3,257		

Inflation and finance

av. ann increase 1989–94

Consumer price			
inflation 1996	122%	Narrow money (M1)	...
Av. ann. inflation 1989–96	84.4%	Broad money	-2.1

Exchange rates

	end 1996		*June 1996*
BGL per $	489.00	Effective rates	*1990 = 100*
BGL per SDR	704.16	– Nominal	...
BGL per Ecu	611.25	– Real	...

Principal exports

	$bn fob		$bn fob
Food, beverages & tobacco	0.9	Iron & steel	0.6
Chemicals	0.8	Total incl. others	**5.1**

Main export destinations

	% of total		% of total
Russia	10.1	Italy	8.2
Germany	8.5	Turkey	7.3
Macedonia, FYR	8.3	Greece	6.9

Principal imports

	$bn cif		$bn cif
Mineral products & fuels	1.3	Non-electrical machinery	0.5
Chemicals	0.6	Total incl. others	**5.1**

Main origins of imports

	% of total		% of total
Russia	28.2	Italy	5.9
Germany	12.6	Greece	4.7

Balance of payments, reserves and debt, $bn

Visible exports fob	5.1	Overall balance	0.4
Visible imports fob	-4.7	Change in reserves	0.0
Trade balance	0.4	Level of reserves	
Invisibles inflows	1.6	end Dec.	0.4
Invisibles outflows	-1.8	No. months of import cover	0.7
Net transfers	0.1	Foreign debt	10.9
Current account balance	0.3	– as % of GDP	92.3
– as % of GDP	2.5	Debt service paid	1.3
Capital balance	-0.1	Debt service ratio	18.8

Family life

No. of households	3.1m	Divorces per 1,000 pop.	1.3
Av. no. per household	2.8	Cost of living, Dec. 1996	
Marriages per 1,000 pop.	4.5	New York = 100	...

a 1990

CAMEROON

Area	475,442 sq km	Currency	CFA franc (CFAfr)
Capital	Yaoundé		

People

Population	13.2m	Life expectancy: men	54.5 yrs
Pop. per sq km	28	women	57.2 yrs
Av. ann. growth		Adult literacy	60.8%
in pop. 1985–95	2.8%	Fertility rate (per woman)	5.3
Pop. under 15	44.2%		
Pop. over 65	3.6%		*per 1,000 pop.*
No. of men per 100 women	98.6	Crude birth rate	39.3
Human Development Index	48.1	Crude death rate	11.9

The economy

GDP	CFAfr4,293bn	GDP per head	$653
GDP	$8.6bn	GDP per head in purchasing	
Av. ann. growth in real		power parity (USA=100)	9
GDP 1985–95	-2.3%		

Origins of GDP[a]		Components of GDP[a]	
	% of total		*% of total*
Agriculture	28.6	Private consumption	71.3
Industry, of which:	24.9	Public consumption	7.2
manufacturing	11.3	Investment	16.8
Services	46.5	Exports	30.0
		Imports	-25.3

Structure of employment[a]

	% of total		*% of labour force*
Agriculture	70	Unemployed 1995	...
Industry	9	Av. ann. rate 1990–94	...
Services	21		

Energy

	'000 TCE		
Total output	8,150	% output exported	77.0
Total consumption	1,815	% consumption imported	1.3
Consumption per head,			
kg coal equivalent	141		

Inflation and finance

Consumer price		*av. ann. change 1989–95*	
inflation 1995	13.9%	Narrow money (M1)	-3.9%
Av. ann. inflation 1989–95	6.5%	Broad money	-1.6%

Exchange rates

	end 1996		*June 1996*
CFAfr per $	523.7	Effective rates	*1990 = 100*
CFAfr per SDR	753.1	– nominal	81.5
CFAfr per Ecu	654.6	– real	66.2

Principal exports[c]

	$m fob		$m fob
Crude oil	565	Cocoa	118
Timber	296	Coffee	116
		Total incl. others	**2,040**

Main export destinations

	% of total		% of total
France	22	Spain	13
Italy	15	Netherlands	8

Principal imports[a]

	$m fob		$m fob
Capital goods	190	Fuel	7
Food	89	Total incl. others	**1,241**

Main origins of imports

	% of total		% of total
France	42	Italy	5
Belgium/Luxembourg	6	United States	4

Balance of payments[c], reserves and debt, $bn

Visible exports fob	1.5	Overall balance	-0.9
Visible imports fob	-1.0	Change in reserves	0.00
Trade balance	0.5	Level of reserves	
Invisibles inflows	0.4	end Dec.	0.02
Invisibles outflows	-1.4	No. months of import cover	0.1
Net transfers	-0.1	Foreign debt	9.4
Current account balance	-0.6	– as % of GDP	124.4
– as % of GDP	-5.8	Debt service paid	0.4
Capital balance	-0.3	Debt service ratio	15.3

Family life

No. of households	1.4m	Divorces per 1,000 pop.	...
Av. no. per household	5.2	Cost of living, Dec. 1996	
Marriages per 1,000 pop.	...	New York = 100	...

a 1994
b 1990
c Fiscal year ending June 30 1995.

CANADA

Area[a]	9,970,610 sq km	Currency	Canadian dollar (C$)
Capital	Ottawa		

People

Population	29.4m	Life expectancy: men		76.1 yrs
Pop. per sq km	3		women	81.8 yrs
Av. ann. growth		Adult literacy		99.0%
in pop. 1985–95	1.3%	Fertility rate (per woman)		1.6
Pop. under 15	20.4%			
Pop. over 65	12.0%			*per 1,000 pop.*
No. of men per 100 women	98.3	Crude birth rate		11.9
Human Development Index	95.1	Crude death rate		7.4

The economy

GDP	C$788bn	GDP per head	$19,512
GDP	$574bn	GDP per head in purchasing	
Av. ann. growth in real		power parity (USA=100)	78
GDP 1985–95	2.2%		

Origins of GDP		Components of GDP	
	% of total		*% of total*
Agriculture	2.8	Private consumption	60.0
Industry, of which:	31.6	Public consumption	19.4
manufacturing	23.3	Investment	18.2
Services	65.6	Exports	37.4
		Imports	-34.9

Structure of employment

	% of total		*% of labour force*
Agriculture	4	Unemployed 1995	9.5
Industry	23	Av. ann. rate 1990–94	10.2
Services	73		

Energy

	'000 TCE		
Total output	482,338	% output exported	45.3
Total consumption	326,655	% consumption imported	18.7
Consumption per head,			
kg coal equivalent	11,209		

Inflation and finance

Consumer price		*av. ann. increase 1989–95*	
inflation 1996	1.6%	Narrow money (M1)	5.9%
Av. ann. inflation 1989–96	2.8%	Broad money	8.6%

Exchange rates

	end 1996		*June 1996*
C$ per $	1.37	Effective rates	*1990 = 100*
C$ per SDR	1.97	– nominal	84.4
C$ per Ecu	1.71	– real	80.7

Principal exports

	$bn fob		$bn fob
Motor vehicles & other		Forest products	25.9
transport equipment	44.9	Energy products	15.2
Machinery & industrial		Agric. products &	
equipment	41.0	foodstuffs	14.6
Industrial supplies	34.2	Total incl. others	**192.1**

Main export destinations

	% of total		% of total
United States	79.6	United Kingdom	1.5
Japan	4.5		

Principal imports

	$bn cif		$bn cif
Machinery & industrial		Consumer goods	18.7
equipment	55.1	Agric. products & foodstuffs	9.8
Motor vehicles & other		Energy products	5.3
transport equipment	36.8		
Industrial supplies	32.8	Total incl. others	**168.0**

Main origins of imports

	% of total		% of total
United States	75.0	United Kingdom	2.1
Japan	3.7		

Balance of payments, reserves and aid, $bn

Visible exports fob	189.9	Capital balance	5.0
Visible imports fob	-167.5	Overall balance	-0.5
Trade balance	22.3	Change in reserves	2.6
Invisibles inflows	34.3	Level of reserves	
Invisibles outflows	-64.9	end Dec.	16.4
Net transfers	-0.4	No. months of import cover	0.8
Current account balance	-8.7	Aid given	2.07
– as % of GDP	-1.5	– as % of GDP	0.38

Family life

No. of households	10.8m	Divorces per 1,000 pop.	2.9
Av. no. per household	2.7	Cost of living, Dec. 1996	
Marriages per 1,000 pop.	7.0	New York = 100	82

a   Including freshwater.

CHILE

Area	756,945 sq km	Currency	Chilean peso (peso)
Capital	Santiago		

People

Population	14.2m	Life expectancy: men	72.3 yrs
Pop. per sq km	19	women	78.3 yrs
Av. ann. growth		Adult literacy	93.8%
in pop. 1985–95	1.7%	Fertility rate (per woman)	2.4
Pop. under 15	29.4%		
Pop. over 65	6.6%		*per 1,000 pop.*
No. of men per 100 women	97.9	Crude birth rate	19.9
Human Development Index	88.2	Crude death rate	5.6

The economy

GDP	23,410bn pesos	GDP per head	$4,163
GDP	$59bn	GDP per head in purchasing	
Av. ann. growth in real		power parity (USA=100)	35
GDP 1985–95	6.8%		

Origins of GDP		Components of GDP	
	% of total		*% of total*
Agriculture	6.9	Private consumption	62.0
Industry, of which:	30.2	Public consumption	8.8
manufacturing	16.8	Investment	27.3
Services	62.9	Exports	29.3
		Imports	-27.4

Structure of employment

	% of total		*% of labour force*
Agriculture	16	Unemployed 1995	4.7
Industry	26	Av. ann. rate 1990–94	5.1
Services	58		

Energy

	'000 TCE		
Total output	7,510	% output exported	1.9
Total consumption	20,299	% consumption imported	69.5
Consumption per head,			
kg coal equivalent	1,445		

Inflation and finance

Consumer price		*av. ann. increase 1989–95*	
inflation 1996	7.4%	Narrow money (M1)	24.1%
Av. ann. inflation 1989–96	14.8%	Broad money	23.7%

Exchange rates

	end 1996		*June 1996*
Peso per $	425.0	Effective rates	*1990 = 100*
Peso per SDR	611.1	– nominal	161.0
Peso per Ecu	531.3	– real	125.8

Principal exports

	$bn fob			$bn fob
Industrial products	6.7	Other mining		1.4
Copper	6.5			
Agricultural & fishing	1.4	Total incl. others		**16.0**

Main export destinations

	% of total		% of total
Japan	17.7	South Korea	5.5
United States	14.4	Germany	5.1
United Kingdom	6.5	Taiwan	4.3
Brazil	6.4		

Principal imports

	$bn cif		$bn cif
Intermediate goods	7.0	Consumer goods	3.1
Capital goods	4.4	Total incl. others	**14.7**

Main origins of imports

	% of total		% of total
United States	24.7	Germany	5.1
Argentina	9.0	Mexico	3.9
Brazil	7.8	South Korea	3.4
Japan	6.6		

Balance of payments, reserves and debt, $bn

Visible exports fob	16.0	Overall balance	1.1
Visible imports fob	-14.7	Change in reserves	1.1
Trade balance	1.4	Level of reserves	
Invisibles inflows	4.0	end Dec.	14.9
Invisibles outflows	-5.6	No. months of import cover	8.8
Net transfers	0.4	Foreign debt	25.6
Current account balance	0.2	– as % of GDP	43.3
– as % of GDP	0.3	Debt service paid	5.2
Capital balance	1.2	Debt service ratio	25.7

Family life

No. of households	3.3m	Divorces per 1,000 pop.	0.4
Av. no. per household	4.4	Cost of living, Dec. 1996	
Marriages per 1,000 pop.	6.6	New York = 100	74

CHINA

Area	9,560,900 sq km	Currency	Yuan
Capital	Beijing		

People

Population	1,220.2m	Life expectancy: men	68.2 yrs
Pop. per sq km	127	women	71.7 yrs
Av. ann. growth		Adult literacy	80.0%
in pop. 1985–94	1.3%	Fertility rate (per woman)	1.8
Pop. under 15	26.3%		
Pop. over 65	6.1%		*per 1,000 pop.*
No. of men per 100 women	106.3	Crude birth rate	16.2
Human Development Index	60.9	Crude death rate	7.1

The economy

GDP	Yuan6,222bn	GDP per head	$610
GDP	$745bn	GDP per head in purchasing	
Av. ann. growth in real		power parity (USA=100)	11
GDP 1985–95	9.5%		

Origins of GDP[a]		Components of GDP[a]	
	% of total		*% of total*
Agriculture	20.5	Private consumption	46.2
Industry, of which:	49.2	Public consumption	12.8
manufacturing	...	Investment	34.7
Services	30.3	Exports	21.7
		Imports	-19.2

Structure of employment[b]

	% of total		*% of labour force*
Agriculture	54	Unemployed[c] 1994	2.8
Industry	23	Av. ann. rate 1990–94	2.5
Services	23		

Energy

	'000 TCE		
Total output	1,142,633	% output exported	4.7
Total consumption	1,092,541	% consumption imported	3.8
Consumption per head,			
kg coal equivalent	920		

Inflation and finance

		av. ann. increase 1989–95	
Consumer price			
inflation 1996	8.3%	Narrow money (M1)	24.6%
Av. ann. inflation 1989–96	11.3%	Broad money	27.6%

Exchange rates

	end 1996		*June 1996*
Yuan per $	8.30	Effective rates	*1990 = 100*
Yuan per SDR	11.93	– nominal	...
Yuan per Ecu	10.38	– real	...

Principal exports

	$bn fob		$bn fob
Clothing & footwear	28.2	Food & tobacco	11.2
Electrical machinery	19.0	Mineral fuels	5.3
Chemicals	11.9	Total incl. others	**148.8**

Main export destinations

	% of total		% of total
Hong Kong	24.1	South Korea	4.7
Japan	18.8	Germany	3.9
United States	16.1	Singapore	2.3

Principal imports

	$bn fob		$bn fob
Machinery	47.0	Vehicles & equipment	5.4
Chemicals	18.3	Fuels	5.1
Textiles	15.8		
Iron & steel	8.0	Total incl. others	**132.1**

Main origins of imports

	% of total		% of total
Japan	22.0	Hong Kong	6.4
United States	12.2	Germany	6.1
Taiwan	11.2	Russia	2.9
South Korea	7.8	Singapore	2.6

Balance of payments, reserves and debt, $bn

Visible exports fob	128.1	Overall balance	22.5
Visible imports fob	-110.1	Change in reserves	22.5
Trade balance	18.1	Level of reserves	
Invisibles inflows	24.3	end Dec.	80.3
Invisibles outflows	-42.2	No. months of import cover	6.3
Net transfers	1.4	Foreign debt	118.1
Current account balance	1.6	- as % of GDP	17.2
- as % of GDP	0.2	Debt service paid	15.1
Capital balance	38.7	Debt service ratio	9.9

Family life

No. of households	357m	Divorces per 1,000 pop.	...
Av. no. per household	3.4	Cost of living, Dec. 1996	
Marriages per 1,000 pop.	...	New York = 100	103

a 1995 estimates.
b 1994
c Urban areas.

COLOMBIA

Area	1,141,748 sq km	Currency	Colombian peso (peso)
Capital	Bogota		

People

Population	35.8m	Life expectancy: men	68.2 yrs
Pop. per sq km	31	women	73.7 yrs
Av. ann. growth		Adult literacy	87.4%
in pop. 1985–95	2.0%	Fertility rate (per woman)	2.7
Pop. under 15	34.3%		
Pop. over 65	4.4%		*per 1,000 pop.*
No. of men per 100 women	98.5	Crude birth rate	23.4
Human Development Index	84	Crude death rate	5.6

The economy

GDP	63,898bn pesos	GDP per head	$1,962
GDP	$70bn	GDP per head in purchasing	
Av. ann. growth in real		power parity (USA=100)	23
GDP 1985–95	4.4%		

Origins of GDP		Components of GDP	
	% of total		*% of total*
Agriculture	20.9	Private consumption	69.1
Industry, of which:	29.2	Public consumption	13.4
manufacturing	20.3	Investment	27.5
Services	49.9	Exports	23.3
		Imports	-33.3

Structure of employment[a]

	% of total		*% of labour force*
Agriculture	1	Unemployed 1993	8.4
Industry	31	Av. ann. rate 1990–93	4.5
Services	68		

Energy

	'000 TCE		
Total output	63,914	% output exported	53.0
Total consumption	34,388	% consumption imported	8.0
Consumption per head,			
kg coal equivalent	995		

Inflation and finance

Consumer price		*av. ann. increase 1991–95*	
inflation 1996	20.8%	Narrow money (M1)	30.6
Av. ann. inflation 1989–96	24.8%	Broad money	31.6

Exchange rates

	end 1996		*June 1996*
Peso per $	1,005	Effective rates	*1990 = 100*
Peso per SDR	1,446	– nominal	86.1
Peso per Ecu	1,256	– real	138.4

Principal exports

	$bn fob		$bn fob
Coffee	1.8	Coal	0.6
Petroleum & products	1.8		
Gold	1.1	Total incl. others	**10.4**

Main export destinations

	% of total		% of total
United States	33.7	EU	24.2
Andean Group[b]	27.9	Japan	3.7

Principal imports

	$bn fob		$bn fob
Industrial supplies	5.7	Consumer goods	2.5
Capital goods	4.8	Total	**12.9**

Main origins of imports

	% of total		% of total
United States	39.1	Andean Group[b]	13.2
EU	16.4	Japan	7.6

Balance of payments, reserves and debt, $bn

Visible exports fob	10.4	Overall balance	0.4
Visible imports fob	-12.9	Change in reserves	0.3
Trade balance	-2.5	Level of reserves	
Invisibles inflows	4.4	end Dec.	8.2
Invisibles outflows	-6.7	No. months of import cover	5.0
Net transfers	0.7	Foreign debt	20.8
Current account balance	-4.1	– as % of GDP	28.2
– as % of GDP	-5.9	Debt service paid	3.8
Capital balance	5.0	Debt service ratio	25.2

Family life

No. of households	8.5m	Divorces per 1,000 pop.	...
Av. no. per household	4.1	Cost of living, Dec. 1996	
Marriages per 1,000 pop.	2.4	New York = 100	71

a 1992, main cities.
b Bolivia, Colombia, Ecuador, Peru, Venezuela.

CÔTE D'IVOIRE

Area	322,463 sq km	Currency	CFA franc (CFAfr)
Capital	Abidjan/Yamoussoukro		

People

Population	13.7m	Life expectancy: men		50.0 yrs
Pop. per sq km	42		women	52.2 yrs
Av. ann. growth		Adult literacy		55.8%
in pop. 1985–95	3.3%	Fertility rate (per woman)		5.1
Pop. under 15	44.8%			
Pop. over 65	2.8%			*per 1,000 pop.*
No. of men per 100 women	104.3	Crude birth rate		37.2
Human Development Index	35.7	Crude death rate		13.8

The economy

GDP	CFAfr4,492bn	GDP per head	$675
GDP	$9bn	GDP per head in purchasing	
Av. ann. growth in real		power parity (USA=100)	6
GDP 1985–95	0.7%		

Origins of GDP[a]		Components of GDP[a]	
	% of total		*% of total*
Agriculture	30.7	Private consumption	65.5
Industry, of which:	19.4	Public consumption	14.8
manufacturing	13.4	Investment	10.9
Services	49.9	Exports	43.1
		Imports	-34.3

Structure of employment[b]

	% of total		*% of labour force*
Agriculture	60	Unemployed 1995	…
Industry	10	Av. ann. rate 1990–94	…
Services	30		

Energy

	'000 TCE		
Total output	614	% output exported	63.7
Total consumption	3,512	% consumption imported	138.0
Consumption per head,			
kg coal equivalent	255		

Inflation and finance

Consumer price		*av. ann. change 1989–95*	
inflation 1995	14%	Narrow money (M1)	7.2%
Av. ann. inflation 1989–95	6.6%	Broad money	6.1%

Exchange rates

	end 1996		*June 1996*
CFAfr per $	523.7	Effective rates	*1990 = 100*
CFAfr per SDR	753.1	– nominal	52.5
CFAfr per Ecu	654.6	– real	83.8

Principal exports

	$m fob		$m fob
Cocoa beans & products	1,106	Petroleum products	366
Timber & products	406	Canned fish	195
Coffee & products	399	Total incl. others	**3,728**

Main export destinations

	% of total		% of total
France	18	Netherlands	8
Germany	8	Italy	8

Principal imports

	$m cif		$m cif
Indusrial imports	877	Fuel	467
Transport equipment	499		
Food & drinks	498	Total incl. others	**2,945**

Main origins of imports

	% of total		% of total
France	32	Ghana	4
Nigeria	20	Germany	4
United States	6		

Balance of payments, reserves and debt, $bn

Visible exports fob	3.9	Overall balance	-0.2
Visible imports fob	-2.5	Change in reserves	0.3
Trade balance	1.5	Level of reserves	
Invisibles inflows	0.6	end Dec.	0.5
Invisibles outflows	-2.0	No. months of import cover	1.5
Net transfers	-0.3	Foreign debt	19.0
Current account balance	-0.3	– as % of GDP	251.7
– as % of GDP	-2.9	Debt service paid	1.0
Capital balance	0.0	Debt service ratio	23.1

Family life

No. of households	2.4m	Divorces per 1,000 pop.	...
Av. no. per household	5.8	Cost of living, Dec. 1996	
Marriages per 1,000 pop.	...	New York = 100	107

a 1994
b 1990

CZECH REPUBLIC

Area	78,864 sq km	Currency	Koruna (Kc)
Capital	Prague		

People

Population	10.3m	Life expectancy: men	69.8 yrs
Pop. per sq km	130	women	76.0 yrs
Av. ann. growth		Adult literacy[a]	99.0%
in pop. 1985–95	nil	Fertility rate (per woman)	1.4
Pop. under 15	18.9%		
Pop. over 65	12.6%		*per 1,000 pop.*
No. of men per 100 women	95.3	Crude birth rate	10.7
Human Development Index[a]	87.2	Crude death rate	12.0

The economy

GDP	Kcs1,062bn	GDP per head	$3,897
GDP	$40bn	GDP per head in purchasing	
Av. ann. growth in real		power parity (USA=100)	36
GDP 1989–95	-3.2%		

Origins of GDP[b]		Components of GDP	
	% of total		*% of total*
Agriculture	5.8	Private consumption	57.3
Industry, of which:	40.7	Public consumption	19.4
manufacturing	...	Investment	27.8
Services	53.5	Exports	59.3
		Imports	-63.8

Structure of employment

	% of total		*% of labour force*
Agriculture	7	Unemployed 1995	3.4
Industry	42	Av. ann. rate 1993–94	3.8
Services	57		

Energy

	'000 TCE		
Total output	42,672	% output exported	27.3
Total consumption	51,207	% consumption imported	45.7
Consumption per head,			
kg coal equivalent	4,974		

Inflation and finance

Consumer price		*av. ann. increase 1994–95*	
inflation 1996	8.8%	Narrow money (M1)	26.6%
Av. ann. inflation 1991–96	20.4%	Broad money	24.8%

Exchange rates

	end 1996		*June 1996*
Kc per $	27.33	Effective rates	*1990 = 100*
Kc per SDR	39.30	– nominal	...
Kc per Ecu	34.16	– real	...

Principal exports

	$bn fob		$bn fob
Manufactured goods	5.5	Raw materials & fuels	1.9
Machinery & industrial		Chemicals	1.8
equipment	4.5	Total incl. others	**17.1**

Main export destinations

	% of total		% of total
Germany	31.8	Austria	6.5
Slovakia	16.2	Poland	5.4

Principal imports

	$bn fob		$bn fob
Machinery & transport		Chemicals	2.8
equipment	7.4	Raw materials & fuels	2.5
Manufactured goods	2.5	Total incl. others	**20.9**

Main origins of imports

	% of total		% of total
Germany	25.8	Russia	8.9
Slovakia	13.1	Austria	6.9

Balance of payments, reserves and debt, $bn

Visible exports fob	21.5	Overall balance	7.5
Visible imports fob	-25.2	Change in reserves	7.7
Trade balance	-3.7	Level of reserves	
Invisibles inflows	7.9	end Dec.	14.6
Invisibles outflows	-6.2	No. months of import cover	5.6
Net transfers	0.6	Foreign debt	16.6
Current account balance	-1.4	– as % of GDP	37.0
– as % of GDP	-3.4	Debt service paid	2.6
Capital balance	8.2	Debt service ratio	10.5

Family life

No. of households	3.4m	Divorces per 1,000 pop.	2.9
Av. no. per household	3.1	Cost of living, Dec. 1996	
Marriages per 1,000 pop.	5.3	New York = 100	67

a 1992
b 1994

DENMARK

Area	43,075 sq km	Currency	Danish krone (DKr)
Capital	Copenhagen		

People

Population	5.2m	Life expectancy: men	73.0 yrs
Pop. per sq km	121	women	78.3 yrs
Av. ann. growth		Adult literacy	99.0%
in pop. 1985–95	0.2	Fertility rate (per woman)	1.8
Pop. under 15	17.5%		
Pop. over 65	15.1%		*per 1,000 pop.*
No. of men per 100 women	97.9	Crude birth rate	13.0
Human Development Index	92.4	Crude death rate	11.8

The economy

GDP	DKr874bn	GDP per head	$29,873
GDP	$156bn	GDP per head in purchasing	
Av. ann. growth in real		power parity (USA=100)	79
GDP 1985–95	1.7%		

Origins of GDP		**Components of GDP**	
	% of total		*% of total*
Agriculture	4.2	Private consumption	53.6
Industry, of which:	28.6	Public consumption	25.1
manufacturing	20.2	Investment	17.3
Services	67.2	Exports	34.5
		Imports	-30.5

Structure of employment

	% of total		*% of labour force*
Agriculture	4	Unemployed 1995	10.3
Industry	27	Av. ann. rate 1990–94	11.2
Services	69		

Energy

	'000 TCE		
Total output	19,695	% output exported	88.0
Total consumption	26,644	% consumption imported	96.6
Consumption per head,			
kg coal equivalent	5,151		

Inflation and finance

Consumer price		*av. ann. increase 1989–95*	
inflation 1996	2.1%	Narrow money (M1)	4.3%
Av. ann. inflation 1989–96	2.4%	Broad money	3.8%

Exchange rates

	end 1996		*June 1996*
DKr per $	5.95	Effective rates	*1990 = 100*
DKr per SDR	8.55	– nominal	107.3
DKr per Ecu	7.44	– real	105.5

Principal exports

	$bn fob		$bn fob
Manufactured goods	34.9	Ships	0.9
Agric. products	6.3		
Energy & products	1.5	Total incl. others	**49.0**

Main export destinations

	% of total		% of total
Germany	22.5	Norway	5.9
Sweden	9.7	France	5.4
United Kingdom	7.9	Netherlands	4.4

Principal imports

	$bn cif		$bn cif
Intermediate goods	20.2	Transport equipment	2.7
Consumer goods	10.8		
Capital goods	4.9	Total incl. others	**43.2**

Main origins of imports

	% of total		% of total
Germany	21.7	United Kingdom	6.6
Sweden	11.7	France	5.2
Netherlands	7.0	Norway	4.9

Balance of payments, reserves and aid, $bn

Visible exports fob	48.9	Capital balance	0.0
Visible imports fob	-42.0	Overall balance	2.4
Trade balance	6.8	Change in reserves	2.0
Invisibles inflows	43.9	Level of reserves	
Invisibles outflows	-48.4	end Dec.	11.8
Net transfers	-1.0	No. months of import cover	1.6
Current account balance	1.4	Aid given	1.62
– as % of GDP	1.0	– as % of GDP	0.96

Family life

No. of households	2.3m	Divorces per 1,000 pop.	2.5
Av. no. per household	2.3	Cost of living, Dec. 1996	
Marriages per 1,000 pop.	6.7	New York = 100	123

EGYPT

Area	1,000,250 sq km	Currency	Egyptian pound (£E)
Capital	Cairo		

People

Population	62.1m	Life expectancy: men	64.7 yrs
Pop. per sq km	62	women	67.3 yrs
Av. ann. growth		Adult literacy	49.8%
in pop. 1985–94	2.2%	Fertility rate (per woman)	3.4
Pop. under 15	38.0%		
Pop. over 65	4.2%		*per 1,000 pop.*
No. of men per 100 women	103.1	Crude birth rate	26.1
Human Development Index	61.1	Crude death rate	7.1

The economy

GDP	£E156bn	GDP per head	$733
GDP	$46bn	GDP per head in purchasing	
Av. ann. growth in real		power parity (USA=100)	14
GDP 1985–95	4.9%		

Origins of GDP[a]		Components of GDP[a]	
	% of total		*% of total*
Agriculture	16.3	Private consumption	72.0
Industry, of which:	22.3	Public consumption	11.1
manufacturing	...	Investment	21.7
Services	61.4	Exports	26.8
		Imports	-31.6

Structure of employment[b]

	% of total		*% of labour force*
Agriculture	35	Unemployed 1994	11.0
Industry	21	Av. ann. rate 1990–94	9.8
Services	44		

Energy

	'000 TCE		
Total output	82,121	% output exported	45.5
Total consumption	40,561	% consumption imported	4.0
Consumption per head,			
kg coal equivalent	658		

Inflation and finance

Consumer price		*av. ann. increase 1989–95*	
inflation 1995	5.8%	Narrow money (M1)	10.5%
Av. ann. inflation 1989–95	13.8%	Broad money	16.9%

Exchange rates

	end 1996		*June 1996*
£E per $	3.39	Effective rates	*1990 = 100*
£E per SDR	4.87	– nominal	...
£E per Ecu	4.24	– real	...

Principal exports[a]

	$m fob		$m fob
Petroleum & products	1,629	Other agric. products	309
Cotton yarn & textiles	926	Raw cotton	306
Industrial goods	548	Total incl. others	**4,447**

Main export destinations

	% of total		% of total
Italy	18.6	United Kingdom	6.6
United States	11.1	Romania	6.2
Germany	6.8	France	4.1

Principal imports[a]

	$m cif		$m cif
Machinery & transport		Chemicals & rubber	1,772
equipment	3,108	Wood, paper & textiles	1,389
Agric. products &		Base metals & manufactures	1,051
foodstuffs	2,760	Total incl. others	**11,280**

Main origins of imports

	% of total		% of total
United States	18.9	France	7.5
Germany	9.6	Japan	5.1
Italy	7.6	United Kingdom	3.8

Balance of payments, reserves and debt, $bn

Visible exports fob	4.7	Overall balance	-1.8
Visible imports fob	-12.3	Change in reserves	2.7
Trade balance	-7.6	Level of reserves	
Invisibles inflows	10.2	end Dec.	17.1
Invisibles outflows	-6.9	No. months of import cover	10.7
Net transfers	4.0	Foreign debt	34.1
Current account balance	-0.3	– as % of GDP	73.3
– as % of GDP	-0.6	Debt service paid	2.4
Capital balance	-1.8	Debt service ratio	14.6

Family life

No. of households	9.7m	Divorces per 1,000 pop.	1.4
Av. no. per household	4.9	Cost of living, Dec. 1996	
Marriages per 1,000 pop.	8.4	New York = 100	88

a   Year ending June 30, 1995.
b   1994

FINLAND

Area	338,145 sq km	Currency	Markka (Fmk)
Capital	Helsinki		

People

Population	5.1m	Life expectancy: men	73.0 yrs
Pop. per sq km	15	women	80.1 yrs
Av. ann. growth		Adult literacy	99%
in pop. 1985–95	0.2%	Fertility rate (per woman)	1.8
Pop. under 15	19.0%		
Pop. over 65	14.1%		*per 1,000 pop.*
No. of men per 100 women	94.9	Crude birth rate	12.0
Human Development Index	93.5	Crude death rate	10.2

The economy

GDP	Fmk459bn	GDP per head	$20,594
GDP	$105bn	GDP per head in purchasing	
Av. ann. growth in real		power parity (USA=100)	66
GDP 1985–95	1.0%		

Origins of GDP		Components of GDP	
	% of total		*% of total*
Agriculture	5.5	Private consumption	54.3
Industry, of which:	32.9	Public consumption	21.5
manufacturing	25.2	Investment	16.5
Services	61.6	Exports	37.5
		Imports	-29.8

Structure of employment

	% of total		*% of labour force*
Agriculture	8	Unemployed 1995	17.1
Industry	27	Av. ann. rate 1990–94	12.0
Services	65		

Energy

	'000 TCE		
Total output	11,708	% output exported[a]	43.4
Total consumption	37,617	% consumption imported[a]	85.6
Consumption per head,			
kg coal equivalent	7,401		

Inflation and finance

Consumer price		*av. ann. increase 1989–95*	
inflation 1996	0.6%	Narrow money (M1)	25.4%
Av. ann. inflation 1989–96	3.0%	Broad money	4.2%

Exchange rates

	end 1996		*June 1996*
Fmk per $	4.64	Effective rates	*1990 = 100*
Fmk per SDR	6.68	– nominal	83.5
Fmk per Ecu	5.80	– real	68.5

Principal exports

	$bn fob		$bn fob
Metals & engineering		Chemicals	3.7
equipment	15.6	Wood & products	3.0
Paper & products	11.0	Total incl. others	**40.0**

Main export destinations

	% of total		% of total
Germany	13.4	United States	6.7
United Kingdom	10.4	Russia	4.8
Sweden	10.1	France	4.6

Principal imports

	$bn cif		$bn cif
Raw materials	15.9	Energy & products	2.1
Consumer goods	5.6		
Capital goods	4.2	Total incl. others	**28.9**

Main origins of imports

	% of total		% of total
Germany	15.6	Russia	7.1
Sweden	11.7	United States	7.1
United Kingdom	8.3	Japan	6.3

Balance of payments, reserves and aid, $bn

Visible exports fob	40.1	Capital balance	-4.0
Visible imports fob	-27.5	Overall balance	-0.4
Trade balance	12.5	Change in reserves	-0.8
Invisibles inflows	10.7	Level of reserves	
Invisibles outflows	-17.3	end Dec.	10.7
Net transfers	-0.3	No. months of import cover	2.8
Current account balance	5.6	Aid given	0.39
– as % of GDP	5.1	– as % of GDP	0.32

Family life

No. of households	2.1m	Divorces per 1,000 pop.	2.7
Av. no. per household	2.4	Cost of living, Dec. 1996	
Marriages per 1,000 pop.	4.6	New York = 100	110

a Energy trade data are distorted by transitory and oil refinery activities.

FRANCE

Area	543,965 sq km	Currency	Franc (FFr)
Capital	Paris		

People

Population	58.1m	Life expectancy: men	74.6 yrs
Pop. per sq km	105	women	82.9 yrs
Av. ann. growth		Adult literacy	99.0%
in pop. 1985–95	0.5%	Fertility rate (per woman)	1.6
Pop. under 15	19.4%		
Pop. over 65	15.2%		*per 1,000 pop.*
No. of men per 100 women	95.0	Crude birth rate	11.6
Human Development Index	93.5	Crude death rate	9.1

The economy

GDP	FFr7,243bn	GDP per head	$24,973
GDP	$1,451bn	GDP per head in purchasing	
Av. ann. growth in real		power parity (USA=100)	78
GDP, 1985–95	2.2%		

Origins of GDP		Components of GDP	
	% of total		*% of total*
Agriculture	2.6	Private consumption	60.2
Industry, of which:	28.6	Public consumption	19.3
manufacturing	...	Investment	18.2
Services	68.8	Exports	23.5
		Imports	-21.1

Structure of employment

	% of total		*% of labour force*
Agriculture	5	Unemployed 1995	11.6
Industry	27	Av. ann. rate 1990–94	10.5
Services	69		

Energy

	'000 TCE		
Total output	159,387	% output exported	20.1
Total consumption	297,614	% consumption imported	63.4
Consumption per head,			
kg coal equivalent	5,151		

Inflation and finance

Consumer price		*av. ann. increase 1989–95*	
inflation 1996	2.0%	Narrow money (M1)	2.5%
Av. ann. inflation 1989–96	2.5%	Broad money	3.7%

Exchange rates

	end 1996		*June 1996*
FFr per $	5.24	Effective rates	*1990 = 100*
FFr per SDR	7.53	– nominal	108.9
FFr per Ecu	6.55	– real	98.7

Principal exports

	$bn fob		$bn fob
Capital equipment	77.6	Motor vehicles & other	
Chemicals	44.9	transport equipment	37.1
Non-durable consumer		Steel & other metals	24.7
goods	43.4		
Agric. products & foodstuffs	42.7	Total incl. others	**286.7**

Main export destinations

	% of total		% of total
Germany	17.7	Spain	7.3
Italy	9.6	United States	5.9
United Kingdom	9.3	Netherlands	4.6
Belgium/Luxembourg	8.5		

Principal imports

	$bn cif		$bn cif
Capital equipment	65.9	Motor vehicles & other	
Chemicals	45.6	transport equipment	31.8
Non-durable consumer		Steel & other metals	25.9
goods	44.4	Energy products	18.4
Agric. products			
& foodstuffs	32.5	Total incl. others	**275.0**

Main origins of imports

	% of total		% of total
Germany	18.5	United States	7.8
Italy	10.0	Spain	6.5
Belgium/Luxembourg	9.0	Netherlands	5.3
United Kingdom	8.0		

Balance of payments, reserves and aid, $bn

Visible exports fob	270.4	Capital balance	-20.6
Visible imports fob	-259.2	Overall balance	0.7
Trade balance	11.2	Change in reserves	0.9
Invisibles inflows	227.8	Level of reserves	
Invisibles outflows	-216.0	end Dec.	58.5
Net transfers	-6.5	No. months of import cover	1.5
Current account balance	16.4	Aid given[a]	8.4
– as % of GDP	1.1	– as % of GDP	0.55

Family life

No. of households	22.8m	Divorces per 1,000 pop.	1.2
Av. no. per household	2.6	Cost of living, Dec. 1996	
Marriages per 1,000 pop.	4.4	New York = 100	129

a Including aid to French overseas territories.

GERMANY

Area	357,868 sq km	Currency	Deutschemark (DM)
Capital	Berlin		

People

Population	81.6m	Life expectancy: men		73.4 yrs
Pop. per sq km	229		women	79.9 yrs
Av. ann. growth		Adult literacy		99.0%
in pop. 1985–95	0.5%	Fertility rate (per woman)		1.3
Pop. under 15	16.0%			
Pop. over 65	15.2%			*per 1,000 pop.*
No. of men per 100 women	95.2	Crude birth rate		9.3
Human Development Index	92	Crude death rate		10.9

The economy

GDP	DM3,227bn	GDP per head	$27,604
GDP	$2,252bn	GDP per head in purchasing	
Av. ann. growth in real		power parity (USA=100)	74
GDP 1985–95[a]	2.8%		

Origins of GNP		**Components of GNP**	
	% of total		*% of total*
Agriculture	1.1	Private consumption	57.0
Industry, of which:	33.4	Public consumption	19.5
manufacturing	...	Investment	22.4
Services	65.5	Exports	23.0
		Imports	-22.0

Structure of employment

	% of total		*% of labour force*
Agriculture	3	Unemployed 1995	8.2
Industry	36	Av. ann. rate 1990–94	8.2
Services	61		

Energy

	'000 TCE		
Total output	200,675	% output exported	15.0
Total consumption	444,978	% consumption imported	68.3
Consumption per head,			
kg coal equivalent	5,475		

Inflation[a] and finance

Consumer price		*av. ann. increase 1989–95*	
inflation 1996	1.5%	Narrow money (M1)	9.8%
Av. ann. inflation 1989–96	2.9%	Broad money	8.0%

Exchange rates

	end 1996		*June 1996*
DM per $	1.55	Effective rates	*1990 = 100*
DM per SDR	2.24	– nominal	108.2
DM per Ecu	2.90	– real	117.0

Principal exports

	$bn fob		$bn fob
Machinery	153.2	Textiles & clothing	21.2
Road vehicles	88.8	Iron & steel	18.4
Chemicals	78.8		
Food, drink & tobacco	25.7	Total incl. others	**523.7**

Main export destinations

	% of total		% of total
France	11.6	United States	7.5
United Kingdom	8.0	Netherlands	7.4
Italy	7.5	Belgium/Luxembourg	6.5

Principal imports

	$bn cif		$bn cif
Machinery	97.6	Food, drink & tobacco	45.7
Road vehicles	47.2	Textiles & clothing	36.8
Chemicals	50.4	Total incl. others	**464.2**

Main origins of imports

	% of total		% of total
France	10.7	United States	7.1
Netherlands	8.4	Belgium/Luxembourg	6.5
Italy	8.3	United Kingdom	6.4

Balance of payments, reserves and aid, $bn

Visible exports fob	523.2	Capital balance	32.6
Visible imports fob	-457.1	Overall balance	7.2
Trade balance	66.1	Change in reserves	8.0
Invisibles inflows	183.3	Level of reserves	
Invisibles outflows	-229.4	end Dec.	121.8
Net transfers	-41.0	No. months of import cover	2.1
Current account balance	-21.0	Aid given	7.5
– as % of GDP	-0.9	– as % of GDP	0.31

Family life

No. of households	35.1m	Divorces per 1,000 pop.	2.0
Av. no. per household	2.3	Cost of living, Dec. 1996	
Marriages per 1,000 pop.	5.3	New York = 100	114

a   Western Germany.

GREECE

Area	131,957 sq km	Currency	Drachma (Dr)
Capital	Athens		

People

Population	10.5m	Life expectancy: men	75.5 yrs
Pop. per sq km	79	women	80.6 yrs
Av. ann. growth		Adult literacy	93.8%
in pop. 1985–95	0.5%	Fertility rate (per woman)	1.4
Pop. under 15	16.8%		
Pop. over 65	15.9%		*per 1,000 pop.*
No. of men per 100 women	97.0	Crude birth rate	10.0
Human Development Index	90.9	Crude death rate	9.9

The economy

GDP	Dr19,923bn	GDP per head	$8,216
GDP	$86bn	GDP per head in purchasing	
Av. ann. growth in real		power parity (USA=100)	43
GDP 1985–95	1.4%		

Origins of GDP[a]		Components of GDP	
	% of total		*% of total*
Agriculture	11.2	Private consumption	74.5
Industry, of which:	25.3	Public consumption	14.1
manufacturing	…	Investment	21.8
Services	63.5	Exports	16.5
		Imports	-26.9

Structure of employment

	% of total		*% of labour force*
Agriculture	20	Unemployed 1995	10.0
Industry	23	Av. ann. rate 1990–94	8.5
Services	57		

Energy

	'000 TCE		
Total output	11,783	% output exported[b]	41.4
Total consumption	33,583	% consumption imported[b]	84.9
Consumption per head,			
kg coal equivalent	3,224		

Inflation and finance

Consumer price		*av. ann. increase 1989–95*	
inflation 1996	8.5%	Narrow money (M1)	18.0%
Av. ann. inflation 1989–96	14.0%	Broad money[b]	13.8%

Exchange rates

	end 1996		*June 1996*
		Effective rates	*1990 = 100*
Dr per $	247.0	Effective rates	
Dr per SDR	355.2	– nominal	67.5
Dr per Ecu	308.8	– real	106.9

Principal exports[c]

	$bn fob		$bn fob
Manufactured products	2.4	Minerals	0.2
Food & beverages	1.4		
Petroleum products	0.6		
Raw materials & industrial supplies	0.3	Total incl. others	**9.4**

Main export destinations[c]

	% of total		% of total
Germany	25.9	France	6.6
United States	17.3	United Kingdom	6.4
Italy	11.3	Netherlands	2.4

Principal imports[c]

	$bn cif		$bn cif
Manufactured consumer goods	7.5	Petroleum	1.2
		Chemicals & products	0.8
Capital goods	4.4	Iron & steel	0.6
Foodstuffs	2.8	Total incl. others	**21.5**

Main origins of imports[b]

	% of total		% of total
Germany	18.3	France	8.2
Italy	15.3	Netherlands	7.3
United States	9.1	United Kingdom	6.7

Balance of payments, reserves and debt, $bn

Visible exports fob	5.9	Overall balance	-0.0
Visible imports fob	-20.3	Change in reserves	0.3
Trade balance	-14.4	Level of reserves	
Invisibles inflows	10.9	end Dec.	16.1
Invisibles outflows	-7.4	No. months of import cover	7.0
Net transfers	8.0	Aid given	0.15
Current account balance	-2.9	– as % of GDP	0.0
– as % of GDP	-3.3		
Capital balance	3.2		

Family life

No. of households	3.7m	Divorces per 1,000 pop.	0.7
Av. no. per household	2.9	Cost of living, Dec. 1996	
Marriages per 1,000 pop.	6.2	New York = 100	97

a   1993
b   Energy trade figures are distorted by transitory and oil refining activities.
c   1994

HONG KONG

Area	1,075 sq km	Currency	Hong Kong dollar (HK$)
Capital	Victoria		

People

Population	6.1m	Life expectancy: men	76.1 yrs
Pop. per sq km	5,859	women	81.8 yrs
Av. ann. growth		Adult literacy	90.0%
in pop. 1985–95	1.2%	Fertility rate (per woman)	1.3
Pop. under 15	19.6%		
Pop. over 65	9.8%		*per 1,000 pop.*
No. of men per 100 women	107.1	Crude birth rate	10.6
Human Development Index	90.9	Crude death rate	6.2

The economy

GDP	HK$1,096bn	GDP per head	$23,245
GDP	$142bn	GDP per head in purchasing	
Av. ann. growth in real		power parity (USA=100)	85
GDP 1985–95	6.7%		

Origins of GDP		Components of GDP	
	% of total		*% of total*
Agriculture	0.1	Private consumption	60.2
Industry, of which:	16.0	Public consumption	8.8
manufacturing	8.8	Investment	34.6
Services	83.9	Exports	149.8
		Imports	-153.2

Structure of employment

	% of total		*% of labour force*
Agriculture	1	Unemployed 1995	3.2
Industry	27	Av. ann. rate 1990–94	1.8
Services	72		

Energy

	'000 TCE		
Total output	nil	% output exported	nil
Total consumption	13,764	% consumption imported	203.6
Consumption per head,			
kg coal equivalent	2,358		

Inflation and finance

Consumer price		*av. ann. increase 1988–95*	
inflation 1996	6.0%	Narrow money (M1)	...
Av. ann. inflation 1989–96	9.1%	Broad money	...

Exchange rates

	end 1996		*June 1996*
HK$ per $	7.74	Effective rates	*1990 = 100*
HK$ per SDR	11.16	– nominal	...
HK$ per Ecu	9.68	– real	...

Principal exports[a]

	$bn fob		$bn fob
Clothing	9.5	Watches, clocks &	
Electrical machinery		photographic equipment	1.8
& apparatus	4.1		
Textiles	1.8	Total incl. others	**29.9**

Main export destinations[b]

	% of total		% of total
China	33.3	Germany	4.3
United States	21.7	United Kingdom	3.2
Japan	6.1	Singapore	2.8

Principal imports

	$bn cif		$bn cif
Consumer goods	72.7	Agric. products & foodstuffs	7.9
Raw materials & semi-		Fuels	3.4
manufactured products	70.2		
Capital goods	38.5	Total incl. others	**192.8**

Main origins of imports

	% of total		% of total
China	36.2	United States	7.7
Japan	14.8	Singapore	5.2
Taiwan	8.7	South Korea	4.9

Balance of payments, reserves and debt, $bn

Visible exports fob	173.7	Overall balance	...
Visible imports cif	-192.8	Change in reserves	7.9
Trade balance	-19.0	Level of reserves	
Invisibles inflows	37.3	end Dec.	57.2
Invisibles outflows	-21.3	No. months of import cover	3.2
Net transfers	...	Foreign debt	18.9
Current account balance	-4.9	– as % of GDP	13.5
– as % of GDP[c]	-3.4	Debt service paid	2.3
Capital balance	...	Debt service ratio	1.1

Family life

No. of households	1.8m	Divorces per 1,000 pop.	1.0
Av. no. per household	3.4	Cost of living, Dec. 1996	
Marriages per 1,000 pop.	6.3	New York = 100	120

a Domestic.
b Including re-exports.
c Including gold imports for industrial use.
Note: Hong Kong became part of China from July 1st 1997.

HUNGARY

Area	93,030 sq km	Currency	Forint (Ft)
Capital	Budapest		

People

Population	10.1m	Life expectancy: men	64.5 yrs
Pop. per sq km	109	women	73.8 yrs
Av. ann. growth		Adult literacy	99.0%
in pop. 1985–95	-0.5%	Fertility rate (per woman)	1.4
Pop. under 15	18.0%		
Pop. over 65	14.0%		*per 1,000 pop.*
No. of men per 100 women	91.8	Crude birth rate	10.2
Human Development Index	85.5	Crude death rate	14.6

The economy

GDP	Ft5,279bn	GDP per head	$4,169
GDP	$42bn	GDP per head in purchasing	
Av. ann. growth in real		power parity (USA=100)	24
GDP 1985–95	-0.9%		

Origins of GDP[a]		Components of GDP[a]	
	% of total		*% of total*
Agriculture	7.3	Private consumption	74.1
Industry, of which:	37.5	Public consumption	13.1
manufacturing	...	Investment	23.0
Services	55.2	Exports	34.6
		Imports	-44.8

Structure of employment

	% of total		*% of labour force*
Agriculture	8	Unemployed 1995	10.3
Industry	33	Av. ann. rate 1992–94	11.0
Services	59		

Energy

	'000 TCE		
Total output	19,836	% output exported	12.8
Total consumption	33,260	% consumption imported	58.5
Consumption per head,			
kg coal equivalent	3,273		

Inflation and finance

Consumer price		*av. ann. increase 1989–95*	
inflation 1996	23.6%	Narrow money (M1)	19.9%
Av. ann. inflation 1989–96	24.4%	Broad money	21.9%

Exchange rates

	end 1996		*June 1996*
			1990 = 100
Ft per $	164.9	Effective rates	
Ft per SDR	237.2	– nominal	48.4
Ft per Ecu	206.1	– real	131.0

Principal exports

	$bn fob		$bn fob
Machinery & transport		Chemicals	1.5
equipment	3.3	Clothing & footwear	1.3
Food & food products	2.3	Total incl. others	**12.9**

Main export destinations

	% of total		% of total
Germany	28.7	Italy	8.5
Austria	10.2	Russia	6.4

Principal imports

	$bn cif		$bn cif
Machinery & transport		Fuels	1.5
equipment	4.8	Food & food products	0.7
Chemicals	2.2	Total incl. others	**15.5**

Main origins of imports

	% of total		% of total
Germany	23.5	Austria	10.8
Russia	11.9	Italy	7.9

Balance of payments, reserves and debt, $bn

Visible exports fob	12.9	Overall balance	5.4
Visible imports fob	-15.3	Change in reserves	5.2
Trade balance	-2.4	Level of reserves	
Invisibles inflows	5.1	end Dec.	12.1
Invisibles outflows	-6.2	No. months of import cover	6.7
Net transfers	1.1	Foreign debt	31.2
Current account balance	-2.5	– as % of GDP	72.8
– as % of GDP	-6.0	Debt service paid	7.0
Capital balance	6.6	Debt service ratio	39.1

Family life

No. of households	3.9m	Divorces per 1,000 pop.	2.1
Av. no. per household	2.6	Cost of living, Dec. 1996	
Marriages per 1,000 pop.	5.3	New York = 100	57

a 1994

INDIA

Area	3,287,263 sq km	Currency	Indian rupee (Rs)
Capital	New Delhi		

People

Population	929.0m	Life expectancy: men	62.1 yrs
Pop. per sq km	283	women	62.7 yrs
Av. ann. growth		Adult literacy	50.6%
in pop. 1985–95	1.9%	Fertility rate (per woman)	3.1
Pop. under 15	35.0%		
Pop. over 65	4.6%		*per 1,000 pop.*
No. of men per 100 women	106.8	Crude birth rate	25.2
Human Development Index	43.6	Crude death rate	9.0

The economy

GDP	Rs10,377bn	GDP per head	$344
GDP	$320bn	GDP per head in purchasing	
Av. ann. growth in real		power parity (USA=100)	5
GDP 1985–95	5.1%		

Origins of GDP[a]		**Components of GDP**[a]	
	% of total		*% of total*
Agriculture	29.4	Private consumption	68.7
Industry, of which:	29.4	Public consumption	10.4
manufacturing	...	Investment	22.9
Services	41.2	Exports	8.6
		Imports	-10.6

Structure of employment

	% of total		*% of labour force*
Agriculture	64	Unemployed 1995	...
Industry	16	Av. ann. rate 1990–94	...
Services	20		

Energy

	'000 TCE		
Total output	296,523	% output exported	nil
Total consumption	343,703	% consumption imported	19.8
Consumption per head,			
kg coal equivalent	374		

Inflation and finance

Consumer price		*av. ann. increase 1989–95*	
inflation 1996	9.0%	Narrow money (M1)	16.9%
Av. ann. inflation 1989–96	9.6%	Broad money	16.3%

Exchange rates

	end 1996		*June 1996*
Rs per $	35.93	Effective rates	*1990 = 100*
Rs per SDR	51.67	– nominal	...
Rs per Ecu	44.91	– real	...

Principal exports[a]

	$bn fob		$bn fob
Gems & jewellery	4.5	Marine products	1.1
Clothing	3.2		
Textiles	2.2	Total incl. others	**26.3**

Main export destinations[a]

	% of total		% of total
United States	19.1	United Kingdom	6.4
Japan	7.7	OPEC	9.2
Germany	6.6		

Principal imports

	$bn cif		$bn cif
Capital goods	7.6	Gems	1.6
Crude oil & products	5.9		
Chemicals	2.9	Total incl. others	**26.7**

Main origins of imports

	% of total		% of total
United States	10.1	United Kingdom	5.4
Germany	7.6	OPEC	21.1
Japan	7.1		

Balance of payments[c], reserves and debt, $bn

Visible exports fob	22.0	Overall balance	4.3
Visible imports fob	-22.5	Change in reserves	-1.4
Trade balance	-0.5	Level of reserves	
Invisibles inflows	5.5	end Dec.	22.9
Invisibles outflows	-10.6	No. months of import cover	5.2
Net transfers	3.8	Foreign debt	93.8
Current account balance	-1.9	– as % of GDP	28.2
– as % of GDP	-0.7	Debt service paid	13.1
Capital balance	7.1	Debt service ratio	28.2

Family life

No. of households	185m	Divorces per 1,000 pop.	...
Av. no. per household	5.0	Cost of living, Dec. 1996	
Marriages per 1,000 pop.	...	New York = 100	45

a   Year ending March 31, 1995.
b   1990
c   1993

INDONESIA

Area	1,919,445 sq km	Currency	Rupiah (Rp)
Capital	Jakarta		

People

Population	197.5m	Life expectancy: men	63.3 yrs
Pop. per sq km	104	women	67.0 yrs
Av. ann. growth		Adult literacy	82.9%
in pop. 1985–95	1.7%	Fertility rate (per woman)	2.6
Pop. under 15	32.9%		
Pop. over 65	4.3%		*per 1,000 pop.*
No. of men per 100 women	99.5	Crude birth rate	23.1
Human Development Index	64.1	Crude death rate	7.6

The economy

GDP	Rp427,234bn	GDP per head	$963
GDP	$190bn	GDP per head in purchasing	
Av. ann. growth in real		power parity (USA=100)	14
GDP 1985–95	6.4%		

Origins of GDP		Components of GDP	
	% of total		*% of total*
Agriculture	17.2	Private consumption	56.0
Industry, of which:	40.4	Public consumption	8.2
manufacturing	24.3	Investment	37.8
Services	42.4	Exports	25.5
		Imports	-27.5

Structure of employment[a]

	% of total		*% of total*
Agriculture	55	Unemployed 1995	…
Industry	14	Av. ann. rate 1990–94	…
Services	31		

Energy

	'000 TCE		
Total output	255,309	% output exported	59.0
Total consumption	90,447	% consumption imported	20.3
Consumption per head,			
kg coal equivalent	465		

Inflation and finance

Consumer price		*av. ann. increase 1989–92*	
inflation 1996	7.9%	Narrow money (M1)	19.0%
Av. ann. inflation 1989–96	8.8%	Broad money	29.7%

Exchange rates

	end 1996		*June 1996*
Rp per $	2,348	Effective rates	*1990 = 100*
Rp per SDR	3,376	– nominal	…
Rp per Ecu	2,935	– real	…

Principal exports

	$bn fob		$bn fob
Petroleum & products	6.4	Plywood	3.5
Textiles & clothing	6.2	Rubber & products	2.2
Natural gas	4.0	Total incl. others	**45.4**

Main export destinations

	% of total		% of total
Japan	27.1	Taiwan	3.9
United States	13.9	China	3.8
Singapore	8.3	Hong Kong	3.6
South Korea	6.4		

Principal imports

	$bn cif		$bn cif
Machinery & transport equipment	16.3	Raw materials	3.6
		Food, drink & tobacco	3.2
Other manufactures	6.7	Fuels	3.0
Chemicals	6.3	Total incl. others	**40.6**

Main origins of imports

	% of total		% of total
Japan	22.7	Singapore	5.8
United States	11.7	Australia	5.0
Germany	6.9	Taiwan	4.5
South Korea	6.0		

Balance of payments, reserves and debt, $bn

Visible exports fob	45.5	Overall balance	1.6
Visible imports fob	-39.8	Change in reserves	1.6
Trade balance	5.7	Level of reserves	
Invisibles inflows	7.0	end Dec.	14.9
Invisibles outflows	-20.6	No. months of import cover	3.0
Net transfers	0.8	Foreign debt	107.8
Current account balance	-7.0	– as % of GDP	56.9
– as % of GDP	-3.7	Debt service paid	16.4
Capital balance	10.4	Debt service ratio	30.9

Family life

No. of households	43.1m	Divorces per 1,000 pop.	0.8
Av. no. per household	4.5	Cost of living, Dec. 1996	
Marriages per 1,000 pop.	7.4	New York = 100	87

a 1992

IRAN

Area	1,648,000 sq km	Currency	Rial (IR)
Capital	Tehran		

People

Population	68.3m	Life expectancy: men	68.5 yrs
Pop. per sq km	41	women	70.0 yrs
Av. ann. growth		Adult literacy	56.0%
in pop. 1985–95	3.4%	Fertility rate (per woman)	4.8
Pop. under 15	44.4%		
Pop. over 65	3.8%		*per 1,000 pop.*
No. of men per 100 women	103.4	Crude birth rate	34.0
Human Development Index	75.4	Crude death rate	6.0

The economy

GDP	IR106,624bn	GDP per head	$898
GDP	$61bn	GDP per head in purchasing	
Av. ann. growth in real		power parity (USA=100)	20
GDP 1985–95	1.3%		

Origins of GDP[a]		Components of GDP[a]	
	% of total		*% of total*
Agriculture	21.3	Private consumption	53.6
Industry, of which:	36.9	Public consumption	15.2
manufacturing	...	Investment	23.2
Services	41.8	Exports	30.1
		Imports	-22.1

Structure of employment[b]

	% of total		*% of labour force*
Agriculture	39	Unemployed 1995	...
Industry	23	Av. ann. rate 1990–94	...
Services	38		

Energy

	'000 TCE		
Total output	317,541	% output exported	61.2
Total consumption	123,550	% consumption imported	6.3
Consumption per head,			
kg coal equivalent	1,879		

Inflation and finance

		av. ann. increase 1989–95	
Consumer price			
inflation 1995	28.9%	Narrow money (M1)	25.2%
Av. ann. inflation 1989–95	24.9%	Broad money	26.2%

Exchange rates

	end 1996		*June 1996*
IR per $	1,749	Effective rates	*1990 = 100*
IR per SDR	2,515	– nominal	...
IR per Ecu	2,186	– real	...

Principal exports[c]

	$bn fob		$bn fob
Oil & gas	14.3	Fruit	0.7
Carpets	1.4	Total incl. others	**18.1**

Main export destinations

	% of total		% of total
Japan	13.8	Germany	4.0
Italy	8.6	Netherlands	3.4
France	6.8	Greece	2.9
South Korea	6.1		

Principal imports[c]

	$bn cif		$bn cif
Raw materials &		Consumer goods	2.2
intermediate goods	12.6		
Capital goods	5.1	Total incl. others	**20.0**

Main origins of imports

	% of total		% of total
Germany	14.7	United Kingdom	4.7
UAE	7.9	Italy	4.6
Japan	5.9	Argentina	4.5
France	5.0		

Balance of payments[d], reserves and debt, $bn

Visible exports fob	18.4	Overall balance	2.9
Visible imports fob	-12.7	Change in reserves	…
Trade balance	5.7	Level of reserves	
Invisibles inflows	0.9	end Dec.	…
Invisibles outflows	-3.1	No. months of import cover	…
Net transfers	…	Foreign debt	21.9
Current account balance	3.5	– as % of GDP[e]	14.7
– as % of GDP	5.7	Debt service paid[f]	4.3
Capital balance	-0.8	Debt service ratio[f]	21.6

Family life

No. of households	10.8m	Divorces per 1,000 pop.	0.7
Av. no. per household	5.2	Cost of living, Dec. 1996	
Marriages per 1,000 pop.	7.4	New York = 100	47

a Iranian year ending March 20, 1995.
b 1990
c Iranian year ending March 20, 1994.
d Iranian year ending March 20, 1996.
e 1992
f 1994

IRAQ

Area	438,317 sq km	Currency	Iraqi dinar (ID)
Capital	Baghdad		

People

Population	20.1m	Life expectancy: men	60.9 yrs
Pop. per sq km	46	women	63.9 yrs
Av. ann. growth		Adult literacy	55.7%
in pop. 1985–95	2.8%	Fertility rate (per woman)	5.3
Pop. under 15	42.8%		
Pop. over 65	3.0%		*per 1,000 pop.*
No. of men per 100 women	103.6	Crude birth rate	36.4
Human Development Index	59.9	Crude death rate	8.5

The economy

GDP	ID5.3bn	GDP per head	$836
GDP	$17bn	GDP per head in purchasing	
Av. ann. growth in real		power parity (USA=100)	...
GDP 1985–95	-9.3%		

Origins of GDP[a]		Components of GDP[a]	
	% of total		*% of total*
Agriculture	5.1	Private consumption	56.1
Industry, of which:	72.9	Public consumption	32.9
manufacturing	11.6	Investment	8.1
Services	22.0	Exports	26.7
		Imports	-23.8

Structure of employment

	% of total		*% of labour force*
Agriculture	...	Unemployed 1995	...
Industry	...	Av. ann. rate 1990–94	...
Services	...		

Energy

	'000 TCE		
Total output	57,432	% output exported	9.7
Total consumption	35,079	% consumption imported	nil
Consumption per head,			
kg coal equivalent	1,761		

Inflation and finance

Consumer price		*av. ann. increase 1989–95*	
inflation 1995	50%	Narrow money (M1)	...
Av. ann. inflation 1989–95	49.0%	Broad money	...

Exchange rates

	end 1996		*June 1996*
ID per $	0.31	Effective rates	*1990 = 100*
ID per SDR	0.45	– nominal	177.3
ID per Ecu	0.39	– real	...

Principal exports[a][b][c]

	$bn fob		$bn fob
Crude oil	14.5	Total incl. others	**14.6**

Main export destinations[b][d]

	% of total		% of total
United States	28.5	Netherlands	7.4
Brazil	9.9	Spain	4.6
Turkey	9.8	France	3.5
Japan	7.8		

Principal imports[b]

	$bn cif		$bn cif
Civilian goods	5.0		
Military goods	2.7	Total incl. others	**7.7**

Main origins of imports[b][d]

	% of total		% of total
Germany	13.3	United Kingdom	8.4
United States	10.7	Japan	4.5
Turkey	9.2	Italy	4.5
France	8.7	Brazil	3.1

Balance of payments[c], reserves and debt, $bn

Visible exports fob	0.8	Overall balance	...
Visible imports fob	-1.2	Change in reserves	...
Trade balance	-0.3	Level of reserves	
Invisibles inflows	...	end Dec.	...
Invisibles outflows	...	No. months of import cover	...
Net transfers	...	Foreign debt	107.2
Current account balance	-0.4	– as % of GDP	638.1
– as % of GDP	...	Debt service	...
Capital balance	...	Debt service ratio	...

Family life

No. of households	2.1m	Divorces per 1,000 pop.	...
Av. no. per household	7.1	Cost of living, Dec. 1996	
Marriages per 1,000 pop.	...	New York = 100	...

a 1989
b Estimate.
c Trade, balance of payments and debt data for Iraq are estimates based on limited
   and inconsistent information.
d 1990

IRELAND

Area	70,282 sq km	Currency	Punt (I£)
Capital	Dublin		

People

Population	3.5m	Life expectancy: men	74.0 yrs
Pop. per sq km	50	women	79.4 yrs
Av. ann. growth		Adult literacy	99.0%
in pop. 1985–95	nil	Fertility rate (per woman)	1.8
Pop. under 15	24.1%		
Pop. over 65	11.3%		*per 1,000 pop.*
No. of men per 100 women	99.7	Crude birth rate	13.0
Human Development Index	91.9	Crude death rate	8.6

The economy

GDP	I£33bn	GDP per head	$14,880
GDP	$53bn	GDP per head in purchasing	
Av. ann. growth in real		power parity (USA=100)	58
GDP 1985–95	4.2%		

Origins of GDP		Components of GDP	
	% of total		*% of total*
Agriculture	8	Private consumption	57
Industry, of which:	38	Public consumption	16
manufacturing	...	Investment	15
Services	54	Exports	78
		Imports	-66

Structure of employment

	% of total		*% of labour force*
Agriculture	12	Unemployed 1995	12.9
Industry	27	Av. ann. rate 1990–94	14.7
Services	61		

Energy

	'000 TCE		
Total output	5,335	% output exported	26.8
Total consumption	15,239	% consumption imported	75.6
Consumption per head,			
kg coal equivalent	4,306		

Inflation and finance

Consumer price		*av. ann. increase 1989–95*	
inflation 1996	1.7%	Narrow money (M1)	9.6%
Av. ann. inflation 1989–96	2.7%	Broad money	12.2%

Exchange rates

	end 1996		*June 1996*
I£ per $	0.59	Effective rates	*1990 = 100*
I£ per SDR	0.86	– nominal	99.3
I£ per Ecu	0.74	– real	...

Principal exports

	$bn fob		$bn fob
Machinery & transport equipment	15.1	Agric. products & foodstuffs	7.7
Chemicals	8.1	Total incl. others	**44.2**

Main export destinations

	% of total		% of total
United Kingdom	25.4	Netherlands	6.9
Germany	14.5	Belgium/Luxembourg	4.4
France	9.5	Italy	3.8
United States	8.3		

Principal imports

	$bn cif		$bn cif
Machinery & transport equipment	13.6	Manufactured goods	3.6
Chemicals	4.1	Total incl. others	**32.6**

Main origins of imports

	% of total		% of total
United Kingdom	35.6	France	3.7
United States	17.7	Netherlands	2.7
Germany	6.9	Italy	1.9
Japan	5.3		

Balance of payments, reserves and aid, $bn

Visible exports fob	43.3	Capital balance	0.1
Visible imports fob	-30.2	Overall balance	2.3
Trade balance	13.1	Change in reserves	2.5
Invisibles inflows	9.8	Level of reserves	
Invisibles outflows	-23.3	end Dec.	8.8
Net transfers	1.8	No. months of import cover	2.0
Current account balance	1.4	Aid given	0.15
– as % of GDP	2.6	– as % of GDP	0.29

Family life

No. of households	0.9m	Divorces per 1,000 pop.	...
Av. no. per household	4.1	Cost of living, Dec. 1996	
Marriages per 1,000 pop.	4.6	New York = 100	100

ISRAEL

Area	20,770 sq km	Currency	New Shekel (NIS)
Capital	Jerusalem		

People

Population	5.5m	Life expectancy: men	75.7 yrs
Pop. per sq km	262	women	79.5 yrs
Av. ann. growth		Adult literacy	95.0%
in pop. 1985–95	2.7%	Fertility rate (per woman)	2.8
Pop. under 15	29.3%		
Pop. over 65	9.5%		*per 1,000 pop.*
No. of men per 100 women	98.6	Crude birth rate	20.3
Human Development Index	90.8	Crude death rate	6.4

The economy

GDP	NIS265bn	GDP per head	$15,905
GDP	$88bn	GDP per head in purchasing	
Av. ann. growth in real		power parity (USA=100)	61
GDP 1985–95	4.7%		

Origins of NDP[a]		Components of GDP	
	% of total		*% of total*
Agriculture	2.4	Private consumption	61.7
Industry, of which:	30.4	Public consumption	29.2
manufacturing	21.5	Investment	26.2
Services	67.2	Exports	32.3
		Imports	-49.4

Structure of employment[b]

	% of total		*% of labour force*
Agriculture	3	Unemployed 1995	6.9
Industry	29	Av. ann. rate 1990–94	9.8
Services	68		

Energy

	'000 TCE		
Total output	39	% output exported[c]	10,700.0
Total consumption	17,799	% consumption imported[c]	132.8
Consumption per head,			
kg coal equivalent	3,261		

Inflation and finance

Consumer price		*av. ann. increase 1989–95*	
inflation 1996	2.5%	Narrow money (M1)	24.1%
Av. ann. inflation 1989–96	12.9%	Broad money	21.7%

Exchange rates

	end 1996		*June 1996*
NIS per $	3.26	Effective rates	*1990 = 100*
NIS per SDR	4.69	– nominal	...
NIS per Ecu	4.08	– real	...

Principal exports

	$bn fob		$bn fob
Industrial	12.3	Agric. products & foodstuffs	0.7
Diamonds	4.6	Total incl. others	**19.0**

Main export destinations

	% of total		% of total
United States	30.1	Germany	5.5
Japan	6.9	Belgium/Luxembourg	5.4
United Kingdom	6.1		

Principal imports

	$bn cif		$bn cif
Investment goods	4.7	Fuel	2.0
Diamonds	4.4		
Consumer goods	3.7	Total incl. others	**29.6**

Main origins of imports

	% of total		% of total
United States	18.6	United Kingdom	8.3
Belgium/Luxembourg	12.1	Italy	7.8
Germany	9.7		

Balance of payments, reserves and debt, $bn

Visible exports fob	19.0	Overall balance	1.3
Visible imports fob	-26.7	Change in reserves	1.3
Trade balance	-7.7	Level of reserves	
Invisibles inflows	9.7	end Dec.	8.1
Invisibles outflows	-13.0	No. months of import cover	2.4
Net transfers	5.6	Foreign debt	28.9
Current account balance	-5.5	– as % of GDP	33.4
– as % of GDP	-6.0	Debt service	5.2
Capital balance	4.5	Debt service ratio	8.1

Family life

No. of households	1.4m	Divorces per 1,000 pop.	1.3
Av. no. per household	3.9	Cost of living, Dec. 1996	
Marriages per 1,000 pop.	6.2	New York = 100	107

a   1993
b   1994
c   Energy trade data are distorted by transitory and oil refining activities.

ITALY

Area	301,245 sq km	Currency	Lira (L)
Capital	Rome		

People

Population	57.2m	Life expectancy: men	75.1 yrs
Pop. per sq km	190	women	81.4 yrs
Av. ann. growth		Adult literacy	97.4%
in pop. 1985–95	0.1%	Fertility rate (per woman)	1.2
Pop. under 15	14.9%		
Pop. over 65	16.1%		*per 1,000 pop.*
No. of men per 100 women	94.6	Crude birth rate	9.1
Human Development Index	91.4	Crude death rate	9.9

The economy

GDP	L1,772,243bn	GDP per head	$19,021
GDP	$1,088bn	GDP per head in purchasing	
Av. ann. growth in real		power parity (USA=100)	74
GDP 1985–95	2.0%		

Origins of GDP		Components of GDP	
	% of total		*% of total*
Agriculture	3.2	Private consumption	62.5
Industry, of which:	27.9	Public consumption	16.5
manufacturing	...	Investment	18.1
Services	68.9	Exports	25.0
		Imports	-22.2

Structure of employment

	% of total		*% of labour force*
Agriculture	8	Unemployed 1995	12.2
Industry	32	Av. ann. rate 1990–94	10.4
Services	60		

Energy

	'000 TCE		
Total output	43,399	% output exported	66.8
Total consumption	225,798	% consumption imported	93.6
Consumption per head,			
kg coal equivalent	3,949		

Inflation and finance

Consumer price		*av. ann. increase 1989–95*	
inflation 1996	4.0%	Narrow money (M1)	6.1%
Av. ann. inflation 1989–96	5.2%	Broad money	8.7%

Exchange rates

	end 1996		*June 1996*
L per $	1,531	Effective rates	*1990 = 100*
L per SDR	2,201	– nominal	76.6
L per Ecu	1,914	– real	80.1

Principal exports

	$bn fob		$bn fob
Industrial & agricultural		Electrical equipment	21.2
machinery	39.4	Chemicals	19.1
Textiles & clothing	26.1	Motor vehicles	17.6
Metal & metal products	24.1	Total incl. others	**229.1**

Main export destinations

	% of total		% of total
Germany	18.7	United Kingdom	6.2
France	13.0	Spain	4.8
United States	7.3	Switzerland	3.8

Principal imports

	$bn cif		$bn cif
Chemicals	29.0	Industrial & agricultural	
Metals & metal products	25.2	machinery	14.7
Electrical equipment	20.3		
Motor vehicles	18.5	Total incl. others	**201.8**

Main origins of imports

	% of total		% of total
Germany	19.1	Netherlands	5.5
France	13.9	United States	4.8
United Kingdom	6.1		

Balance of payments, reserves and aid, $bn

Visible exports fob	231.3	Capital balance	-1.6
Visible imports fob	-187.3	Overall balance	2.8
Trade balance	44.1	Change in reserves	2.9
Invisibles inflows	99.0	Level of reserves	
Invisibles outflows	-112.7	end Dec.	60.7
Net transfers	-4.6	No. months of import cover	2.4
Current account balance	25.7	Aid given	1.62
– as % of GDP	2.4	– as % of GDP	0.15

Family life

No. of households	22.3m	Divorces per 1,000 pop.	0.5
Av. no. per household	2.6	Cost of living, Dec. 1996	
Marriages per 1,000 pop.	4.9	New York = 100	96

JAPAN

Area	377,727 sq km	Currency	Yen (¥)
Capital	Tokyo		

People

Population	125.1m	Life expectancy: men	76.9 yrs
Pop. per sq km	331	women	82.9 yrs
Av. ann. growth		Adult literacy	99.0%
in pop. 1985–95	0.3%	Fertility rate (per woman)	1.5
Pop. under 15	16.2%		
Pop. over 65	14.2%		*per 1,000 pop.*
No. of men per 100 women	96.5	Crude birth rate	10.3
Human Development Index	93.8	Crude death rate	8.2

The economy

GDP	¥466,914bn	GDP per head	$39,687
GDP	$4,964bn	GDP per head in purchasing	
Av. ann. growth in real		power parity (USA=100)	82
GDP 1985–95	3.1%		

Origins of NDP[a]		Components of GDP	
	% of total		*% of total*
Agriculture	2.1	Private consumption	60.2
Industry, of which:	38.3	Public consumption	9.8
manufacturing	24.5	Investment	28.6
Services	59.6	Exports	9.4
		Imports	-7.9

Structure of employment

	% of total		*% of labour force*
Agriculture	6	Unemployed 1995	3.2
Industry	34	Av. ann. rate 1990–94	2.4
Services	60		

Energy

	'000 TCE		
Total output	121,775	% output exported[b]	9.8
Total consumption	621,323	% consumption imported[b]	89.9
Consumption per head,			
kg coal equivalent	4,978		

Inflation and finance

Consumer price		*av. ann. increase 1989–95*	
inflation 1996	0.1%	Narrow money (M1)	6.3%
Av. ann. inflation 1989–96	1.5%	Broad money	4.3%

Exchange rates

	end 1996		*June 1996*
¥ per $	116.0	Effective rates	*1990 = 100*
¥ per SDR	166.8	– nominal	134.6
¥ per Ecu	145.0	– real	135.5

Principal exports

	$bn fob		$bn fob
Motor vehicles	52.9	Iron & steel products	17.7
Office machinery	30.7		
Chemicals	30.1		
Scientific & optical equipment	18.5	Total incl. others	**443.0**

Main export destinations

	% of total		% of total
United States	27.3	Hong Kong	6.3
South Korea	7.0	Singapore	5.2
Taiwan	6.5	China	5.0

Principal imports

	$bn cif		$bn cif
Mineral fuels	53.4	Chemicals	24.6
Agric. products & foodstuffs	50.9	Wood	10.0
Textiles	24.6	Total incl. others	**336.1**

Main origins of imports

	% of total		% of total
United States	22.4	Australia	4.3
China	10.7	Taiwan	4.3
South Korea	5.1	Indonesia	4.3

Balance of payments, reserves and aid, $bn

Visible exports fob	429.3	Capital balance	-66.7
Visible imports fob	-297.2	Overall balance	58.6
Trade balance	132.1	Change in reserves	57.5
Invisibles inflows	257.8	Level of reserves	
Invisibles outflows	-270.9	end Dec.	192.6
Net transfers	-7.8	No. months of import cover	4.1
Current account balance	111.3	Aid given	14.49
– as % of GDP	2.2	– as % of GDP	0.28

Family life

No. of households	40.5m	Divorces per 1,000 pop.	1.4
Av. no. per household	3.1	Cost of living, Dec. 1996	
Marriages per 1,000 pop.	6.3	New York = 100	171

a 1994
b Energy trade data are distorted by transitory and oil refining activities.

KENYA

Area	582,646 sq km	Currency	Kenyan shilling (KSh)
Capital	Nairobi		

People

Population	27.2m	Life expectancy: men	52.3 yrs
Pop. per sq km	47	women	55.7 yrs
Av. ann. growth		Adult literacy	75.7%
in pop. 1985–95	3.2%	Fertility rate (per woman)	4.9%
Pop. under 15	46.0%		
Pop. over 65	2.9%		*per 1,000 pop.*
No. of men per 100 women	100.3	Crude birth rate	36.9
Human Development Index	47.3	Crude death rate	11.3

The economy

GDP	KSh391bn	GDP per head	$279
GDP	$7.6bn	GDP per head in purchasing	5
Av. ann. growth in real		power parity (USA=100)	
GDP 1985–95	3.6%		

Origins of GDP		Components of GDP	
	% of total		*% of total*
Agriculture	29.7	Private consumption	69.4
Industry, of which:	...	Public consumption	15.0
manufacturing	11.1	Investment	22.0
Other	59.2	Exports	33.1
		Imports	-39.5

Structure of employment

	% of total		*% of labour force*
Agriculture	80	Unemployed 1995	...
Industry	7	Av. ann. rate 1990–94	...
Services	13		

Energy

	'000 TCE		
Total output	697	% output exported[a]	92.8
Total consumption	3,293	% consumption imported[a]	112.6
Consumption per head,			
kg coal equivalent	120		

Inflation and finance

Consumer price		*av. ann. increase 1989–95*	
inflation 1996	8.8%	Narrow money (M1)	20.2%
Av. ann. inflation 1989–96	19.6%	Broad money	23.6%

Exchange rates

	end 1996		*June 1996*
KSh per $	55.02	Effective rates	*1990 = 100*
KSh per SDR	79.12	– nominal	...
KSh per Ecu	68.78	– real	...

Principal exports

	$m fob		$m fob
Tea	350	Petroleum products	85
Coffee	281		
Horticultural products	207	Total incl. others	**1,878**

Main export destinations

	% of total		% of total
Uganda	15.8	United Kingdom	10.0
Tanzania	13.0	Germany	7.6

Principal imports

	$m cif		$m cif
Industrial machinery	507	Iron & steel	200
Motor vehicles & chassis	363		
Petroleum & products	225	Total incl. others	**2,949**

Main origins of imports

	% of total		% of total
United Kingdom	12.6	Germany	6.8
Japan	11.0	UAE	6.7

Balance of payments, reserves and debt, $bn

Visible exports fob	1.9	Overall balance	-0.1
Visible imports fob	-2.7	Change in reserves	-0.2
Trade balance	-0.7	Level of reserves	
Invisibles inflows	1.1	end Dec.	0.4
Invisibles outflows	-1.2	No. months of import cover	1.2
Net transfers	0.5	Foreign debt	7.4
Current account balance	-0.4	– as % of GDP	97.7
– as % of GDP	-5.3	Debt service paid	0.8
Capital balance	0.2	Debt service ratio	25.7

Family life

No. of households	3.0m	Divorces per 1,000 pop.	…
Av. no. per household	5.1	Cost of living, Dec. 1996	
Marriages per 1,000 pop.	…	New York = 100	58

a Energy trade data are distorted by transitory and oil refining activities.
b 1993

MALAYSIA

Area	332,665 sq km	Currency	Malaysian dollar/ringgit
Capital	Kuala Lumpur		(M$)

People

Population	20.1m	Life expectancy: men		69.9yrs
Pop. per sq km	61	women		74.3yrs
Av. ann. growth		Adult literacy		80.0%
in pop. 1985–95	2.5%	Fertility rate (per woman)		3.2
Pop. under 15	38.0%			
Pop. over 65	3.9%		*per 1,000 pop.*	
No. of men per 100 women	101.8	Crude birth rate		25.2
Human Development Index	82.6	Crude death rate		4.8

The economy

GDP	M$195bn	GDP per head	$3,889
GDP	$78bn	GDP per head in purchasing	
Av. ann. growth in real		power parity (USA=100)	33
GDP 1985–95	7.6%		

Origins of GDP

	% of total
Agriculture	13.6
Industry, of which:	44.9
manufacturing	33.1
Services	41.5

Components of GDP

	% of total
Private consumption	49.8
Public consumption	12.7
Investment	40.7
Exports	94.3
Imports	-97.6

Structure of employment

	% of total		*% of labour force*
Agriculture	20	Unemployed 1995	2.8
Industry	32	Av. ann. rate 1990–94	3.8
Services	48		

Energy

	'000 TCE		
Total output	78,780	% output exported	59.8
Total consumption	45,113	% consumption imported	38.8
Consumption per head,			
kg coal equivalent	2,291		

Inflation and finance

		av. ann. increase 1989–95	
Consumer price			
inflation 1996	3.5%	Narrow money (M1)	19.1%
Av. ann. inflation 1989–96	3.8%	Broad money	18.6%

Exchange rates

	end 1996		*June 1996*
M$ per $	2.53	Effective rates	*1990 = 100*
M$ per SDR	3.64	– nominal	114.9
M$ per Ecu	3.16	– real	108.3

Principal exports

	$bn fob		$bn fob
Electronics & electrical machinery	38.8	Textiles, clothing & footwear	2.6
		Chemicals & products	2.5
Palm oil	4.1	Timber	2.4
Petroleum & LNG	3.9	Total incl. others	**74.1**

Main export destinations

	% of total		% of total
United States	20.7	Hong Kong	5.4
Singapore	20.3	United Kingdom	4.0
Japan	12.7	Thailand	3.9

Principal imports

	$bn cif		$bn cif
Manufacturing supplies	30.2	Consumer durables	2.3
Machinery & transport equipment	13.2	Food, beverages & tobacco	2.2
Metal products	4.7	Total incl. others	**77.8**

Main origins of imports

	% of total		% of total
Japan	27.3	Taiwan	5.1
United States	16.3	Germany	4.4
Singapore	12.4	South Korea	4.1

Balance of payments[a], reserves and debt, $bn

Visible exports fob	56.9	Overall balance	-3.2
Visible imports fob	-55.3	Change in reserves	-1.6
Trade balance	1.6	Level of reserves	
Invisibles inflows	8.9	end Dec.	24.7
Invisibles outflows	-14.8	No. months of import cover	3.2
Net transfers	0.2	Foreign debt	34.4
Current account balance	-4.1	as % of GDP	42.6
– as % of GDP	-6.0	Debt service paid	6.5
Capital balance	1.5	Debt service ratio	7.8

Family life

No. households	4.0m	Divorces per 1,000 pop.	...
Av. no. per household	4.9	Cost of living, Dec. 1996	
Marriages per 1,000 pop.	3.2	New York = 100	79

a   1994

MEXICO

Area	1,972,545 sq km	Currency	Mexican peso (PS)
Capital	Mexico City		

People

Population	91.1m	Life expectancy: men		69.5 yrs
Pop. per sq km	47	women		75.5 yrs
Av. ann. growth		Adult literacy		88.6%
in pop. 1985–95	1.9%	Fertility rate (per woman)		2.8
Pop. under 15	35.5%			
Pop. over 65	4.3%		*per 1,000 pop.*	
No. of men per 100 women	98.3	Crude birth rate		24.6
Human Development Index	84.5	Crude death rate		5.1

The economy

GDP	1,958bn New pesos	GDP per head	$3,342
GDP	$305bn	GDP per head in purchasing	24
Av. ann. growth in real		power parity (USA=100)	
GDP 1985–95	2.0%		

Origins of GDP		Components of GDP	
	% of total		*% of total*
Agriculture	7.6	Private consumption	67.3
Industry, of which:	32.6	Public consumption	10.4
manufacturing	22.6	Investment	19.4
Services	59.8	Exports	24.0
		Imports	-21.1

Structure of employment

	% of total		*% of labour force*
Agriculture	25	Unemployed 1995	4.7
Industry	21	Av. ann. rate 1990–94	2.3
Services	54		

Energy

	'000 TCE		
Total output	283,065	% output exported	37.0
Total consumption	186,573	% consumption imported	7.7
Consumption per head,			
kg coal equivalent	2,031		

Inflation and finance

Consumer price		*av. ann. increase 1989–95*	
inflation 1996	34.4%	Narrow money (M1)	32.3%
Av. ann. inflation 1989–96	21.0%	Broad money	44.1%

Exchange rates

	end 1996		*June 1996*
PS per $	7.87	Effective rates	*1990 = 100*
PS per SDR	11.31	– nominal	...
PS per Ecu	9.84	– real	...

Principal exports

	$bn fob		$bn fob
Manufactured products	66.6	Agricultural products	4.0
Crude oil & products	8.4	Total incl. others	**79.5**

Main export destinations

	% of total		% of total
United States	83.4	Spain	1.0
Canada	2.5	Switzerland	0.8
Japan	1.2		

Principal imports

	$bn cif		$bn cif
Intermediate goods	58.4	Consumer goods	5.3
Capital goods	8.7	Total	**72.5**

Main origins of imports

	% of total		% of total
United States	74.3	Canada	1.9
Japan	5.0	France	1.4
Germany	3.7		

Balance of payments, reserves and debt, $bn

Visible exports fob	79.5	Overall balance	-15.3
Visible imports fob	-72.5	Change in reserves	10.6
Trade balance	7.1	Level of reserves	
Invisibles inflows	14.0	end Dec.	17.0
Invisibles outflows	-25.7	No. months of import cover	2.1
Net transfers	4.0	Foreign debt	165.7
Current account balance	-0.7	– as % of GDP	69.9
– as % of GDP	-0.2	Debt service paid	23.6
Capital balance	-11.8	Debt service ratio	24.2

Family life

No. of households	19.0m	Divorces per 1,000 pop.	0.6
Av. no. per household	5.0	Cost of living, Dec. 1996	
Marriages per 1,000 pop.	7.3	New York = 100	64

MOROCCO

Area	446,550 sq km	Currency	Dirham (Dh)
Capital	Rabat		

People

Population	26.5m	Life expectancy: men	64.8 yrs
Pop. per sq km	59	women	68.5 yrs
Av. ann. growth		Adult literacy	41.7%
in pop. 1985–95	2.1%	Fertility rate (per woman)	3.1
Pop. under 15	36.3%		
Pop. over 65	4.2%		*per 1,000 pop.*
No. of men per 100 women	100.2	Crude birth rate	25.3
Human Development Index	53.4	Crude death rate	6.7

The economy

GDP	Dh256bn	GDP per head	$1,114
GDP	$30bn	GDP per head in purchasing	
Av. ann. growth in real		power parity (USA=100)	12
GDP 1985–95	3.8%		

Origins of GDP		**Components of GDP**	
	% of total		*% of total*
Agriculture	11.3	Private consumption	67.6
Industry, of which:	30.4	Public consumption	18.4
manufacturing	18.8	Investment	21.0
Services	58.3	Exports	22.6
		Imports	-29.6

Structure of employment[a]

	% of total		*% of labour force*
Agriculture	4	Unemployed 1992	16.0
Industry	33	Av. ann. rate 1990–92	16.1
Services	63		

Energy

	'000 TCE		
Total output	798	% output exported	nil
Total consumption	12,345	% consumption imported	105.6
Consumption per head,			
kg coal equivalent	466		

Inflation and finance

Consumer price		*av. ann. increase 1989–95*	
inflation 1995	6.1%	Narrow money (M1)	10.0%
Av. ann. inflation 1989–95	5.7%	Broad money	11.4%

Exchange rates

	end 1996		*June 1996*
Dh per $	8.80	Effective rates	*1990 = 100*
Dh per SDR	12.65	– nominal	119.2
Dh per Ecu	11.00	– real	114.0

Principal exports

	$bn fob		$bn fob
Agricultural products &		Mineral ores	0.5
foodstuffs	1.5	Capital goods	0.2
Semi-finished goods	1.2		
Consumer goods	1.1	Total incl. others	**4.8**

Main export destinations

	% of total		% of total
France	29.7	India	6.6
Spain	9.4	Italy	5.5
Japan	7.7		

Principal imports

	$bn cif		$bn cif
Semi-manufactured goods	2.1	Energy & fuels	1.2
Industrial equipment	1.9	Raw materials	1.1
Agric. products & foodstuffs	1.4	Total incl. others	**8.6**

Main origins of imports

	% of total		% of total
France	21.8	Germany	6.3
Spain	8.5	Italy	5.7
United States	6.5		

Balance of payments, reserves and debt, $bn

Visible exports fob	6.9	Overall balance	-0.8
Visible imports fob	-9.3	Change in reserves	-0.7
Trade balance	-2.4	Level of reserves	
Invisibles inflows	2.3	end Dec.	3.9
Invisibles outflows	-3.6	No. months of import cover	3.6
Net transfers	2.3	Foreign debt	22.1
Current account balance	-1.5	– as % of GDP	71.0
– as % of GDP	-5.1	Debt service paid	3.5
Capital balance	0.1	Debt service ratio	32.1

Family life

No. of households	3.4m	Divorces per 1,000 pop.	...
Av. no. per household	5.9	Cost of living, Dec. 1996	
Marriages per 1,000 pop.	...	New York = 100	...

a 1992

NETHERLANDS

Area[a]	41,526 sq km	Currency	Guilder (Fl)
Capital	Amsterdam		

People

Population	15.5m	Life expectancy: men	75.0 yrs
Pop. per sq km	379	women	80.6 yrs
Av. ann. growth		Adult literacy	99.0%
in pop. 1985–95	0.7%	Fertility rate (per woman)	1.6
Pop. under 15	18.3%		
Pop. over 65	13.2%		*per 1,000 pop.*
No. of men per 100 women	98.0	Crude birth rate	11.9
Human Development Index	93.8	Crude death rate	8.8

The economy

GDP	Fl596bn	GDP per head	$23,966
GDP	$371bn	GDP per head in purchasing	
Av. ann. growth in real		power parity (USA=100)	74
GDP 1985–95	2.6%		

Origins of GDP		Components of GDP	
	% of total		*% of total*
Agriculture	3.4	Private consumption	59.9
Industry, of which:	29.7	Public consumption	14.3
manufacturing	...	Investment	19.4
Services	66.9	Exports	53.3
		Imports	-46.9

Structure of employment

	% of total		*% of labour force*
Agriculture	4	Unemployed 1995	6.5
Industry	23	Av. ann. rate 1990–94	6.0
Services	73		

Energy

	'000 TCE		
Total output	102,621	% output exported[c]	108.7
Total consumption	111,117	% consumption imported[c]	119.9
Consumption per head,			
kg coal equivalent	7,217		

Inflation and finance

Consumer price		*av. ann. increase 1989–95*	
inflation 1996	2.1%	Narrow money (M1)	6.5%
Av. ann. inflation 1989–96	2.6%	Broad money	5.5%

Exchange rates

	end 1996		*June 1996*
Fl per $	1.74	Effective rates	*1990 = 100*
Fl per SDR	2.51	– nominal	106.7
Fl per Ecu	2.18	– real	96.6

Principal exports

	$bn fob		$bn fob
Machinery & transport equipment	42.9	Fuels	11.5
		Raw materials, oils & fats	7.5
Food, drink & tobacco	30.5		
Chemicals & plastics	29.4	Total incl. others	**177.4**

Main export destinations

	% of total		% of total
Germany	28.6	United Kingdom	9.7
Belgium/Luxembourg	12.9	Italy	5.6
France	11.1		

Principal imports

	$bn cif		$bn cif
Machinery & transport equipment	46.5	Fuels	10.9
		Textiles & clothing	9.6
Chemicals & plastics	18.8		
Food, drink & tobacco	16.9	Total incl. others	**157.7**

Main origins of imports

	% of total		% of total
Germany	23.4	United States	8.0
Belgium/Luxembourg	11.8	France	7.4
United Kingdom	10.1		

Balance of payments, reserves and aid, $bn

Visible exports fob	173.3	Capital balance	-8.7
Visible imports fob	-154.0	Overall balance	-1.9
Trade balance	19.3	Change in reserves	-0.7
Invisibles inflows	77.7	Level of reserves	
Invisibles outflows	-74.4	end Dec.	47.2
Net transfers	-6.3	No. months of import cover	2.5
Current account balance	16.2	Aid given	3.23
– as % of GDP	4.8	– as % of GDP	0.81

Family life

No. of households	6.4m	Divorces per 1,000 pop.	2.0
Av. no. per household	2.4	Cost of living, Dec. 1996	
Marriages per 1,000 pop.	5.2	New York = 100	111

a   Includes water.
b   1992
c   Energy trade data are distorted due to transitory and oil refining activities.

NEW ZEALAND

Area	270,534 sq km	Currency New Zealand dollar (NZ$)
Capital	Wellington	

People

Population	3.6m	Life expectancy: men	74.7 yrs
Pop. per sq km	13	women	79.7 yrs
Av. ann. growth		Adult literacy	99.0%
in pop. 1985–95	0.9%	Fertility rate (per woman)	2.0
Pop. under 15	23.2%		
Pop. over 65	11.4%		*per 1,000 pop.*
No. of men per 100 women	97.7	Crude birth rate	15.4
Human Development Index	92.7	Crude death rate	7.9

The economy

GDP	NZ$79bn	GDP per head	$14,506
GDP	$52bn	GDP per head in purchasing	
Av. ann. growth in real		power parity (USA=100)	61
GDP 1985–95	1.2%		

Origins of GDP[a]		Components of GDP[a]	
	% of total		*% of total*
Agriculture	7.8	Private consumption	61.9
Industry, of which:	25.3	Public consumption	15.6
manufacturing	19.0	Investment	22.7
Services	66.9	Exports	32.6
		Imports	-32.9

Structure of employment

	% of total		*% of labour force*
Agriculture	10	Unemployed 1995	6.3
Industry	25	Av. ann. rate 1990–94	9.0
Services	65		

Energy

	'000 TCE		
Total output	16,133	% output exported	15.8
Total consumption	19,304	% consumption imported	32.7
Consumption per head,			
kg coal equivalent	5,467		

Inflation and finance

Consumer price		*av. ann. increase 1989–95*	
inflation 1996	2.0%	Narrow money (M1)	12.4%
Av. ann. inflation 1989–96	3.0%	Broad money	21.4%

Exchange rates

	end 1996		*June 1996*
NZ$ per $	1.42	Effective rates	*1990 = 100*
NZ$ per SDR	2.04	– nominal	111.5
NZ$ per Ecu	1.78	– real	105.8

Principal exports

	$bn fob		$bn fob
Dairy produce	1.8	Fruit & vegetables	0.8
Forest products	1.7	Wool	0.8
Meat	1.6	Total incl. others	**13.7**

Main export destinations

	% of total		% of total
Australia	20.4	United States	10.0
Japan	16.2	United Kingdom	6.1

Principal imports

	$bn cif		$bn cif
Machinery	2.1	Mineral fuels	0.7
Vehicles & aircraft	2.0		
Electrical machinery	1.4	Total incl. others	**14.0**

Main origins of imports

	% of total		% of total
Australia	21.8	Japan	13.7
United States	18.6	United Kingdom	5.9

Balance of payments, reserves and aid, $bn

Visible exports fob	13.5	Capital balance	1.8
Visible imports fob	-12.6	Overall balance	0.3
Trade balance	0.9	Change in reserves	0.7
Invisibles inflows	5.1	Level of reserves	
Invisibles outflows	-9.8	end Dec.	4.4
Net transfers	0.1	No. months of import cover	2.4
Current account balance	-3.8	Aid given	0.12
– as % of GDP	-7.3	– as % of GDP	0.23

Family life

No. of households	1.2m	Divorces per 1,000 pop.	2.7
Av. no. per household	2.9	Cost of living, Dec. 1996	
Marriages per 1,000 pop.	6.3	New York = 100	94

a   Year ending June 30, 1995.

NIGERIA

Area	923,768 sq km	Currency	Naira (N)
Capital	Abuja		

People

Population	111.7m	Life expectancy: men	50.8 yrs
Pop. per sq km	121	women	54.0 yrs
Av. ann. growth		Adult literacy	54.1%
in pop. 1985–95	3.0%	Fertility rate (per woman)	6.0
Pop. under 15	45.5%		
Pop. over 65	2.8%		*per 1,000 pop.*
No. of men per 100 women	98.3	Crude birth rate	42.3
Human Development Index	40.0	Crude death rate	13.9

The economy

GDP	N613bn	GDP per head	$254
GDP	$28bn	GDP per head in purchasing	
Av. ann. growth in real		power parity (USA=100)	5
GDP 1985–95	4.2%		

Origins of GDP		**Components of GDP**	
	% of total		*% of total*
Agriculture	36.8	Private consumption	86.8
Industry, of which:	19.3	Public consumption	3.3
manufacturing	6.9	Investment	6.4
Services	43.9	Exports	15.5
		Imports	-12.0

Structure of employment[a]

	% of total		*% of labour force*
Agriculture	43	Unemployed 1995	...
Industry	7	Av. ann. rate 1990–94	...
Services	50		

Energy

	'000 TCE		
Total output	143,875	% output exported	79.7
Total consumption	22,678	% consumption imported	14.5
Consumption per head,			
kg coal equivalent	209		

Inflation and finance

Consumer price		*av. ann. increase 1989–95*	
inflation 1995	72.8%	Narrow money (M1)	39.7%
Av. ann. inflation 1989–95	41.3%	Broad money	34.9%

Exchange rates

	end 1996		*June 1996*
N per $	22.00	Effective rates	*1990 = 100*
N per SDR	31.68	– nominal	26.6
N per Ecu	27.50	– real	151.1

Principal exports

	$bn fob		$bn fob
Petroleum	10.4	Rubber	0.1
Cocoa beans & products	0.1	Total incl. others[b]	**10.6**

Main export destinations

	% of total		% of total
United States	39.4	Germany	4.9
Spain	8.9	India	4.9
France	6.3		

Principal imports

	$bn cif		$bn cif
Machinery & transport equipment	2.6	Agric products & foodstuffs	1.1
Chemicals	2.5		
Manufactured goods	2.2	Total incl. others[b]	**9.3**

Main origins of imports

	% of total		% of total
United Kingdom	13.4	France	8.2
United States	11.8	Netherlands	5.7
Germany	10.9		

Balance of payments[c], reserves and debt, $bn

Visible exports fob	9.5	Overall balance	-1.9
Visible imports fob	-6.5	Change in reserves	0.1
Trade balance	2.9	Level of reserves	
Invisibles inflows	0.4	end Dec.	1.7
Invisibles outflows	-6.0	No. months of import cover	1.5
Net transfers	0.5	Foreign debt	35.0
Current account balance	-2.1	– as % of GDP	140.5
– as % of GDP	-7.1	Debt service paid	1.6
Capital balance	0.3	Debt service ratio	12.3

Family life

No. households	21.9m	Divorces per 1,000 pop.	...
Av. no. per household	5.1	Cost of living, Dec. 1996	
Marriages per 1,000 pop.	...	New York = 100	...

a 1990
b Valued at unitary exchange rate (weighted average of official and market rates).
c 1994

NORWAY

Area	323,878 sq km	Currency	Norwegian krone (Nkr)
Capital	Oslo		

People

Population	4.3m	Life expectancy: men	74.8 yrs
Pop. per sq km	13	women	80.6 yrs
Av. ann. growth		Adult literacy	99.0%
in pop. 1985–95	0.4%	Fertility rate (per woman)	1.9
Pop. under 15	19.4%		
Pop. over 65	15.9%		*per 1,000 pop.*
No. of men per 100 women	98.2	Crude birth rate	13.4
Human Development Index	93.7	Crude death rate	10.7

The economy

GDP	Nkr862bn	GDP per head	$31,412
GDP	$136bn	GDP per head in purchasing	
Av. ann. growth in real		power parity (USA=100)	81
GDP 1985–95	2.5%		

Origins of GDP		Components of GDP	
	% of total		*% of total*
Agriculture	2.4	Private consumption	49.4
Industry, of which:	27.6	Public consumption	20.7
manufacturing	...	Investment	23.9
Services	70.0	Exports	38.3
		Imports	-32.3

Structure of employment

	% of total		*% of labour force*
Agriculture	5	Unemployed 1995	4.9
Industry	23	Av. ann. rate 1990–94	5.6
Services	72		

Energy

	'000 TCE		
Total output	241,339	% output exported	87.1
Total consumption	32,158	% consumption imported	21.4
Consumption per head,			
kg coal equivalent	7,441		

Inflation and finance

Consumer price		*av. ann. increase 1989–95*	
inflation 1996	1.3%	Narrow money (M1)	9.7%
Av. ann. inflation 1989–96	2.7%	Broad money	4.8%

Exchange rates

	end 1996		*June 1996*
Nkr per $	6.44	Effective rates	*1990 = 100*
Nkr per SDR	9.26	– nominal	98.5
Nkr per Ecu	8.05	– real	103.0

Principal exports

	$bn fob		$bn fob
Oil, gas & products	17.9	Fish & fish products	3.2
Non-ferrous metals	3.4		
Machinery incl. electrical	3.3	Total incl. others	**42.1**

Main export destinations

	% of total		% of total
United Kingdom	19.8	Netherlands	9.1
Germany	12.7	France	7.8
Sweden	9.8		

Principal imports

	$bn cif		$bn cif
Machinery incl. electrical	8.5	Iron & steel	1.4
Road vehicles	2.6	Clothing	1.4
Food, drink & tobacco	2.0	Total incl. others	**34.2**

Main origins of imports

	% of total		% of total
Sweden	15.4	Denmark	7.5
Germany	13.8	United States	6.6
United Kingdom	9.7		

Balance of payments[a], reserves and aid, $bn

Visible exports fob	34.9	Capital balance	-1.3
Visible imports fob	-26.6	Overall balance	1.5
Trade balance	8.3	Change in reserves	3.5
Invisibles inflows	15.9	Level of reserves	
Invisibles outflows	-19.0	end Dec.	23.0
Net transfers	-1.6	No. months of import cover	4.9
Current account balance	3.6	Aid given	1.24
– as % of GDP	3.2	– as % of GDP	0.87

Family life

No. households	1.8m	Divorces per 1,000 pop.	2.5
Av. no. per household	2.4	Cost of living, Dec. 1996	
Marriages per 1,000 pop.	4.8	New York = 100	140

a 1994

PAKISTAN

Area	803,940 sq km	Currency	Pakistan rupee (PRs)
Capital	Islamabad		

People

Population	136.3m	Life expectancy: men	62.9 yrs
Pop. per sq km	171	women	65.1 yrs
Av. ann. growth		Adult literacy	36.4%
in pop. 1985–95	3.0%	Fertility rate (per woman)	5.0
Pop. under 15	42.7%		
Pop. over 65	3.1%		*per 1,000 pop.*
No. of men per 100 women	107.2	Crude birth rate	36.1
Human Development Index	44.2	Crude death rate	7.8

The economy

GDP	PRs1,899bn	GDP per head	$440
GDP	$60bn	GDP per head in purchasing	
Av. ann. growth in real		power parity (USA=100)	8
GDP 1985–95	5.0%		

Origins of GDP[a]		Components of GDP[b]	
	% of total		*% of total*
Agriculture	25.6	Private consumption	71.9
Industry, of which:	...	Public consumption	12.1
manufacturing	17.8	Investment	19.0
Services	...	Exports	15.6
		Imports	-18.8

Structure of employment[a]

	% of total		*% of labour force*
Agriculture	50	Unemployed 1994	4.8
Industry	17	Av. ann. rate 1990–94	5.0
Services	33		

Energy

	'000 TCE		
Total output	28,787	% output exported	1.4
Total consumption	45,346	% consumption imported	40.6
Consumption per head,			
kg coal equivalent	332		

Inflation and finance

Consumer price		*av. ann. increase 1989–95*	
inflation 1996	10.4%	Narrow money (M1)	14.5%
Av. ann. inflation 1989–96	10.3%	Broad money	16.5%

Exchange rates

	end 1996		*June 1996*
PRs per $	40.22	Effective rates	*1990 = 100*
PRs per SDR	57.84	– nominal	...
PRs per Ecu	50.28	– real	...

Principal exports[a]

	$bn fob		$bn fob
Cotton yarn	1.5	Garments & hosiery	0.6
Cotton fabrics	1.1		
Knitwear	0.7	Total incl. others	**8.1**

Main export destinations

	% of total		% of total
United States	15.0	Japan	6.7
Hong Kong	7.5	Germany	6.4
United Kingdom	6.8	UAE	4.4

Principal imports[a]

	$bn cif		$bn cif
Machinery	2.4	Edible oils	1.0
Chemicals	1.6	Motor vehicles	0.4
Petroleum & products	1.6	Total incl. others	**10.4**

Main origins of imports

	% of total		% of total
Japan	10.7	Germany	6.2
United States	9.2	Kuwait	5.6
Malaysia	8.4	Saudi Arabia	4.9

Balance of payments[c], reserves and debt, $bn

Visible exports fob	7.1	Overall balance	1.3
Visible imports fob	-9.3	Change in reserves	-1.2
Trade balance	-2.2	Level of reserves	
Invisibles inflows	1.9	end Dec.	2.5
Invisibles outflows	-4.3	No. months of import cover	2.1
Net transfers	2.9	Foreign debt	30.2
Current account balance	-1.8	– as % of GDP	49.5
– as % of GDP	-3.2	Debt service paid	3.1
Capital balance	3.0	Debt service ratio	26.9

Family life

No. households	19.4m	Divorces per 1,000 pop.	...
Av. no. per household	6.7	Cost of living, Dec. 1996	
Marriages per 1,000 pop.	...	New York = 100	54

a Fiscal year ending June 30, 1995.
b Fiscal year ending June 30, 1994.
c 1994

PERU

Area	1,285,216 sq km	Currency	Nuevo Sol (New Sol)
Capital	Lima		

People

Population	23.5m	Life expectancy: men	65.9 yrs
Pop. per sq km	19	women	70.9 yrs
Av. ann. growth		Adult literacy[a]	87.8%
in pop. 1985–94	1.9%	Fertility rate (per woman)	3.0
Pop. under 15	35.9%		
Pop. over 65	4.4%		*per 1,000 pop.*
No. of men per 100 women	98.7	Crude birth rate	24.9
Human Development Index	69.4	Crude death rate	6.4

The economy

GDP	New Soles 124bn	GDP per head	$2,338
GDP	$55bn	GDP per head in purchasing	
Av. ann. growth in real		power parity (USA=100)	14
GDP 1985–95	1.3%		

Origins of GDP		Components of GDP	
	% of total		*% of total*
Agriculture	12.2	Private consumption	73.1
Industry, of which:	39.3	Public consumption	8.2
manufacturing	23.5	Investment	23.8
Services	48.5	Exports	11.6
		Imports	-16.7

Structure of employment[b]

	% of total		*% of labour force*
Agriculture	36	Unemployed 1995	7.1
Industry	18	Av. ann. rate 1991–94	8.5
Services	46		

Energy

	'000 TCE		
Total output	10,899	% output exported	29.2
Total consumption	10,648	% consumption imported	29.1
Consumption per head,			
kg coal equivalent	456		

Inflation and finance

		av. ann. increase 1989–95	
Consumer price			
inflation 1996	11.5%	Narrow money (M1)	286%
Av. ann. inflation 1989–96	289%	Broad money	324.1%

Exchange rates

	end 1996		*June 1996*
New Soles per $	2.60	Effective rates	*1990 = 100*
New Soles per SDR	3.74	– nominal	…
New Soles per Ecu	3.25	– real	…

Principal exports

	$bn fob		$bn fob
Copper	1.2	Gold	0.5
Fish & fish products	1.0	Textiles	0.4
Agricultural products	0.6	Total incl. others	**5.6**

Main export destinations

	% of total		% of total
United States	17.3	China	6.5
Japan	9.1	United Kingdom	6.0
Germany	7.4		

Principal imports

	$bn fob		$bn fob
Industrial supplies	3.2	Consumer goods	1.8
Capital goods	2.4	Total incl. others	**7.7**

Main origins of imports

	% of total		% of total
United States	26.7	Chile	7.5
Colombia	7.8	Brazil	5.4

Balance of payments, reserves and debt, $bn

Visible exports fob	5.6	Overall balance	-1.1
Visible imports fob	-7.7	Change in reserves	1.2
Trade balance	-2.1	Level of reserves	
Invisibles inflows	1.8	end Dec.	8.7
Invisibles outflows	-4.4	No. months of import cover	8.5
Net transfers	0.5	Foreign debt	30.8
Current account balance	-4.2	– as % of GDP	54.1
– as % of GDP	-7.7	Debt service paid	1.2
Capital balance	1.9	Debt service ratio	15.3

Family life

No. of households	5.1m	Divorces per 1,000 pop.	...
Av. no. per household	4.7	Cost of living, Dec. 1996	
Marriages per 1,000 pop.	6.0	New York = 100	73

---

a   Excluding indigenous jungle population.
b   1990

PHILIPPINES

Area	300,000 sq km	Currency	Philippine peso (P)
Capital	Manila		

People

Population	67.8m	Life expectancy: men	66.6 yrs
Pop. per sq km	226	women	70.2 yrs
Av. ann. growth		Adult literacy	94.2%
in pop. 1985–95	2.2%	Fertility rate (per woman)	3.6
Pop. under 15	38.5%		
Pop. over 65	3.4%		*per 1,000 pop.*
No. of men per 100 women	101.3	Crude birth rate	28.4
Human Development Index	66.5	Crude death rate	5.7

The economy

GDP	P1,851bn	GDP per head	$1,059
GDP	$72bn	GDP per head in purchasing	
Av. ann. growth in real		power parity (USA=100)	11
GDP 1985–95	3.3%		

Origins of GDP		**Components of GDP**	
	% of total		*% of total*
Agriculture	21.7	Private consumption	74.1
Industry, of which:	32.2	Public consumption	8.9
manufacturing	23.0	Investment	22.3
Services	46.1	Exports	36.6
		Imports	-43.5

Structure of employment

	% of total		*% of labour force*
Agriculture	44	Unemployed 1995	8.4
Industry	16	Av. ann. rate 1990–94	8.6
Services	40		

Energy

	'000 TCE		
Total output	9,571	% output exported	7.8
Total consumption	28,217	% consumption imported	78.8
Consumption per head,			
kg coal equivalent	426		

Inflation and finance

Consumer price		*av. ann. increase 1989–95*	
inflation 1996	8.4%	Narrow money (M1)	18.0%
Av. ann. inflation 1989–96	10.8%	Broad money	22.6%

Exchange rates

	end 1996		*June 1996*
P per $	26.29	Effective rates	*1990 = 100*
P per SDR	37.80	– nominal	108.4
P per Ecu	32.86	– real	131.2

Principal exports

	$bn fob		$bn fob
Electrical & electronic equipment	7.4	Machinery & transport equipment	0.7
Clothing	2.6	Copper	0.5
Coconut products	0.8	Total incl. others	**17.4**

Main export destinations

	% of total		% of total
United States	35.3	United Kingdom	5.3
Japan	15.7	Hong Kong	4.7
Singapore	5.7	Netherlands	4.6

Principal imports

	$bn cif		$bn cif
Electrical equipment parts	3.8	Telecom & electrical machinery	3.2
Semi-processed manufactures	3.6	Total incl. others	**26.4**

Main origins of imports

	% of total		% of total
Japan	22.4	Taiwan	5.4
United States	18.9	South Korea	5.1
Saudi Arabia	6.2	Hong Kong	4.8
Singapore	5.9		

Balance of payments, reserves and debt, $bn

Visible exports fob	17.4	Overall balance	1.2
Visible imports fob	-26.4	Change in reserves	0.6
Trade balance	-8.9	Level of reserves	
Invisibles inflows	15.4	end Dec.	7.8
Invisibles outflows	-9.3	No. months of import cover	2.6
Net transfers	0.9	Foreign debt	39.4
Current account balance	-2.0	– as % of GDP	51.5
– as % of GDP	-2.8	Debt service paid	5.3
Capital balance	5.3	Debt service ratio	16.4

Family life

No. of households	12.8m	Divorces per 1,000 pop.	...
Av. no. per household	5.4	Cost of living, Dec. 1996	
Marriages per 1,000 pop.	6.0	New York = 100	68

POLAND

Area	312,683 sq km	Currency	Zloty (Zl)
Capital	Warsaw		

People

Population	38.6m	Life expectancy: men	66.7 yrs
Pop. per sq km	119	women	75.7 yrs
Av. ann. growth		Adult literacy	99.0%
in pop. 1985–95	0.4%	Fertility rate (per woman)	1.7
Pop. under 15	24.9%		
Pop. over 65	11.0%		*per 1,000 pop.*
No. of men per 100 women	94.9	Crude birth rate	11.9
Human Development Index	81.9	Crude death rate	10.7

The economy

GDP	Zl262bn	GDP per head	$2,797
GDP	$108bn	GDP per head in purchasing	
Av. ann. growth in real		power parity (USA=100)	20
GDP 1985–95	0.2%		

Origins of GDP		Components of GDP	
	% of total		*% of total*
Agriculture	6.6	Private consumption	63.7
Industry, of which:	28.9	Public consumption	17.8
manufacturing	...	Accumulation	18.5
Services	64.5	Exports	...
		Imports	...

Structure of employment

	% of total		*% of labour force*
Agriculture	22	Unemployed 1995	14.9
Industry	32	Av. ann. rate 1990–94	12.8
Services	46		

Energy

	'000 TCE		
Total output	134,558	% output exported	21.0
Total consumption	134,448	% consumption imported	22.3
Consumption per head,			
kg coal equivalent	3,507		

Inflation and finance

Consumer price		*av. ann. increase 1989–95*	
inflation 1996	19.0%	Narrow money (M1)	86.6%
Av. ann. inflation 1989–96	88.5%	Broad money	92.0%

Exchange rates

	end 1996		*June 1996*
Zl per $	2.87	Effective rates	*1990 = 100*
Zl per SDR	4.13	– nominal	39.8
Zl per Ecu	3.59	– real	194.1

Principal exports

	$bn fob		$bn fob
Machinery & equipment	4.4	Chemicals	1.7
Light industry products	2.5	Paper & wood	1.7
Metals	2.4	Total incl. others	**17.2**

Main export destinations

	% of total		% of total
Germany	38.3	United Kingdom	3.9
Russia	5.6	France	3.4
Netherlands	5.4	United States	3.4
Italy	4.7		

Principal imports

	$bn fob		$bn fob
Machinery & equipment	7.3	Oil & gas	2.3
Chemicals	4.1	Metals	1.1
Food & agric. products	4.0		
Light industry	2.3	Total incl. others	**21.6**

Main origins of imports

	% of total		% of total
Germany	26.6	France	4.9
Italy	8.4	Netherlands	4.5
Russia	6.8	United States	3.9
United Kingdom	5.1		

Balance of payments, reserves and debt, $bn

Visible exports fob	23.5	Overall balance	9.8
Visible imports fob	-26.7	Change in reserves	8.9
Trade balance	-3.2	Level of reserves	
Invisibles inflows	9.7	end Dec.	15.0
Invisibles outflows	-10.2	No. months of import cover	4.9
Net transfers	-0.5	Foreign debt	42.3
Current account balance	-4.2	– as % of GDP	36.1
– as % of GDP	-3.9	Debt service paid	4.1
Capital balance	14.2	Debt service ratio	12.2

Family life

No. of households	11.6m	Divorces per 1,000 pop.	0.7
Av. no. per household	3.3	Cost of living, Dec. 1996	
Marriages per 1,000 pop.	5.4	New York = 100	69

PORTUGAL

Area	88,940 sq km	Currency	Escudo (Esc)
Capital	Lisbon		

People

Population	9.8m	Life expectancy: men	71.8 yrs
Pop. per sq km	106	women	78.9 yrs
Av. ann. growth		Adult literacy	86.2%
in pop. 1985–95	-0.1%	Fertility rate (per woman)	1.5
Pop. under 15	17.8%		
Pop. over 65	14.8%		*per 1,000 pop.*
No. of men per 100 women	92.9	Crude birth rate	11.2
Human Development Index	87.8	Crude death rate	10.9

The economy

GDP	Esc14,658bn	GDP per head	$9,851
GDP	$97bn	GDP per head in purchasing	
Av. ann. growth in real		power parity (USA=100)	47
GDP 1985–95	3.2%		

Origins of GDP		Components of GDP	
	% of total		*% of total*
Agriculture	6.2	Private consumption	65.7
Industry, of which:	36.4	Public consumption	19.4
manufacturing	...	Investment	25.0
Services	57.4	Exports	27.2
		Imports	-37.3

Structure of employment

	% of total		*% of labour force*
Agriculture	11	Unemployed 1995	7.1
Industry	32	Av. ann. rate 1990–94	5.0
Services	56		

Energy

	'000 TCE		
Total output	1,443	% output exported[a]	412.3
Total consumption	20,975	% consumption imported[a]	132.2
Consumption per head,			
kg coal equivalent	2,134		

Inflation and finance

Consumer price		*av. ann. increase 1989–95*	
inflation 1996	3.1%	Narrow money (M1)	11.5%
Av. ann. inflation 1989–96	8.1%	Broad money	14.1%

Exchange rates

	end 1996		*June 1996*
			1990 = 100
Esc per $	156.4	Effective rates	
Esc per SDR	224.9	– nominal	95.8
Esc per Ecu	195.5	– real	114.8

Principal exports

	$bn fob		$bn fob
Machinery	3.6	Clothing	2.4
Textiles	2.8	Shoes	1.8
Vehicles & transport equipment	2.4	Total incl. others	**22.8**

Main export destinations

	% of total		% of total
Germany	21.6	United Kingdom	11.1
Spain	14.7	Netherlands	5.2
France	14.0	United States	3.3

Principal imports

	$bn cif		$bn cif
Machinery	6.6	Food products	2.8
Vehicles & transport equipment	4.5	Textiles	2.2
Chemicals	3.5	Total incl. others	**32.6**

Main origins of imports

	% of total		% of total
Spain	20.8	Italy	8.4
Germany	14.4	United Kingdom	6.6
France	11.9	Netherlands	4.5

Balance of payments, reserves and debt, $bn

Visible exports fob	23.9	Overall balance	-0.3
Visible imports fob	-32.4	Change in reserves	0.4
Trade balance	-8.5	Level of reserves	
Invisibles inflows	11.7	end Dec.	22.1
Invisibles outflows	-10.6	No. months of import cover	6.3
Net transfers	7.1	Aid given	0.27
Current account balance	-0.2	– as % of GDP	0.27
– as % of GDP	-0.2		
Capital balance	3.2		

Family life

No. of households	3.2m	Divorces per 1,000 pop.	1.4
Av. no. per household	3.0	Cost of living, Dec. 1996	
Marriages per 1,000 pop.	6.7	New York = 100	89

a Energy trade data are distorted by transitory and oil refining activities.

ROMANIA

˙Area	237,500 sq km	Currency	Leu (L)
Capital	Bucharest		

People

Population	22.7m	Life expectancy: men	66.0 yrs
Pop. per sq km	96	women	73.2 yrs
Av. ann. growth		Adult literacy	69.9%
in pop. 1985–95	nil	Fertility rate (per woman)	1.4
Pop. under 15	20.5%		
Pop. over 65	11.8%		*per 1,000 pop.*
No. of men per 100 women	97.0	Crude birth rate	11.0
Human Development Index	73.8	Crude death rate	11.6

The economy

GDP	L67,098bn	GDP per head	$1,473
GDP	$33bn	GDP per head in purchasing	
Av. ann. growth in real		power parity (USA=100)	16
GDP 1985–95	-3.0%		

Origins of GDP

	% of total
Agriculture	20.0
Industry, of which:	39.9
manufacturing	...
Services	40.1

Components of GDP

	% of total
Private consumption	66.1
Public consumption	12.5
Investment	26.1
Exports	18.9
Imports	-23.7

Structure of employment

	% of total		% of labour force
Agriculture	40	Unemployed 1995	8.7
Industry	31	Av. ann. rate 1991–94	8.0
Services	29		

Energy

	'000 TCE		
Total output	43,997	% output exported	16.3
Total consumption	28,313	% consumption imported	9.0
Consumption per head,			
kg coal equivalent	2,533		

Inflation and finance

Consumer price		*av. ann. increase 1989–95*	
inflation 1996	57%	Narrow money (M1)	63.9%
Av. ann. inflation 1989–96	88.3%	Broad money	71.5%

Exchange rates

	end 1996		June 1996
		Effective rates	1990 = 100
L per $	4,035.0		
L per SDR	5,802.2	– nominal	...
L per Ecu	5,043.8	– real	...

Principal exports

	$bn fob		$bn fob
Textiles & footwear	1.9	Chemicals	0.7
Basic metals & products	1.5		
Mineral products	0.8	Total incl. others	**7.5**

Main export destinations

	% of total		% of total
Germany	17.8	Turkey	4.5
Italy	15.6	China	3.0
France	5.7	Netherlands	3.0

Principal imports

	$bn cif		$bn cif
Fuels & minerals	2.4	Food products	0.6
Machinery & equipment	1.8		
Chemicals	0.8	Total incl. others	**9.4**

Main origins of imports

	% of total		% of total
Germany	17.1	France	5.2
Italy	13.2	United States	4.2
Russia	12.6	Egypt	4.1

Balance of payments, reserves and debt, $bn

Visible exports fob	7.5	Overall balance	-0.5
Visible imports fob	-8.8	Change in reserves	-0.5
Trade balance	-1.2	Level of reserves	
Invisibles inflows	1.6	end Dec.	2.6
Invisibles outflows	-2.0	No. months of import cover	2.9
Net transfers	0.4	Foreign debt	6.7
Current account balance	-1.3	– as % of GDP	19.5
– as % of GDP	-4.0	Debt service paid	1.0
Capital balance	1.0	Debt service ratio	10.6

Family life

No. of households	7.7m	Divorces per 1,000 pop.	1.4
Av. no. per household	3.0	Cost of living, Dec. 1996	
Marriages per 1,000 pop.	6.8	New York = 100	62

RUSSIA[a]

Area	17,075,400 sq km	Currency	Rouble (Rb)
Capital	Moscow		

People

Population	148.5m	Life expectancy: men	58.0 yrs
Pop. per sq km	9	women	71.5 yrs
Av. ann. growth		Adult literacy	98.7%
in pop. 1985–95	0.4%	Fertility rate (per woman)	1.4
Pop. under 15	21.1%		
Pop. over 65	12.0%		*per 1,000 pop.*
No. of men per 100 women	88.2	Crude birth rate	9.6
Human Development Index	80.4	Crude death rate	14.5

The economy

GDP	Rb1,513,588bn	GDP per head	$2,236
GDP	$332bn	GDP per head in purchasing	
Av. ann. growth in real		power parity (USA=100)	17
GDP 1990–95	-14.1%		

Origins of GDP		Components of GDP	
	% of total		*% of total*
Agriculture	6.3	Private consumption	49.4
Industry, of which:	37.4	Public consumption	18.1
manufacturing	...	Investment	25.5
Services	56.3	Exports	26.3
		Imports	-20.0

Structure of employment

	% of total		*% of labour force*
Agriculture	16	Unemployed 1995	8.3
Industry	36	Av. ann. rate 1992–94	5.9
Services	48		

Energy

	'000 TCE		
Total output	1,384,012	% output exported	34.4
Total consumption	883,595	% consumption imported	4.4
Consumption per head,			
kg coal equivalent	5,996		

Inflation and finance

Consumer price		*av. ann. increase 1988–92*	
inflation 1996	47.7%	Narrow money (M1)	...
Av. ann. inflation 1991–96	191.9%	Broad money	...

Exchange rates

	end 1996		*June 1996*
Rb per $	5,560	Effective rates	*1990 = 100*
Rb per SDR	7,995	– nominal	...
Rb per Ecu	6,950	– real	...

Principal exports

	$ bn		$ bn
Fuels & raw materials	31.3	Chemicals & rubber	7.4
Metals	14.8		
Machinery & equipment	7.7	Total incl. others	**77.4**

Main export destinations

	% of total		% of total
Ukraine	8.9	United States	6.6
Germany	7.9	China	4.4
Switzerland	4.8	Italy	4.3

Principal imports

	$ bn		$ bn
Machinery & equipment	15.3	Metals	3.4
Food products	12.9		
Chemicals & rubber	4.9	Total incl. others	**46.4**

Main origins of imports

	% of total		% of total
Ukraine	14.3	United States	5.7
Germany	14.1	Finland	4.4
Kazakhstan	5.9		

Balance of payments, reserves and debt, $bn

Visible exports fob	81.5	Overall balance	-11.1
Visible imports fob	-59.0	Change in reserves	10.8
Trade balance	22.5	Level of reserves	
Invisibles inflows	16.7	end Dec.	18.0
Invisibles outflows	-28.1	No. months of import cover	2.5
Net transfers	0.2	Foreign debt	120.5
Current account balance	11.3	– as % of GDP	37.6
– as % of GDP	3.2	Debt service paid	6.3
Capital balance	-12.9	Debt service ratio	6.6

Family life

No. of households	52.3m	Divorces per 1,000 pop.	4.3
Av. no. per household	2.8	Cost of living, Dec. 1996	
Marriages per 1,000 pop.	7.3	New York = 100	120

a For selected data on Ukraine and other ex-Soviet republics, see page 192.

SAUDI ARABIA

Area	2,200,000 sq km	Currency	Riyal (SR)
Capital	Riyadh		

People

Population	18.3m	Life expectancy: men	69.9 yrs
Pop. per sq km	8	women	73.4 yrs
Av. ann. growth		Adult literacy	64.1%
in pop. 1985–95	3.7%	Fertility rate (per woman)	5.9
Pop. under 15	41.6%		
Pop. over 65	2.7%		*per 1,000 pop.*
No. of men per 100 women	126.8	Crude birth rate	34.3
Human Development Index	77.1	Crude death rate	4.2

The economy

GDP	SR502bn	GDP per head	$7,315
GDP	$134bn	GDP per head in purchasing	
Av. ann. growth in real		power parity (USA=100)	...
GDP 1985–95	3.7%		

Origins of GDP[a]		Components of GDP[a]	
	% of total		*% of total*
Agriculture	7.0	Private consumption	43.8
Industry, of which:	50.3	Public consumption	27.0
manufacturing	8.6	Investment	19.7
Services	42.7	Exports	39.3
		Imports	-29.8

Structure of employment[b]

	% of total		*% of labour force*
Agriculture	19	Unemployed 1995	...
Industry	20	Av. ann. rate 1990–94	...
Services	61		

Energy

	'000 TCE		
Total output	656,067	% output exported	77.4
Total consumption	100,676	% consumption imported	0.0
Consumption per head,			
kg coal equivalent	5,769		

Inflation and finance

		av. ann. increase 1989–95	
Consumer price			
inflation 1995	5.0%	Narrow money (M1)	4.7%
Av. ann. inflation 1989–95	2.0%	Broad money	4.4%

Exchange rates

	end 1996		*June 1996*
SR per $	3.75	Effective rates	*1990 = 100*
SR per SDR	5.39	– nominal	100.2
SR per Ecu	4.69	– real	93.8

Principal exports

	$bn fob		$bn fob
Crude oil & refined		Petrochemicals	3.9
petroleum	41.4	Total incl. others	**46.6**

Main export destinations

	% of total		% of total
Japan	17.6	Singapore	6.9
United States	14.7	France	4.5
South Korea	9.7	Netherlands	3.5

Principal imports

	$bn cif		$bn cif
Machinery	6.1	Chemical products	2.2
Transport equipment	4.1	Textiles & clothing	2.1
Agric. products & foodstuffs	3.2	Total incl. others	**28.1**

Main origins of imports

	% of total		% of total
United States	21.4	Japan	7.7
United Kingdom	8.7	Switzerland	5.1
Germany	7.8	France	4.9

Balance of payments, reserves and debt[a], $bn

Visible exports fob	50.0	Overall balance	1.2
Visible imports fob	-25.7	Change in reserves	1.3
Trade balance	24.4	Level of reserves	
Invisibles inflows	8.5	end Dec.	10.4
Invisibles outflows	-20.5	No. months of import cover	2.7
Net transfers	-17.6	Foreign debt	20.0
Current account balance	-5.3	– as % of GDP	16.0
– as % of GDP	-4.0	Debt service	2.4
Capital balance	9.3	Debt service ratio	4.5

Family life

No. of households	...	Divorces per 1,000 pop.	...
Av. no. per household	...	Cost of living, Dec. 1996	
Marriages per 1,000 pop.	...	New York = 100	74

a 1994
b 1990

SINGAPORE

Area	639 sq km	Currency	Singapore dollar (S$)
Capital	Singapore		

People

Population	3.3m	Life expectancy: men	75.1 yrs
Pop. per sq km	5,354	women	79.5 yrs
Av. ann. growth		Adult literacy	92.0%
in pop. 1985–95	2.1%	Fertility rate (per woman)	1.8
Pop. under 15	22.5%		
Pop. over 65	6.3%		*per 1,000 pop.*
No. of men per 100 women	101.5	Crude birth rate	15.7
Human Development Index	88.1	Crude death rate	5.0

The economy

GDP	S$113bn	GDP per head	$23,995
GDP	$80bn	GDP per head in purchasing	
Av. ann. growth in real		power parity (USA=100)	84
GDP 1985–95	8.2%		

Origins of GDP		Components of GDP	
	% of total		*% of total*
Agriculture	0.2	Private consumption	41.7
Industry, of which:	37.1	Public consumption	9.3
manufacturing	28.0	Investment	34.9
Services	62.7	Exports less imports	15.6

Structure of employment

	% of total		*% of labour force*
Agriculture	0	Unemployed 1995	2.7
Industry	31	Av. ann. rate 1990–94	2.3
Services	69		

Energy

	'000 TCE		
Total output	...	% output exported	...
Total consumption	27,290	% consumption imported[a]	383.7
Consumption per head,			
kg coal equivalent	9,674		

Inflation and finance

Consumer price		*av. ann. increase 1989–95*	
inflation 1996	1.7%	Narrow money (M1)	11.3%
Av. ann. inflation 1989–96	2.5%	Broad money	13.5%

Exchange rates

	end 1996		*June 1996*
S$ per $	1.40	Effective rates	*1990 = 100*
S$ per SDR	2.01	– nominal	123.7
S$ per Ecu	1.75	– real	...

Principal exports

	$bn fob		$bn fob
Machinery & equipment	77.5	Agric. products & foodstuffs	2.5
Mineral fuels	9.8	Crude materials	1.7
Manufactured products	7.5		
Chemicals	7.0	Total incl. others	**118.3**

Main export destinations

	% of total		% of total
United States	19.2	Thailand	5.8
Malaysia	18.2	Germany	3.4
Hong Kong	8.6	United Kingdom	2.6
Japan	7.8		

Principal imports

	$bn cif		$bn cif
Machinery & equipment	71.9	Agric. products & foodstuffs	3.6
Manufactured products	13.5	Crude minerals	1.5
Mineral fuels	10.0		
Chemicals	8.0	Total incl. others	**124.5**

Main origins of imports

	% of total		% of total
Japan	21.1	South Korea	4.3
Malaysia	15.5	Taiwan	4.1
United States	15.0	Germany	3.5
Thailand	5.2		

Balance of payments, reserves and debt[b], $bn

Visible exports fob	119.0	Overall balance	8.6
Visible imports fob	-117.4	Change in reserves	10.5
Trade balance	1.6	Level of reserves	
Invisibles inflows	40.4	end Dec.	68.7
Invisibles outflows	-26.1	No. months of import cover	5.7
Net transfers	-0.9	Foreign debt	5.5
Current account balance	15.1	– as % of GDP	10.0
– as % of GDP	18.9	Debt service	0.6
Capital balance	-6.9	Debt service ratio	0.6

Family life

No. of households	0.8m	Divorces per 1,000 pop.	1.3
Av. no. per household	3.7	Cost of living, Dec. 1996	
Marriages per 1,000 pop.	8.8	New York = 100	115

a Energy trade data are distorted by transitory and oil refining activities.
b 1993.

SLOVAKIA

Area	49,035 sq km	Currency	Koruna (Kc)
Capital	Bratislava		

People

Population	5.3m	Life expectancy: men	67.0 yrs
Pop. per sq km	109	women	75.8 yrs
Av. ann. growth		Adult literacy	…
in pop. 1985–95	0.4%	Fertility rate (per woman)	1.5
Pop. under 15	24.7%		
Pop. over 65	10.7%		*per 1,000 pop.*
No. of men per 100 women	95.2	Crude birth rate	11.7
Human Development Index	86.4	Crude death rate	10.5

The economy

GDP	Kc475bn	GDP per head	$2,969
GDP	$16bn	GDP per head in purchasing	
Av. ann. growth in real		power parity (USA=100)	13
GDP 1989–95	-3.7%		

Origins of GDP[a]		Components of GDP[a]	
	% of total		*% of total*
Agriculture	5.3	Private consumption	48.1
Industry, of which:	49.7	Public consumption	23.1
manufacturing	…	Investment	14.0
Services	44.9	Exports	76.5
		Imports	-61.7

Structure of employment

	% of total		*% of labour force*
Agriculture	9	Unemployed 1995	13.1
Industry	37	Av. ann. rate 1990–94	13.7
Services	54		

Energy

	'000 TCE		
Total output	6,486	% output exported	36.0
Total consumption	21,726	% consumption imported	87.5
Consumption per head,			
kg coal equivalent	4,074		

Inflation and finance

Consumer price		*av. ann. increase 1994–95*	
inflation 1996	5.8%	Narrow money (M1)	13.3
Av. ann. inflation 1991–96	29.7%	Broad money	17.9

Exchange rates

	end 1996		*June 1996*
Kc per $	31.90	Effective rates	*1990 = 100*
Kc per SDR	45.86	– nominal	…
Kc per Ecu	39.88	– real	…

Principal exports

	$bn fob		$bn fob
Machinery & industrial		Manufactured goods	1.1
equipment	1.6	Raw materials	0.4
Chemicals	1.2	Total incl. others	**8.6**

Main export destinations

	% of total		% of total
EU	37.4	Czech Republic	35.2

Principal imports

	$bn fob		$bn fob
Machinery & transport		Intermediate manufactured	
equipment	2.5	goods	1.5
Fuels	1.6	Total incl. others	**8.8**

Main origins of imports

	% of total		% of total
EU	34.7	Czech Republic	27.5

Balance of payments, reserves and debt, $bn

Visible exports fob	8.6	Overall balance	1.8
Visible imports fob	-8.5	Change in reserves	1.7
Trade balance	0.0	Level of reserves	
Invisibles inflows	2.6	end Dec.	3.9
Invisibles outflows	-2.1	No. months of import cover	4.2
Net transfers	0.1	Foreign debt	5.8
Current account balance	0.6	– as % of GDP	33.5
– as % of GDP	2.5	Debt service paid	1.1
Capital balance	1.2	Debt service ratio	9.7

Family life

No. of households	1.8m	Divorces per 1,000 pop.	1.5
Av. no. per household	2.9	Cost of living, Dec. 1996	
Marriages per 1,000 pop.	6.4	New York = 100	...

a 1994

SOUTH AFRICA

Area	1,225,815 sq km	Currency	Rand (R)
Capital	Pretoria		

People

Population	41.5m	Life expectancy: men	62.3 yrs
Pop. per sq km	34	women	68.3 yrs
Av. ann. growth		Adult literacy	81.0%
in pop. 1985–95	2.3%	Fertility rate (per woman)	3.8
Pop. under 15	37.3%		
Pop. over 65	4.4%		*per 1,000 pop.*
No. of men per 100 women	98.7	Crude birth rate	29.7
Human Development Index	64.9	Crude death rate	7.9

The economy

GDP	R475bn	GDP per head	$3,157
GDP	$131bn	GDP per head in purchasing	
Av. ann. growth in real		power parity (USA=100)	19
GDP 1985–95	1.0%		

Origins of GDP		Components of GDP	
	% of total		*% of total*
Agriculture	4.6	Private consumption	60.3
Industry, of which:	37.0	Public consumption	20.6
manufacturing	25.2	Investment	19.0
Services	58.4	Exports	24.9
		Imports	-24.8

Structure of employment[a]

	% of total		*% of labour force*
Agriculture	14	Unemployed 1995	4.5
Industry	32	Av. ann. rate 1990–94	4.4
Services	54		

Energy

	'000 TCE		
Total output	145,452	% output exported	29.8
Total consumption	126,281	% consumption imported	19.2
Consumption per head,			
kg coal equivalent	2,726		

Inflation and finance

		av. ann. increase 1993–95	
Consumer price			
inflation 1996	7.5%	Narrow money (M1)	18.3%
Av. ann. inflation 1989–96	11.6%	Broad money	13.4%

Exchange rates

	end 1996		*June 1996*
R per $	4.68	Effective rates	*1990 = 100*
R per SDR	6.73	– nominal	69.5
R per Ecu	5.85	– real	89.0

Principal exports[b]

	$bn fob		$bn fob
Gold	6.4	Food, drink & tobacco	2.1
Base metals	3.1		
Diamonds	2.7	Total incl. others	**25.1**

Main export destinations

	% of total		% of total
Italy	7.8	Germany	5.5
Japan	7.3	United Kingdom	5.0
United States	6.6		

Principal imports

	$bn cif		$bn cif
Machinery & transport		Chemicals	2.7
equipment	10.2	Food, drink & tobacco	1.0
Manufactured goods	2.8	Total incl. others	**23.4**

Main origins of imports

	% of total		% of total
Germany	15.9	Japan	9.8
United Kingdom	11.5	Italy	4.5
United States	10.9		

Balance of payments, reserves and debt, $bn

Visible exports fob	27.9	Overall balance	2.5
Visible imports fob	-27.1	Change in reserves	1.2
Trade balance	0.7	Level of reserves	
Invisibles inflows	5.6	end Dec.	4.5
Invisibles outflows	-9.9	No. months of import cover	1.4
Net transfers	0.0	Foreign debt	30.9
Current account balance	-3.5	– as % of GDP	23.2
– as % of GDP	-2.7	Debt service	3.5
Capital balance	5.3	Debt service ratio	10.4

Family life

No. of households	8.2m	Divorces per 1,000 pop.	0.4
Av. no. per household	5.0	Cost of living, Dec. 1996	
Marriages per 1,000 pop.	...	New York = 100	60

a	1990
b	1994

SOUTH KOREA

Area	99,274 sq km	Currency	Won (W)
Capital	Seoul		

People

Population	44.9m	Life expectancy: men	68.8 yrs
Pop. per sq km	454	women	76.0 yrs
Av. ann. growth		Adult literacy	96.8%
in pop. 1985–95	1.0%	Fertility rate (per woman)	1.7
Pop. under 15	23.3%		
Pop. over 65	5.6%		*per 1,000 pop.*
No. of men per 100 women	101.5	Crude birth rate	15.0
Human Development Index	88.6	Crude death rate	6.4

The economy

GDP	W335,502bn	GDP per head	$9,689
GDP	$435bn	GDP per head in purchasing	
Av. ann. growth in real		power parity (USA=100)	42
GDP 1985–95	8.7%		

Origins of GDP		**Components of GDP**	
	% of total		*% of total*
Agriculture	6.5	Private consumption	52.9
Industry, of which:	44.0	Public consumption	10.4
manufacturing	29.9	Investment	37.1
Services	49.5	Exports	33.2
		Imports	-34.2

Structure of employment

	% of total		*% of labour force*
Agriculture	11	Unemployed 1995	2.0
Industry	40	Av. ann. rate 1990–94	2.5
Services	49		

Energy

	'000 TCE		
Total output	27,073	% output exported	62.6
Total consumption	168,089	% consumption imported	108.0
Consumption per head,			
kg coal equivalent	3,772		

Inflation and finance

Consumer price		*av. ann. increase 1989–95*	
inflation 1996	5.0%	Narrow money (M1)	19.6%
Av. ann. inflation 1989–96	6.3%	Broad money	17.8%

Exchange rates

	end 1996		*June 1996*
W per $	844	Effective rates	*1990 = 100*
W per SDR	1,214	– nominal	...
W per Ecu	1,055	– real	...

Principal exports

	$bn fob		$bn fob
Electronic components	19.4	Ships	5.5
Textiles	10.1	Clothing & accessories	5.0
Cars	7.2	Total incl. others	**125.1**

Main export destinations

	% of total		% of total
United States	19.3	China	7.6
Japan	13.6	Germany	4.8
Hong Kong	8.5		

Principal imports

	$bn cif		$bn cif
Machinery & transport equipment	49.4	Raw materials	11.7
		Food & live animals	5.9
Mineral fuels & lubricants	19.0		
Chemicals	13.2	Total incl. others	**135.1**

Main origins of imports

	% of total		% of total
Japan	24.1	Germany	4.9
United States	22.5	Saudi Arabia	4.0
China	5.7		

Balance of payments, reserves and debt, $bn

Visible exports fob	123.2	Overall balance	7.0
Visible imports fob	-127.9	Change in reserves	7.0
Trade balance	-4.7	Level of reserves	
Invisibles inflows	23.9	end Dec.	32.8
Invisibles outflows	-32.5	No. months of import cover	2.5
Net transfers	0.4	Foreign debt	74.6
Current account balance	-8.3	– as % of GDP	16.4
– as % of GDP	-1.9	Debt service paid	10.6
Capital balance	16.7	Debt service ratio	7.0

Family life

No. of households	13.3m	Divorces per 1,000 pop.	1.0
Av. no. per household	3.4	Cost of living, Dec. 1996	
Marriages per 1,000 pop.	7.5	New York = 100	110

SPAIN

Area	504,782 sq km	Currency	Peseta (Pta)
Capital	Madrid		

People

Population	39.6m	Life expectancy: men	74.5 yrs
Pop. per sq km	79	women	81.5 yrs
Av. ann. growth		Adult literacy	99.0%
in pop. 1985–95	0.3%	Fertility rate (per woman)	1.2
Pop. under 15	16.6%		
Pop. over 65	15.0%		*per 1,000 pop.*
No. of men per 100 women	96.3	Crude birth rate	9.7
Human Development Index	93.3	Crude death rate	9.4

The economy

GDP	Pta66,335bn	GDP per head	$13,434
GDP	$532bn	GDP per head in purchasing	
Av. ann. growth in real		power parity (USA=100)	54
GDP 1985–95	2.9%		

Origins of GDP		Components of GDP	
	% of total		*% of total*
Agriculture	3.3	Private consumption	62.1
Industry, of which:	34.2	Public consumption	16.4
manufacturing	...	Investment	21.2
Services	62.4	Exports	23.7
		Imports	-23.6

Structure of employment

	% of total		*% of labour force*
Agriculture	9	Unemployed 1995	22.9
Industry	30	Av. ann. rate 1990–94	19.6
Services	61		

Energy

	'000 TCE		
Total output	39,923	% output exported[a]	31.6
Total consumption	119,223	% consumption imported[a]	91.1
Consumption per head,			
kg coal equivalent	3,013		

Inflation and finance

Consumer price		*av. ann. increase 1989–95*	
inflation 1996	3.6%	Narrow money (M1)	8.0%
Av. ann. inflation 1989–96	5.4%	Broad money	10.0%

Exchange rates

	end 1996		*June 1996*
Pta per $	131.3	Effective rates	*1990 = 100*
Pta per SDR	188.8	– nominal	80.3
Pta per Ecu	164.1	– real	87.4

Principal exports

	$bn fob		$bn fob
Raw materials & intermediate products	40.0	Capital goods	11.7
Consumer goods	38.5	Total incl. others	**89.4**

Main export destinations

	% of total		% of total
France	20.5	United Kingdom	8.0
Germany	15.4	United States	4.1
Italy	9.1		

Principal imports

	$bn cif		$bn cif
Raw materials & intermediate products (excl. fuels)	59.8	Capital goods	18.0
		Energy products	9.5
Consumer goods	27.5	Total incl. others	**113.4**

Main origins of imports

	% of total		% of total
France	17.1	United Kingdom	7.8
Germany	15.3	United States	6.4
Italy	9.1		

Balance of payments, reserves and aid, $bn

Visible exports fob	92.6	Capital balance	1.6
Visible imports fob	-110.3	Overall balance	-6.5
Trade balance	-17.7	Change in reserves	-7.0
Invisibles inflows	53.4	Level of reserves	
Invisibles outflows	-39.5	end Dec.	40.5
Net transfers	5.1	No. months of import cover	1.4
Current account balance	1.3	Aid given	1.35
– as % of GDP	0.2	– as % of GDP	0.24

Family life

No. of households	15.2m	Divorces per 1,000 pop.	0.2
Av. no. per household	2.6	Cost of living, Dec. 1996	
Marriages per 1,000 pop.	5.0	New York = 100	99

a Energy trade data are distorted by transitory and oil refining activities.

SWEDEN

Area	449,964 sq km	Currency	Swedish krona (Skr)
Capital	Stockholm		

People

Population	8.8m	Life expectancy: men	76.2 yrs
Pop. per sq km	20	women	80.8 yrs
Av. ann. growth		Adult literacy	99.0%
in pop. 1985–95	0.5%	Fertility rate (per woman)	1.8
Pop. under 15	18.8%		
Pop. over 65	17.3%		*per 1,000 pop.*
No. of men per 100 women	97.8	Crude birth rate	11.9
Human Development Index	93.3	Crude death rate	11.2

The economy

GDP	Skr1,498bn	GDP per head	$23,864
GDP	$210bn	GDP per head in purchasing	
Av. ann. growth in real		power parity (USA=100)	69
GDP 1985–95	1.0%		

Origins of GDP		Components of GDP	
	% of total		*% of total*
Agriculture	2.3	Private consumption	52.2
Industry, of which:	29.8	Public consumption	25.9
manufacturing	24.3	Investment	15.6
Services	67.9	Exports	40.8
		Imports	-34.5

Structure of employment

	% of total		*% of labour force*
Agriculture	3	Unemployed 1997	7.7
Industry	26	Av. ann. rate 1990–94	5.2
Services	71		

Energy

	'000 TCE		
Total output	34,806	% output exported	37.5
Total consumption	59,369	% consumption imported	70.0
Consumption per head,			
kg coal equivalent	6,794		

Inflation and finance

Consumer price		*av. ann. increase 1989–95*	
inflation 1996	0.5%	Narrow money (M1)	...
Av. ann. inflation 1989–96	4.7%	Broad money	3.8%

Exchange rates

	end 1996		*June 1996*
Skr per $	6.87	Effective rates	*1990 = 100*
Skr per SDR	9.88	– nominal	90.0
Skr per Ecu	8.06	– real	84.5

Principal exports

	$bn fob		$bn fob
Machinery incl.		Transport equipment	11.7
electricals	24.4	Chemicals	7.1
Wood products, pulp &		Iron & steel	4.8
paper	12.6	Total incl. others	**79.0**

Main export destinations

	% of total		% of total
Germany	11.1	United States	6.7
United Kingdom	8.5	Denmark	5.8
Norway	6.8	Finland	4.0

Principal imports

	$bn cif		$bn cif
Machinery incl.		Food, beverages & tobacco	4.1
electricals	20.3	Mineral fuels	4.1
Chemicals	7.3	Clothing, footwear & textiles	2.7
Transport equipment	6.0	Total incl. others	**64.3**

Main origins of imports

	% of total		% of total
Germany	16.1	Denmark	5.9
United Kingdom	8.4	Finland	5.5
United States	7.5	Norway	5.3

Balance of payments, reserves and aid, $bn

Visible exports fob	79.2	Capital balance	-2.7
Visible imports fob	-63.2	Overall balance	-1.2
Trade balance	16.0	Change in reserves	0.3
Invisibles inflows	29.9	Level of reserves	
Invisibles outflows	-38.2	end Dec.	25.9
Net transfers	-3.0	No. months of import cover	3.1
Current account balance	4.6	Aid given	1.70
– as % of GDP	2.2	– as % of GDP	0.77

Family life

No. of households	3.9m	Divorces per 1,000 pop.	2.5
Av. no. per household	2.3	Cost of living, Dec. 1996	
Marriages per 1,000 pop.	3.8	New York = 100	123

SWITZERLAND

Area	41,293 sq km	Currency	Swiss franc (SFr)
Capital	Berne		

People

Population	7.2m	Life expectancy: men	75.3 yrs
Pop. per sq km	174	women	81.8 yrs
Av. ann. growth		Adult literacy	99.0%
in pop. 1985–95	0.9%	Fertility rate (per woman)	1.5
Pop. under 15	17.4%		
Pop. over 65	14.3%		*per 1,000 pop.*
No. of men per 100 women	98.1	Crude birth rate	10.9
Human Development Index	92.6	Crude death rate	9.1

The economy

GDP	SFr338bn	GDP per head	$39,913
GDP	$286bn	GDP per head in purchasing	
Av. ann. growth in real		power parity (USA=100)	96
GDP 1985–95	1.6%		

Origins of GDP[a]		Components of GDP	
	% of total		*% of total*
Agriculture	3.1	Private consumption	58.5
Industry, of which:	34.7	Public consumption	14.2
manufacturing	…	Investment	23.2
Services	62.2	Exports	35.2
		Imports	-31.3

Structure of employment

	% of total		*% of labour force*
Agriculture	4	Unemployed 1995	3.3
Industry	48	Av. ann. rate 1991–94	3.1
Services	48		

Energy

	'000 TCE		
Total output	13,959	% output exported	30.9
Total consumption	32,219	% consumption imported	73.2
Consumption per head,			
kg coal equivalent	4,499		

Inflation and finance

Consumer price		*av. ann. increase 1989–95*	
inflation 1996	0.8%	Narrow money (M1)	1.9%
Av. ann. inflation 1989–96	3.1%	Broad money	4.2%

Exchange rates

	end 1996		*June 1996*
SFr per $	1.35	Effective rates	*1990 = 100*
SFr per SDR	1.94	– nominal	110.7
SFr per Ecu	1.69	– real	114.1

Principal exports

	$bn fob		$bn fob
Machinery	23.2	Metals & metal manufactures	7.1
Chemicals	20.0	Textiles & clothing	3.4
Precision instruments,			
watches & jewellery	12.7	Total incl. others	**78.0**

Main export destinations

	% of total		% of total
Germany	23.4	Italy	7.8
France	9.7	United Kingdom	5.2
United States	8.4	Japan	3.9

Principal imports

	$bn cif		$bn cif
Machinery	17.4	Textiles, clothing & shoes	6.7
Chemicals	11.0	Precision instruments,	
Motor vehicles	9.0	watches & jewellery	4.7
Metals & metals manufactures	7.6		
Agricultural products	6.8	Total incl. others	**76.9**

Main origins of imports

	% of total		% of total
Germany	34.8	United States	5.8
France	11.7	United Kingdom	4.4
Italy	10.5	Japan	3.3

Balance of payments, reserves and aid, $bn

Visible exports fob	97.1	Capital balance	-18.5
Visible imports fob	-93.9	Overall balance	0.1
Trade balance	3.2	Change in reserves	2.0
Invisibles inflows	57.7	Level of reserves	
Invisibles outflows	-35.2	end Dec.	68.6
Net transfers	-4.1	No. months of import cover	6.4
Current account balance	21.6	Aid given	1.08
– as % of GDP	7.6	– as % of GDP	0.34

Family life

No. of households	3.0m	Divorces per 1,000 pop.	2.2
Av. no. per household	2.4	Cost of living, Dec. 1996	
Marriages per 1,000 pop.	5.8	New York = 100	133

a 1990
b Based on index of manufacturing output.

TAIWAN

Area	36,179 sq km	Currency	Taiwan dollar (T$)
Capital	Taipei		

People

Population	21.3m	Life expectancy: men	...
Pop. per sq km[a]	592	women	...
Av. ann. growth		Adult literacy	...
in pop. 1985–95	1.0%	Fertility rate (per woman)	1.8
Pop. under 15	24.0%		
Pop. over 65	7.7%		*per 1,000 pop.*
No. of men per 100 women	106.0	Crude birth rate	15.2
Human Development Index	...	Crude death rate	5.3

The economy

GDP	T$7,020bn	GDP per head	$12,214
GDP	$260bn	GDP per head in purchasing	
Av. ann. growth in real		power parity (USA=100)	...
GDP 1985–95	6.6%		

Origins of GDP		Components of GDP	
	% of total		*% of total*
Agriculture	3.5	Private consumption	59.2
Industry, of which:	36.3	Public consumption	14.4
manufacturing	28.2	Investment	23.4
Services	60.2	Exports	48.3
		Imports	-46.3

Structure of employment

	% of total		*% of labour force*
Agriculture	11	Unemployed 1995	1.8
Industry	39	Av. ann. rate 1990–94	1.6
Services	50		

Energy

	'000 TCE		
Total output	...	% output exported	3.3
Total consumption	...	% consumption imported	76.7
Consumption per head,			
kg coal equivalent	...		

Inflation and finance

		av. ann. increase 1989–95	
Consumer price			
inflation 1996	3.1%	Narrow money (M1)	7.2%
Av. ann. inflation 1989–96	3.8%	Broad money	14.2%

Exchange rates

	end 1996		*June 1996*
			1990 = 100
T$ per $	27.50	Effective rates	
T$ per SDR	39.60	– nominal	...
T$ per Ecu	34.38	– real	...

Principal exports

	$bn fob		$bn fob
Machinery & electrical		Plastic & rubber articles	8.1
equipment	48.8	Vehicles, aircraft & ships	5.4
Textiles & clothing	15.6		
Base metals & manufactures	10.0	Total incl. others	**111.6**

Main export destinations

	% of total		% of total
United States	23.6	Germany	3.4
Hong Kong	23.4	Netherlands	2.9
Japan	11.8	Thailand	2.7
Singapore	3.9	Malaysia	2.6

Principal imports

	$bn cif		$bn cif
Machinery & electrical		Precision instruments, clocks	
equipment	34.4	& watches	4.2
Metals	12.9	Crude petroleum	3.8
Chemicals	11.6		
Vehicles, aircraft & ships	6.0	Total incl. others	**103.7**

Main origins of imports

	% of total		% of total
Japan	29.2	Singapore	2.9
United States	20.0	Malaysia	2.9
Germany	5.5	Australia	2.5
South Korea	4.2	Indonesia	2.1

Balance of payments, reserves and debt, $bn

Visible exports fob	110.7	Overall balance	-3.9
Visible imports fob	-97.1	Change in reserves	-2.1
Trade balance	13.6	Level of reserves	
Invisibles inflows	23.8	end Dec.	91.0
Invisibles outflows	-29.5	No. months of import cover	8.6
Net transfers	-2.9	Foreign debt	27.0
Current account balance	5.0	– as % of GDP	10.4
– as % of GDP	1.9	Debt service	2.1
Capital balance	-9.3	Debt service ratio	1.6

Family life

No. of households	5.7m	Divorces per 1,000 pop.	...
Av. no. per household	3.7	Cost of living, Dec. 1996	
Marriages per 1,000 pop.	7.9	New York = 100	112

THAILAND

Area	513,115 sq km	Currency	Baht (Bt)
Capital	Bangkok		

People

Population	58.2m	Life expectancy: men	66.3 yrs
Pop. per sq km	114	women	72.3 yrs
Av. ann. growth		Adult literacy	93.8%
in pop. 1985–95	1.3%	Fertility rate (per woman)	1.7
Pop. under 15	27.9%		
Pop. over 65	5.0%		*per 1,000 pop.*
No. of men per 100 women	100.0	Crude birth rate	16.7
Human Development Index	83.2	Crude death rate	6.6

The economy

GDP	Bt3,986bn	GDP per head	$2,741
GDP	$160bn	GDP per head in purchasing	
Av. ann. growth in real		power parity (USA=100)	28
GDP 1985–95	9.4%		

Origins of GDP		Components of GDP	
	% of total		*% of total*
Agriculture	10.9	Private consumption	54.5
Industry, of which:	39.5	Public consumption	9.7
manufacturing[a]	30.2	Investment	42.9
Services	49.6	Exports	41.1
		Imports	-48.0

Structure of employment[b]

	% of total		*% of labour force*
Agriculture	48	Unemployed 1993	1.5
Industry	15	Av. ann. rate 1990–93	2.0
Services	37		

Energy

	'000 TCE		
Total output	24,439	% output exported	6.6
Total consumption	62,431	% consumption imported	64.7
Consumption per head,			
kg coal equivalent	1,073		

Inflation and finance

Consumer price		*av. ann. increase 1989–95*	
inflation 1996	6.0%	Narrow money (M1)	14.7%
Av. ann. inflation 1989–96	5.2%	Broad money	19.4%

Exchange rates

	end 1996		*June 1996*
		Effective rates	*1990 = 100*
Bt per $	25.61	Effective rates	1990 = 100
Bt per SDR	36.83	– nominal	...
Bt per Ecu	32.01	– real	...

Principal exports

	$bn fob		$bn fob
Textiles & clothing	5.7	Plastic products	2.5
Computers & parts	5.3	Footwear	2.3
Integrated circuits	2.5	Total incl. others	**56.6**

Main export destinations

	% of total		% of total
United States	17.8	Hong Kong	5.2
Japan	16.8	Germany	2.9
Singapore	14.1		

Principal imports

	$bn cif		$bn cif
Capital goods	32.2	Petroleum & products	4.5
Raw materials & intermediates	20.7		
Consumer goods	7.3	Total incl. others	**71.8**

Main origins of imports

	% of total		% of total
Japan	30.6	Germany	5.3
United States	12.0	Taiwan	4.8
Singapore	5.9		

Balance of payments, reserves and debt, $bn

Visible exports fob	55.4	Overall balance	7.2
Visible imports fob	-63.4	Change in reserves	6.7
Trade balance	-8.0	Level of reserves	
Invisibles inflows	18.6	end Dec.	36.9
Invisibles outflows	-24.7	No. months of import cover	5.0
Net transfers	0.5	Foreign debt	56.8
Current account balance	-13.6	– as % of GDP	34.9
– as % of GDP	-8.5	Debt service paid	7.5
Capital balance	21.9	Debt service ratio	10.2

Family life

No. of households	13.0m	Divorces per 1,000 pop.	0.7
Av. no. per household	4.6	Cost of living, Dec. 1996	
Marriages per 1,000 pop.	8.4	New York = 100	82

a   Includes mining and quarrying.
b   1991

TURKEY

Area	779,452 sq km	Currency	Turkish Lira (L)
Capital	Ankara		

People

Population	60.8m	Life expectancy: men	66.5 yrs
Pop. per sq km	78	women	71.7 yrs
Av. ann. growth		Adult literacy	81.1%
in pop. 1985–95	1.9%	Fertility rate (per woman)	2.5
Pop. under 15	31.2%		
Pop. over 65	5.1%		*per 1,000 pop.*
No. of men per 100 women	102.4	Crude birth rate	21.9
Human Development Index	71.1	Crude death rate	6.5

The economy

GDP	L7,747,805bn	GDP per head	$2,785
GDP	$169bn	GDP per head in purchasing	
Av. ann. growth in real		power parity (USA=100)	21
GDP 1985–95	4.1%		

Origins of GDP		Components of GDP	
	% of total		*% of total*
Agriculture	14.9	Private consumption	69.0
Industry, of which:	33.9	Public consumption	7.6
manufacturing	...	Investment	28.1
Services	51.2	Exports	22.1
		Imports	-26.8

Structure of employment

	% of total		*% of labour force*
Agriculture	48	Unemployed 1995	6.6
Industry	21	Av. ann. rate 1990–94	8.0
Services	31		

Energy

	'000 TCE		
Total output	26,655	% output exported	1.2
Total consumption	70,254	% consumption imported	69.2
Consumption per head,			
kg coal equivalent	1,156		

Inflation and finance

Consumer price		*av. ann. increase 1989–95*	
inflation 1996	81.2%	Narrow money (M1)	66.1%
Av. ann. inflation 1989–96	75.6%	Broad money	83.2%

Exchange rates

	end 1996		*June 1996*
L per $	107,775	Effective rates	*1990 = 100*
L per SDR	154,976	– nominal	...
L per Ecu	134,719	– real	...

Principal exports

	$bn fob		$bn fob
Clothing & textiles	8.3	Processed food & tobacco	1.6
Iron, steel & metals	2.7		
Vegetables, fruit & nuts	2.0	Total incl. others	**21.6**

Main export destinations

	% of total		% of total
Germany	23.3	Russia	5.7
United States	7.0	United Kingdom	5.3
Italy	6.7	France	4.8

Principal imports

	$bn cif		$bn cif
Machinery	8.0	Chemicals	4.3
Minerals	4.9	Vehicles	3.6
Metals	4.5	Total incl. others	**35.7**

Main origins of imports

	% of total		% of total
Germany	15.5	France	. 5.6
United States	10.4	United Kingdom	5.1
Italy	8.9	Saudi Arabia	3.9

Balance of payments, reserves and debt, $bn

Visible exports fob	22.0	Overall balance	4.7
Visible imports fob	-35.2	Change in reserves	5.3
Trade balance	-13.2	Level of reserves	
Invisibles inflows	16.1	end Dec.	13.9
Invisibles outflows	-9.7	No. months of import cover	3.7
Net transfers	4.5	Foreign debt	73.6
Current account balance	-2.3	– as % of GDP	44.1
– as % of GDP	-1.4	Debt service paid	11.5
Capital balance	4.7	Debt service ratio	27.7

Family life

No. of households	14.4m	Divorces per 1,000 pop.	0.5
Av. no. per household	4.2	Cost of living, Dec. 1996	
Marriages per 1,000 pop.	8.0	New York = 100	...

UKRAINE

Area	603,700 sq km	Currency	Hryvna
Capital	Kiev		

People

Population	51.6m	Life expectancy: men	63.6 yrs
Pop. per sq km	86	women	74.0 yrs
Av. ann. growth		Adult literacy	95.0%
in pop. 1985–95	0.2%	Fertility rate (per woman)	1.4
No. of men per 100 women	86.7		per 1,000 pop.
Human Development Index	71.9	Crude birth rate[a]	9.7
		Crude death rate[a]	13.8

The economy

GDP	$84.1bn	GDP per head	$1,625
Av. ann. growth in real		GDP per head in purchasing	
GDP 1989–95	-11.9%	power parity (USA=100)	9

Origins of GDP		**Components of GDP**	
	% of total		% of total
Agriculture	13.2	Private consumption	51.5
Industry	34.4	Public consumption	18.3
Construction	9.3	Net investment	34.2
Other	43.1	Net exports	-4.0

Inflation and exchange rates

			end 1996
Consumer price			
inflation 1996	80%	Hryvna per $	1.77
Av. ann. inflation 1989–96	327%	Hryvna per Ecu	2.21

Principal exports

	$ bn		$ bn
Metals	4.7	Machinery	1.6
Chemicals	1.8	Agricultural produce	1.3
Food industry	1.6	Total incl. others	**14.2**

Main export destinations

	% of total		% of total
Russia	43.1	Belarus	3.6
United States	4.9	China	3.6
Germany	4.1		

Principal imports

	$ bn		$ bn
Mineral products	9.4	Metals	0.8
Machinery & equipment	2.5		
Chemicals	0.9	Total incl. others	**16.9**

Main origins of imports

	% of total		% of total
Russia	52.3	Germany	5.3
Turkmenistan	7.89	Switzerland	2.6

EX-SOVIET REPUBLICS

	Area '000 sq km	Population m	Population[a] per sq km	Capital	Currency
Armenia	29.8	3.62	122	Yerevan	Dram
Azerbaijan	86.6	7.53	87	Baku	Manat
Belarus	207.6	10.35	50	Minsk	Rouble
Estonia	45.2	1.49	33	Tallinn	Kroon
Georgia	69.7	5.45	78	Tbilisi	Lari
Kazakhstan	2,717.3	16.82	6	Alma-Ata	Tenge
Kirgizstan	198.5	4.46	22	Bishkek	Som
Latvia	63.7	2.54	39	Riga	Lat
Lithuania	65.2	3.74	57	Vilnius	Lit
Moldova	33.7	4.44	132	Kishinev	Leu
Tajikistan	143.1	5.83	41	Dushanbe	Rouble
Turkmenistan	488.1	4.01	8	Ashkhabad	Manat
Uzbekistan	447.4	22.76	51	Tashkent	Som

People

	Av. ann. pop. growth 1985–95	Pop. under 15 %	Male life expect.[a] yrs	Birth rate[a]	Death rate[a]	Human Dev. Index
Armenia	0.8	28.6	67.2	13	7.5	68
Azerbaijan	1.2	32.2	66.5	19	6.6	67
Belarus	0.3	21.7	64.4	10	12.1	79
Estonia	-0.2	20.5	63.9	9	13.1	75
Georgia	0.3	23.7	68.5	14	9.5	65
Kazakhstan	0.6	29.8	62.8	18	8.5	74
Kirgizstan	1.0	36.9	63.4	26	7.4	66
Latvia	-0.2	20.6	62.5	10	13.8	82
Lithuania	0.5	21.7	64.9	11	11.6	72
Moldova	0.5	26.4	63.5	14	10.8	66
Tajikistan	2.5	42.0	64.2	30	6.9	62
Turkmenistan	2.4	39.4	61.2	29	7.6	70
Uzbekistan	2.3	39.9	64.3	28	6.6	68

The economy

	GDP $bn	GDP Per head $	GDP PPP USA = 100	Agric. as % of GDP	Exports of goods $m	Imports of goods $m	Foreign debt $m
Armenia	2.8	758	8	48.6	271	674	374
Azerbaijan	3.6	478	5	31.1	485	710	321
Belarus	21.4	2,063	16	13.9	4,621	5,149	1,648
Estonia	4.3	2,858	16	8.6	1,861	2,554	309
Georgia	2.4	433	5	68.0	347	690	1,189
Kazakhstan	22.1	1,317	11	12.3	5,200	5,400	3,712
Kirgizstan	3.2	708	7	34.7	409	672	610
Latvia	5.7	2,251	12	7.8	1,368	1,947	462
Lithuania	7.1	1,892	15	8.1	2,706	3,404	802
Moldova	4.0	901	…	47.7	741	773	691
Tajikistan	2.0	339	3	19.0	657	628	665
Turkmenistan	4.1	1,012	…	11.3	2,008	1,472	393
Uzbekistan	22.0	966	9	28.5	3,805	3,598	1,630

a 1995–2000.

UNITED KINGDOM

Area	242,534 sq km	Currency	Pound (£)
Capital	London		

People

Population	58.1m	Life expectancy: men	74.5 yrs
Pop. per sq km	238	women	79.8 yrs
Av. ann. growth		Adult literacy	99.0%
in pop. 1985–95	0.3%	Fertility rate (per woman)	1.7
Pop. under 15	19.3%		
Pop. over 65	15.8%		*per 1,000 pop.*
No. of men per 100 women	96.0	Crude birth rate	11.9
Human Development Index	92.4	Crude death rate	11.1

The economy

GDP	£694bn	GDP per head	$18,849
GDP	$1,095bn	GDP per head in purchasing	
Av. ann. growth in real		power parity (USA=100)	71
GDP 1985–95	2.2%		

Origins of GDP		Components of GDP	
	% of total		*% of total*
Agriculture	2.0	Private consumption	63.7
Industry, of which:	27.1	Public consumption	21.3
manufacturing	21.8	Investment	15.7
Services	70.9	Exports	28.3
		Imports	-29.0

Structure of employment

	% of total		*% of labour force*
Agriculture	2	Unemployed 1995	8.5
Industry	26	Av. ann. rate 1990–94	9.0
Services	72		

Energy

	'000 TCE		
Total output	347,703	% output exported	41.7
Total consumption	310,996	% consumption imported	34.7
Consumption per head,			
kg coal equivalent	5,333		

Inflation and finance

Consumer price		*av. ann. increase 1989–95*	
inflation 1996	2.4%	Narrow money (M1)	8.8%
Av. ann. inflation 1989–96	4.6%	Broad money	8.8%

Exchange rates

	end 1996		*June 1996*
£ per $	0.59	Effective rates	*1990 = 100*
£ per SDR	0.85	– nominal	86.0
£ per Ecu	0.74	– real	88.4

Principal exports

	$bn fob		$bn fob
Finished manufactured products	132.2	Fuels	14.6
		Basic materials	4.6
Semi-manufactured products	68.6		
Food, beverages & tobacco	17.6	Total incl. others	**240.5**

Main export destinations

	% of total		% of total
Germany	13.8	Netherlands	8.0
United States	11.8	Belgium/Luxembourg	5.4
France	9.9	Ireland	5.0

Principal imports

	$bn cif		$bn cif
Finished manufactured products	142.3	Basic materials	10.2
		Fuels	8.8
Semi-manufactured products	71.1		
Food, beverages & tobacco	24.1	Total incl. others	**258.8**

Main origins of imports

	% of total		% of total
Germany	15.5	Netherlands	6.8
United States	12.1	Japan	5.7
France	9.7	Italy	4.9

Balance of payments, reserves and aid, $bn

Visible exports fob	240.4	Capital balance	0.2
Visible imports fob	-258.8	Overall balance	-1.0
Trade balance	-18.4	Change in reserves	1.1
Invisibles inflows	218.3	Level of reserves	
Invisibles outflows	-193.6	end Dec.	49.1
Net transfers	-11.0	No. months of import cover	1.3
Current account balance	-4.6	Aid given	3.16
– as % of GDP	-0.6	– as % of GDP	0.28

Family life

No. of households	21.3m	Divorces per 1,000 pop.	3.0
Av. no. per household	2.7	Cost of living, Dec. 1996	
Marriages per 1,000 pop.	5.9	New York = 100	105

UNITED STATES

Area	9,372,610 sq km	Currency	US dollar ($)
Capital	Washington DC		

People

Population	267.1m	Life expectancy: men		73.4 yrs
Pop. per sq km	29	women		80.1 yrs
Av. ann. growth		Adult literacy		99.0%
in pop. 1985–95	1.0%	Fertility rate (per woman)		2.0
Pop. under 15	22.0%			
Pop. over 65	12.6%			*per 1,000 pop.*
No. of men per 100 women	97.1	Crude birth rate		13.8
Human Development Index	94	Crude death rate		8.7

The economy

GDP	$7,100bn	GDP per head	$26,580
Av. ann. growth in real		GDP per head in purchasing	
GDP 1985–95	2.5%	power parity (USA=100)	100

Origins of GDP[a]		Components of GDP	
	% of total		*% of total*
Agriculture	1.9	Private consumption	67.9
Industry, of which:	23.4	Public consumption	18.7
manufacturing	17.9	Investment	14.7
Services	74.9	Exports	11.1
		Imports	-12.4

Structure of employment

	% of total		*% of labour force*
Agriculture	3	Unemployed 1995	5.6
Industry	24	Av. ann. rate 1990–94	6.6
Services	73		

Energy

	'000 TCE		
Total output	2,447,502	% output exported	4.7
Total consumption	2,968,744	% consumption imported	24.8
Consumption per head,			
kg coal equivalent	11,391		

Inflation and finance

Consumer price		*av. ann. increase 1989–95*	
inflation 1996	2.9%	Narrow money (M1)	4.9%
Av. ann. inflation 1989–96	3.6%	Broad money	3.2%

Exchange rates

	end 1996		*June 1996*
$ per SDR	1.44	Effective rates	*1990 = 100*
$ per Ecu	1.25	– nominal	97.1
		– real	97.7

Principal exports

	$bn fob		$bn fob
Capital goods, excl. vehicles	233.8	Vehicles & products	61.8
Industrial supplies	146.4	Food & beverages	50.5
Consumer goods, excl. vehicles	64.4	Total incl. others	**575.9**

Main export destinations

	% of total		% of total
Canada	22.2	South Korea	4.2
Japan	11.0	Germany	3.8
Mexico	8.0	Taiwan	3.2
United Kingdom	4.9		

Principal imports

	$bn fob		$bn fob
Capital goods, excl. vehicles	221.4	Vehicles & products	124.8
Industrial supplies	183.8	Food & beverages	33.2
Consumer goods, excl. vehicles	160.0	Total incl. others	**749.4**

Main origins of imports

	% of total		% of total
Canada	19.8	Germany	4.9
Japan	16.5	Taiwan	3.9
Mexico	8.3	United Kingdom	3.6
China	6.1		

Balance of payments, reserves and aid, $bn

Visible exports fob	577.8	Capital balance	20.8
Visible imports fob	-749.8	Overall balance	-95.9
Trade balance	-172.0	Change in reserves	12.4
Invisibles inflows	391.4	Level of reserves	
Invisibles outflows	-332.5	end Dec.	176.0
Net transfers	-35.2	No. months of import cover	2.0
Current account balance	-148.2	Aid given	7.37
– as % of GDP	-2.1	– as % of GDP	0.10

Family life

No. of households	100.3m	Divorces per 1,000 pop.	4.6
Av. no. per household	2.6	Cost of living, Dec. 1996	
Marriages per 1,000 pop.	9.1	New York = 100	100

a 1994

VENEZUELA

Area	912,050 sq km	Currency	Bolivar (Bs)
Capital	Caracas		

People

Population	21.8m	Life expectancy: men	70.0 yrs
Pop. per sq km	24	women	75.7 yrs
Av. ann. growth		Adult literacy	89.0%
in pop. 1985–95	2.5%	Fertility rate (per woman)	3.0
Pop. under 15	36.2%		
Pop. over 65	4.1%		*per 1,000 pop.*
No. of men per 100 women	101.5	Crude birth rate	24.9
Human Development Index	85.9	Crude death rate	4.7

The economy

GDP	Bs11,495bn	GDP per head	$2,993
GDP	$65bn	GDP per head in purchasing	
Av. ann. growth in real		power parity (USA=100)	29
GDP 1985–95	3.1%		

Origins of GDP		Components of GDP	
	% of total		*% of total*
Agriculture	5.5	Private consumption	62.9
Industry, of which:	40.8	Public consumption	10.2
manufacturing	16.2	Investment	20.2
Services	53.7	Exports	29.3
		Imports	-22.6

Structure of employment

	% of total		*% of labour force*
Agriculture	13	Unemployed 1995	10.3
Industry	24	Av. ann. rate 1990–94	8.5
Services	63		

Energy

	'000 TCE		
Total output	261,262	% output exported	65.7
Total consumption	80,072	% consumption imported	0.4
Consumption per head,			
kg coal equivalent	3,746		

Inflation and finance

Consumer price		*av. ann. increase 1989–95*	
inflation 1996	99.9%	Narrow money (M1)	37.5%
Av. ann. inflation 1989–96	54.5%	Broad money	41.9%

Exchange rates

	end 1996		*June 1996*
Bs per $	477	Effective rates	*1990 = 100*
Bs per SDR	685	– nominal	15.7
Bs per Ecu	596	– real	104.7

Principal exports

	$bn fob		$bn fob
Petroleum & products	14.4		
Metals	1.5	Total incl. others	**18.9**

Main export destinations

	% of total		% of total
United States	49.2	Brazil	3.9
Colombia	6.4	Germany	2.6

Principal imports

	$bn fob		$bn fob
Machinery & transport equipment	4.0	Agricultural products	1.3
Chemicals	1.8	Total incl. others	**10.8**

Main origins of imports

	% of total		% of total
United States	42.1	Germany	4.9
Colombia	7.6	Japan	4.2

Balance of payments, reserves and debt, $bn

Visible exports fob	18.9	Overall balance	-1.0
Visible imports fob	-11.6	Change in reserves	-1.7
Trade balance	7.3	Level of reserves	
Invisibles inflows	3.5	end Dec.	10.7
Invisibles outflows	-8.7	No. months of import cover	6.3
Net transfers	0.1	Foreign debt	35.8
Current account balance	2.3	– as % of GDP	49.0
– as % of GDP	3.4	Debt service paid	4.9
Capital balance	-2.7	Debt service ratio	21.7

Family life

No. households	3.9m	Divorces per 1,000 pop.	1.0
Av. no. per household	5.6	Cost of living, Dec. 1996	
Marriages per 1,000 pop.	5.4	New York = 100	57

ZAIRE

Area	2,345,410 sq km	Currency	Zaire (Z)
Capital	Kinshasa		

People

Population	45.5m	Life expectancy: men	51.3 yrs
Pop. per sq km	19	women	54.5 yrs
Av. ann. growth		Adult literacy	74.0%
in pop. 1985–95	3.7%	Fertility rate (per woman)	6.2
Pop. under 15	47.2%		
Pop. over 65	2.8%		*per 1,000 pop.*
No. of men per 100 women	97.7	Crude birth rate	44.9
Human Development Index	37.1	Crude death rate	13.5

The economy

GDP	Z37,227bn	GDP per head	$117
GDP	$5.3bn	GDP per head in purchasing	
Av. ann. growth in real		power parity (USA=100)	2
GDP 1985–95	-4.7%		

Origins of GDP[a]		Components of GDP[b]	
	% of total		*% of total*
Agriculture	53.4	Private consumption	68.8
Industry, of which:	15.6	Public consumption	21.7
manufacturing	5.5	Investment	6.9
Services	31.2	Exports	21.6
		Imports	-19.0

Structure of employment

	% of total		*% of labour force*
Agriculture	...	Unemployed 1995	...
Industry	...	Av. ann. rate 1990–94	...
Services	...		

Energy

	'000 TCE		
Total output	2,693	% output exported	63.3
Total consumption	2,359	% consumption imported	68.5
Consumption per head,			
kg coal equivalent	55		

Inflation and finance

Consumer price		*av. ann. increase 1989–95*	
inflation 1995	659%	Narrow money (M1)	1,109%
Av. ann. inflation 1989–95	1,208%	Broad money	1,143%

Exchange rates

	end 1996		*June 1996*
Z per $	112,652	Effective rates	1990 = 100
Z per SDR	162,089	– nominal	...
Z per Ecu	140,815	– real	82.5

Principal exports[a]

	$m fob		$m fob
Diamonds	451	Copper & cobalt	184
Coffee	247	Total incl. others	**1,028**

Main export destinations

	% of total		% of total
Belgium/Luxembourg	37	Italy	10
United States	17	South Africa	8

Principal imports[a]

	$m fob		$m fob
Consumer goods	232	Energy products	85
Capital goods	116		
Raw materials	93	Total incl. others	**581**

Main origins of imports

	% of total		% of total
Belgium/Luxembourg	15	Hong Kong	8
South Africa	11	United States	7

Balance of payments[d], reserves and debt, $bn

Visible exports fob	2.1	Overall balance	-0.8
Visible imports fob	-1.5	Change in reserves	0.0
Trade balance	0.6	Level of reserves	
Invisibles inflows	0.2	end Dec.	0.2
Invisibles outflows	-1.5	No. months of import cover[d]	1.0
Net transfers	0.1	Foreign debt	13.1
Current account balance	-0.6	– as % of GDP	255.2
– as % of GDP	-7.9	Debt service paid	0.03
Capital balance	-0.2	Debt service ratio[d]	15.1

Family life

No. of households	5.7m	Divorces per 1,000 pop.	...
Av. no. per household	5.4	Cost of living, Dec. 1996	
Marriages per 1,000 pop.	...	New York = 100	...

a 1994
b 1992
c 1986
d 1990
Note: at the time of going to press Zaire had been renamed the Democratic Republic of Congo but had not been officially recognised by many countries.

ZIMBABWE

Area	390,759 sq km	Currency	Zimbabwe dollar (Z$)
Capital	Harare		

People

Population	11.2m	Life expectancy: men	47.6 yrs
Pop. per sq km	29	women	49.4 yrs
Av. ann. growth		Adult literacy	84.0%
in pop. 1985–95	2.9%	Fertility rate (per woman)	4.7
Pop. under 15	44.3%		
Pop. over 65	2.7%		*per 1,000 pop.*
No. of men per 100 women	98.5	Crude birth rate	37.1
Human Development Index	53.4	Crude death rate	14.6

The economy

GDP	Z$51bn	GDP per head	$530
GDP	$5.9bn	GDP per head in purchasing	
Av. ann. growth in real		power parity (USA=100)	8
GDP 1985–95	2.3%		

Origins of GDP[a]		**Components of GDP[b]**	
	% of total		*% of total*
Agriculture	13.6	Private consumption	51.5
Industry, of which:	30.1	Public consumption	27.2
manufacturing	22.9	Investment	28.5
Services	56.3	Exports	32.6
		Imports	-34.9

Structure of employment[c]

	% of total		*% of labour force*
Agriculture	68	Unemployed 1995	...
Industry	8	Av. ann. rate 1990–94	...
Services	24		

Energy

	'000 TCE		
Total output	5,760	% output exported	0.5
Total consumption	7,650	% consumption imported	23.4
Consumption per head,			
kg coal equivalent	695		

Inflation and finance

		av. ann. increase 1989–95	
Consumer price			
inflation 1996	21.4%	Narrow money (M1)	32.0%
Av. ann. inflation 1989–96	23.5%	Broad money	24.9%

Exchange rates

	end 1996		*June 1996*
Z$ per $	10.83	Effective rates	*1990 = 100*
Z$ per SDR	15.58	– nominal	...
Z$ per Ecu	13.54	– real	...

Principal exports

	$m fob		$m fob
Tobacco	472	Nickel	88
Gold	249		
Ferro-alloys	214	Total incl. others	**2,089**

Main export destinations[d]

	% of total		% of total
South Africa	13.5	Germany	7.9
United Kingdom	10.1	Japan	7.7

Principal imports

	$m fob		$m fob
Machinery & transport equipment	1,126	Petroleum products & electricity	239
Manufactured products	451		
Chemicals	366	Total incl. others	**2,629**

Main origins of imports

	% of total		% of total
South Africa	40.9	Japan	6.1
United Kingdom	7.0	United States	6.1

Balance of payments[e], reserves and debt, $bn

Visible exports fob	2.0	Overall balance	-0.1
Visible imports fob	-1.8	Change in reserves	0.3
Trade balance	0.2	Level of reserves	
Invisibles inflows	0.4	end Dec.	0.9
Invisibles outflows	-1.0	No. months of import cover	2.8
Net transfers	0.0	Foreign debt	4.9
Current account balance	-0.4	– as % of GDP	78.9
– as % of GDP	-7.8	Debt service paid	0.7
Capital balance	0.3	Debt service ratio[e]	25.6

Family life

No. of households	0.1m	Divorces per 1,000 pop.	...
Av. no. per household	...	Cost of living, Dec. 1996	
Marriages per 1,000 pop.	...	New York = 100	53

a	1994
b	1991
c	1990
d	Excluding gold.
e	1994

Glossary

Balance of payments The record of a country's transactions with the rest of the world. The **current account** of the balance of payments consists of: visible trade (goods); "invisible" trade (services and income); private transfer payments (eg, remittances from those working abroad); official transfers (eg, payments to international organisations, famine relief). Visible imports and exports are normally compiled on rather different definitions to those used in the trade statistics (shown in principal imports and exports) and therefore the statistics do not match. The **capital account** consists of long- and short-term transactions relating to a country's assets and liabilities (eg, loans and borrowings). Adding the current to the capital account gives the **overall balance**. This is compensated by net monetary movements and changes in reserves. In practice methods of statistical recording are neither complete nor accurate and an errors and omissions item, sometimes quite large, will appear. In the country pages of this book this item is included in the overall balance. **Changes in reserves** exclude revaluation effects and are shown without the practice often followed in balance of payments presentations of reversing the sign.

CFA Communauté Financière Africaine. Its members, most of the francophone African nations, share a common currency, the CFA franc, which is maintained at a fixed rate of 1FFr = 100 CFAfr by the French treasury.

Cif/fob Measures of the value of merchandise trade. Imports include the cost of "carriage, insurance and freight" (cif) from the exporting country to the importing. The value of exports des not include these elements and is recorded 'free on board' (fob). Balance of payments statistics are generally adjusted so that both exports and imports are shown fob; the cif elements are included in invisibles.

Commonwealth of Independent States All former Soviet Union Republics, excluding Estonia, Latvia and Lithuania. It was established January 1 1992; Azerbaijan joined in September 1993 and Georgia in December 1993.

Crude birth rate The number of live births in a year per 1,000 population. The crude rate will automatically be relatively high if a large proportion of the population is of childbearing age.

Crude death rate The number of deaths in a year per 1,000 population. Also affected by the population's age structure.

Debt, foreign Financial obligations owed by a country to the rest of the world and repayable in foreign currency. **Debt service paid** is the sum of principal repayments and interest payments actually made. **The debt service ratio** is debt service expressed as a percentage of the country's earnings from exports of goods and services.

EU European Union. Members are: Belgium, Denmark, France, Germany, Greece, Ireland, Italy, Luxembourg, Netherlands, Portugal, Spain and the United Kingdom and, since January 1 1995, Austria, Finland and Sweden.

Ecu European currency unit. An accounting measure used within the EU and composed of a weighted basket of the currencies of 12 EU members.

Effective exchange rate This measures a currency's depreciation (figures below 100) or appreciation (figures over 100) from a base date against a trade weighted basket of the currencies of the country's main trading partners.

Efta European Free Trade Association. An organisation of West European states that are not members of the European Union. Members are: Austria, Finland,

Iceland, Liechtenstein, Norway, Sweden and Switzerland.

Fertility rate The average number of children born to a woman who completes her childbearing years.

GDP Gross domestic product. The sum of all output produced by economic activity within a country. GNP (gross national product) includes net income from abroad eg, rent, profits.

Import cover The number of months of imports covered by reserves, ie reserves ÷ ¹⁄₁₂ annual imports (visibles and invisibles).

Inflation The annual rate at which prices are increasing. The most common measure and the one shown here is the increase in the consumer price index.

Life expectancy The average length of time a baby born today can expect to live.

Literacy is defined by UNESCO as the ability to read and write a simple sentence, but definitions can vary from country to country.

Money supply A measure of the "money" available to buy goods and services. Various definitions exist. The measures shown here are based on definitions used by the IMF and may differ from measures used nationally. Narrow money (M1) consists of cash in circulation and demand deposits (bank deposits that can be withdrawn on demand). "Quasi-money" (time, savings and foreign currency deposits) is added to this to create broad money.

NMP Net material product. The equivalent measure to GDP used in Eastern Europe and certain other economies. It differs from GDP in excluding certain services and in deducting capital consumption. In general, NMP is between 80-90% of GDP.

OECD Organisation for Economic Co-operation and Development. The "rich countries" club was established in 1961 to promote economic growth and the expansion of world trade. It is based in Paris and now has 29 members.

Opec Organisation of Petroleum Exporting Countries. Set up in 1960 and based in Vienna, Opec is mainly concerned with oil pricing and production issues. Members are; Algeria, Ecuador, Gabon, Indonesia, Iran, Iraq, Kuwait, Libya, Nigeria, Qatar, Saudi Arabia, UAE and Venezuela.

PPP Purchasing power parity. PPP statistics adjust for cost of living differences by replacing normal exchange rates with rates designed to equalise the prices of a standard "basket"of goods and services. These are used to obtain PPP estimates of GDP per head. PPP estimates are normally shown on a scale of 1 to 100, taking the United States, where the average standard of living is highest, as 100.

Real terms Figures adjusted to exclude the effect of inflation.

Reserves The stock of gold and foreign currency held by a country to finance any calls that may be made for the settlement of foreign debt.

SDR Special drawing right. The reserve currency, introduced by the IMF in 1970, was intended to replace gold and national currencies in settling international transactions. The IMF uses SDRs for book-keeping purposes and issues them to member countries. Their value is based on a basket of the five most widely traded currencies: the US dollar, Deutschemark, pound sterling, Japanese yen and French franc.

Sources

Airports Council International, *Worldwide Airport Traffic Report*

Asian Studies Centre, The Heritage Foundation, *US and Asia Statistical Handbook*

BP, *Statistical Review of World Energy*

British Mountaineering Council

Corporate Resources Group, *Quality of Living Report*

The Economist Intelligence Unit, *Cost of Living Survey*

The Economist Intelligence Unit, *Country Forecasts*

The Economist Intelligence Unit, *Country Reports*

The Economist Intelligence Unit, *Global Outlook – Business Environment Rankings*

Euromonitor, *International Marketing Data and Statistics*

Euromonitor, *European Marketing Data and Statistics*

Europa Publications, *The Europa World Yearbook*

European Bank for Reconstruction and Development, *Transition Report*

FAO, *Production Yearbook*

Financial Times Business Information, *The Banker*

Gold Fields Mineral Services Ltd.

The Howard League for Penal Reform

ILO, *Year Book of Labour Statistics*

IMF, *Balance of Payments Statistics Yearbook*

IMF, *Direction of Trade*

IMF, *International Financial Statistics*

IMF, *World Economic Outlook*

International Cocoa Organisation, *Quarterly Bulletin of Cocoa Statistics*

International Civil Aviation Organisation, *Civil Aviation Statistics of the World*

International Coffee Organisation

International Cotton Advisory Committee, *Bulletin*

International Criminal Police Organisation (Interpol), *International Crime Statistics*

International Finance Corporation, *Emerging Stock Markets Factbook*

International Road Federation, *World Road Statistics*

International Rubber Study Group, *Rubber Statistical Bulletin*

International Federation of the Phonographic Industry

International Grains Council, *The Grain Market Report*

International Sugar Organisation, *Sugar Yearbook*

International Tea Committee, *Annual Bulletin of Statistics*

International Telecommunication Union, *World Telecommunication Development Report*

International Wool Textile Organisation

Lloyd's Register, *Statistical Tables*

Journal de la Marine Marchande et du Transport Multimodal

Network Wizards

OECD, *Economic Outlook*

OECD, *Environmental Data*

Penal Reform International

ISTA Mielke, *Oil World*

Taiwan Statistical Data Book

The Times, *Atlas of the World*

Time Inc Magazines, *Fortune International*

The World Almanac

UN, *Demographic Yearbook*

UN, *Energy Statistics Yearbook*

UN, *Statistical Chart on World Families*

UN, *World Population Prospects*

UN Development Programme, *Human Development Report*

UNESCO, *Statistical Yearbook*

Union International des Chemins de Fer, *Statistiques Internationales des Chemins de Fer*

US Department of Agriculture, *Rice Report*

WHO, *Weekly Epidemiological Record*

WHO, *World Health Statistics*

World Bank, *Atlas*

World Bank, *Global Development Finance*

World Bank, *World Development Report*

World Bureau of Metal Statistics, *World Metal Statistics*

World Economic Forum, *The Global Competitiveness Report 1997*

World Resources Institute, *World Resources*

World Tourist Organisation, *Yearbook of Tourism Statistics*

World Trade Organisation, *Annual Report*

List of countries

Whenever data is available, the world rankings consider 171 countries: all those which had, in 1995, a population of at least 1m or a GDP/GNP of at least $1bn. Here is a list of them.

	Population '000	GDP $m		Population '000	GDP $m
Afghanistan	19,661	...	Eritrea	3,171	...
Albania[a]	3,383	1,229	Estonia	1,488	4,252
Algeria	28,109	44,609	Ethiopia	56,404	5,722
Angola[a]	10,816	4,400	Fiji	784	1,895
Argentina	34,768	278,431	Finland	5,107	105,174
Armenia	3,632	2,752	France	58,104	1,451,051
Australia	17,866	337,909	Gabon	1,076	3,759
Austria	8,045	216,547	Gambia, The	1,111	354
Azerbaijan	7,531	3,601	Georgia	5,450	2,358
Bahamas	279	3,297	Germany	81,594	2,252,343
Bahrain	557	4,525	Ghana	17,338	6,719
Bangladesh	118,229	28,599	Greece	10,454	85,885
Barbados	261	1,745	Guadeloupe	424	2,071
Belarus	10,352	21,356	Guatemala	10,621	14,255
Belgium	10,127	250,710	Guinea	7,349	3,593
Benin	5,409	2,034	Guinea-Bissau	1,069	265
Bermuda	63	1,914	Haiti	7,124	1,777
Bhutan	1,770	295	Honduras	5,654	3,566
Bolivia	7,414	5,905	Hong Kong	6,123	142,332
Bosnia	3,569	...	Hungary	10,106	42,129
Botswana	1,450	4,381	Iceland	269	6,686
Brazil	159,015	579,787	India	929,005	319,660
Brunei[a]	293	3,975	Indonesia	197,460	190,105
Bulgaria	8,509	11,225	Iran	68,365	61,400
Burkina Faso	10,479	2,417	Iraq	20,095	16,800
Burundi	6,064	984	Ireland	3,546	52,765
Cambodia	10,024	2,718	Israel	5,525	87,875
Cameroon	13,192	8,615	Italy	57,204	1,088,085
Canada	29,402	573,695	Jamaica	2,468	3,803
CAR	3,273	1,123	Japan	125,068	4,963,587
Chad	6,335	1,144	Jordan	5,373	6,354
Chile	14,210	59,151	Kazakhstan	16,817	22,143
China	1,220,224	744,890	Kenya	27,150	7,583
Colombia	35,814	70,263	Kirgizstan	4,460	3,158
Congo	2,593	1,784	Kuwait	1,691	28,941
Costa Rica	3,424	8,884	Laos	4,882	1,694
Côte d'Ivoire	13,694	9,248	Latvia	2,536	5,708
Croatia	4,505	15,508	Lebanon	3,009	10,673
Cuba	10,964	13,750	Lesotho	2,027	1,519
Cyprus	745	8,580	Liberia[b]	2,123	14,850
Czech Republic	10,263	39,990	Libya	5,407	40,148
Denmark	5,223	156,027	Lithuania	3,736	7,070
Dominican Rep	7,823	11,390	Luxembourg	407	16,876
Ecuador	11,460	15,997	Macau[c]	430	3,456
Egypt	62,096	45,507	Macedonia, FYR	2,156	1,813
El Salvador	5,662	9,057	Madagascar	14,874	3,178

	Population	GDP		Population	GDP
	'000	$m		'000	$m
Malawi	9,673	1,623	Serbia,		
Malaysia	20,140	78,321	Montenegro	10,251	15,900
Mali	10,795	2,410	Sierra Leone	4,195	762
Malta	367	3,363	Singapore	3,327	79,831
Martinique	380	...	Slovakia	5,338	15,848
Mauritania	2,274	1,049	Slovenia	1,925	16,328
Mauritius	1,117	3,815	Somalia	9,491	...
Mexico	91,145	304,596	South Africa	41,465	130,918
Moldova	4,437	3,996	South Korea	44,909	435,137
Mongolia	2,463	767	Spain	39,627	532,347
Morocco	26,524	29,545	Sri Lanka	17,928	12,616
Mozambique	17,260	1,353	Sudan	26,707	8,500
Myanmar	45,106	108,148	Suriname	427	360
Namibia	1,536	3,098	Swaziland	857	1,171
Nepal	21,456	4,391	Sweden	8,788	209,720
Netherlands	15,482	371,039	Switzerland	7,166	286,014
Netherlands			Syria	14,203	15,780
Antilles	194	1,321	Taiwan	21,304	260,200
New Zealand	3,561	51,655	Tajikistan	5,828	1,976
Nicaragua	4,123	1,659	Tanzania	29,685	3,703
Niger	9,151	1,961	Thailand	58,242	159,630
Nigeria	111,721	28,411	Togo	4,085	1,266
North Korea	22,097	22,300	Trinidad & Tob	1,287	4,851
Norway	4,332	136,077	Tunisia	8,987	16,369
Oman	2,207	10,578	Turkey	60,838	169,452
Pakistan	136,257	59,991	Turkmenistan	4,075	4,125
Panama	2,631	7,235	UAE	2,210	42,806
Papua New			Uganda	19,689	4,668
Guinea	4,301	4,976	Ukraine	51,757	84,084
Paraguay	4,828	8,158	United Kingdom	58,079	1,094,734
Peru	23,532	55,019	United States	267,115	7,100,007
Philippines	67,839	71,865	Uruguay	3,186	16,458
Poland	38,557	107,829	Uzbekistan	22,762	21,979
Portugal	9,815	96,689	Venezuela	21,844	65,382
Puerto Rico	3,701	28,370	Vietnam	73,793	17,634
Qatar	548	7,448	West Bank		
Réunion	655	...	and Gaza	2,267	3,351
Romania	22,728	33,488	Yemen	15,027	4,044
Russia	148,460	331,948	Zaire	45,453	5,313
Rwanda	5,184	1,128	Zambia	8,081	3,605
Saudi Arabia	18,255	133,540	Zimbabwe	11,190	5,933
Senegal	8,312	5,070			

a 1994
b Estimate.
c 1992